Becoming Apostolic

Brill's Studies in Catholic Theology

Edited by

Philip Endean (*Centre Sèvres – Facultés jésuites de Paris*)
Paul van Geest (*Tilburg University, Erasmus University, KU Leuven*)
Paul Murray (*University of Durham*)
Marcel Sarot (*Tilburg University*)

VOLUME 14

The titles published in this series are listed at *brill.com/bsct*

Becoming Apostolic

Conversations with Older Roman Catholic Sisters

By

Catherine Sexton

BRILL

LEIDEN | BOSTON

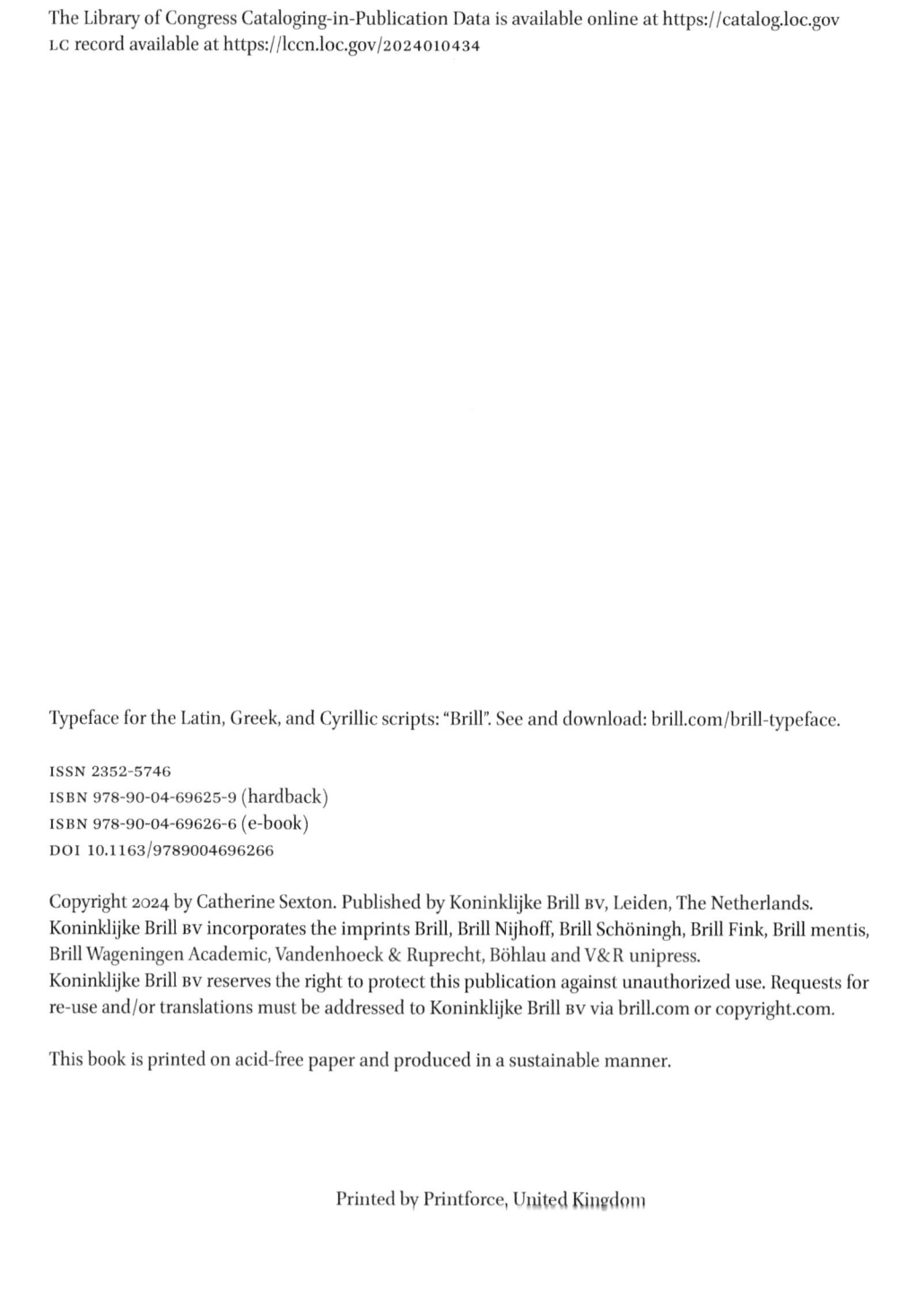

Cover illustration: EP/8/LP/5/2/1: Hands Images Project 2, Clasped Hands. With the permission of the Society of the Holy Child Jesus.

The Library of Congress Cataloging-in-Publication Data is available online at https://catalog.loc.gov
LC record available at https://lccn.loc.gov/2024010434

Typeface for the Latin, Greek, and Cyrillic scripts: "Brill". See and download: brill.com/brill-typeface.

ISSN 2352-5746
ISBN 978-90-04-69625-9 (hardback)
ISBN 978-90-04-69626-6 (e-book)
DOI 10.1163/9789004696266

Copyright 2024 by Catherine Sexton. Published by Koninklijke Brill BV, Leiden, The Netherlands.
Koninklijke Brill BV incorporates the imprints Brill, Brill Nijhoff, Brill Schöningh, Brill Fink, Brill mentis, Brill Wageningen Academic, Vandenhoeck & Ruprecht, Böhlau and V&R unipress.
Koninklijke Brill BV reserves the right to protect this publication against unauthorized use. Requests for re-use and/or translations must be addressed to Koninklijke Brill BV via brill.com or copyright.com.

This book is printed on acid-free paper and produced in a sustainable manner.

Printed by Printforce, United Kingdom

Contents

Acknowledgments IX
Abbreviations X

1 **Women in Apostolic Religious Life** 1
   1.1 Introduction 1
   1.2 From Active to Semi-monastic Life: the Historical Context before the Second Vatican Council (1962–65) 2
   1.3 The Second Vatican Council and Apostolic Religious Life 4
   1.4 Implications for the Women in This Study 6
   1.5 The Significance of the United States' Context for the Discourse on Religious Life in the United Kingdom 9
   1.6 United States Writing: Two Articulations of Apostolic Life for Women 11
   1.7 Discourse on Religious Life in the United Kingdom, 2000–18 14
      1.7.1 *Recurring Concerns and Themes* 17
   1.8 Rationale for This Study 21
   1.9 Structure of This Book 23

2 **Treading on Holy Ground: Listening for Absent Voices** 26
   2.1 Introduction 26
   2.2 Theoretical Basis for Research Design 26
      2.2.1 *An Approach to Interpretation: Hermeneutical Phenomenology* 26
      2.2.2 *A Feminist Approach* 28
   2.3 The Centrality of Women's Experience and Attendant Challenges 30
   2.4 Reflexivity 31
   2.5 My Engagement with Religious Life 33
   2.6 Insider/Outsider Stance 33
   2.7 Method as Holy Listening and Sacred Reading 36
      2.7.1 *Introduction* 36
      2.7.2 *Laying the Groundwork for Listening* 37
         2.7.2.1 Choice of Research Methods 37
         2.7.2.2 Criteria for Selection of Congregations 38
         2.7.2.3 Profile of Interview Participants 39
   2.8 Holy Listening: Encounters with Religious Women 40
      2.8.1 *The Interviews: a Third Presence in the Space in Between* 41

    2.8.2   *After the Interviews: the Process of Data Analysis*   43
           2.8.2.1   The First Component of Method: Choosing the Voice-Centred Relational Method (VCRM)   43
           2.8.2.2   The Four Readings of the VCRM   45
  2.9   The Second Component of the Method: Listening for the Voice through Sacred Reading   48
    2.9.1   *Theoretical Considerations*   50
  2.10 The Third Component of the Method: Thematic Analysis   54
  2.11 Conclusion   55

3 **Framing the Apostolic Becoming**   56
  3.1   Introduction   56
  3.2   Making Meaning of Vocation   56
    3.2.1   *The Call Narratives*   56
    3.2.2   *Context*   57
    3.2.3   *The Lure of the Missions*   59
    3.2.4   *Family Influence*   61
    3.2.5   *A Call to an Occupation?*   62
    3.2.6   *A Call to Serve? An Apostolic Impulse?*   64
    3.2.7   *A Call to God*   65
  3.3   Narratives of a Changed Understanding   66
    3.3.1   *From Corporate Apostolates to Individualized Ministries*   67
    3.3.2   *The Rise of the Justice and Peace Paradigm*   69
    3.3.3   *The Missionary Context*   70
    3.3.4   *Back to the United Kingdom*   71
  3.4   Naming Their Way of Life   73
    3.4.1   *Name and Identity*   80
  3.5   Conclusion   81

4 **Becoming Apostolic as Themselves**   84
  4.1   Introduction   84
  4.2   The Context   85
  4.3   Free to Become Oneself   86
  4.4   First Set of Narratives: Claiming and Asserting Identity   88
    4.4.1   *Resisting Externally Ascribed Identities*   89
    4.4.2   *Resisting Internally Ascribed Identities*   92
  4.5   Second Set of Narratives: Fulfilment and Frustration   94
    4.5.1   *Examples of Thwarted Desire*   97

- 4.6 Using Voice to Exercise Personal Agency: from Obedience to Discernment   99
- 4.7 Encouraged to Be Themselves   104
  - 4.7.1 *A Concern with Freedom*   107
  - 4.7.2 *From Self-Denial to Self-Gift*   110
- 4.8 Conclusion   111

5 Being With and Being For   112
- 5.1 Introduction   112
- 5.2 Context   113
- 5.3 Ways of Being Apostolic   114
  - 5.3.1 *Evangelizing*   114
  - 5.3.2 *Availability in the Everyday*   116
- 5.4 Facing towards Others   120
- 5.5 Ministry as Gift: Fit for Purpose?   123
  - 5.5.1 *Ministry as Gift*   124
  - 5.5.2 *Reciprocity*   128
- 5.6 Self-Gift   132
- 5.7 Conclusion   134

6 Ministry in Old Age: Apostolic to the Very End   135
- 6.1 Introduction   135
- 6.2 Ministry in Old Age   135
  - 6.2.1 *Ambivalence towards Old Age and Inactivity*   136
    - 6.2.1.1 Contextual Influences   140
  - 6.2.2 *In Defence of Dependency and Passivity*   142
- 6.3 Forms of Ministry in Later Life   144
- 6.4 Ministry of Presence   144
  - 6.4.1 *Contexts for Ministry of Presence*   145
  - 6.4.2 *Expressions of Presence*   147
  - 6.4.3 *Towards a Sacramental Theology of Presence*   149
  - 6.4.4 *Presence as Incarnational*   151
  - 6.4.5 *Raising Up the Ordinary*   155
- 6.5 Ministry to Each Other in Community: Sacramentality of Relationships   158
- 6.6 Ministry with and for Their Carers   160
- 6.7 Obedience of Detachment and Relinquishment   163
  - 6.7.1 *Obedient to the End*   166
- 6.8 Conclusion   169

7 **Theologies That Speak to All?** 170
    7.1   Theology for Ageing Religious or for Apostolic Religious Life More Widely? 170
    7.2   Theology of Religious Life or Theology for All Those Ageing? 178

Bibliography 181
Index 204

Acknowledgments

This work originally began life as a PhD thesis. I am deeply grateful to my two supervisors: Amy Daughton and Susan O'Brien for their generosity, wisdom and firm guidance, and their belief in this Project. Susan brought her own commitment to and knowledge of religious life. Amy was both exceptionally generous with her time and conversation: appropriately challenging, as well as offering real support at difficult times.

Thanks also goes to Sr Gemma Simmonds CJ, who suggested the idea of my pursuing a Doctorate, and to her warm encouragement and conversation over the years. Thank you too to Sr Judith Lancaster SHCJ for being an intellectual and spiritual accompanier and sounding board over many, many years, and similarly Carmen Mangion who shared her enthusiasm and knowledge over coffee in the British Library.

I would like to thank the Margaret Beaufort Institute of Theology, Cambridge for being such a welcoming and stimulating place to study for a doctorate, and Karen Kilby and Paul Murray of the Centre for Catholic Studies at Durham University, who encouraged me to take the final step towards publishing this work.

Thanks to Jane Brearley for always providing helpful comments on the text and for her wit and wisdom.

Most of all I would like to express my enormous appreciation to the five congregations who saw the potential in this project: the Society of the Holy Child Jesus; the Sisters of St Joseph of Peace; the Canonesses of the Holy Sepulchre; the Sisters of the Passion and Cross and the Poor Servants of the Mother of God. They were generous in their recommendations of this research to their sisters. Finally, I want to thank the twelve women themselves and all they have offered me. Sadly, several of these good women have died since making their contributions to this work. They nonetheless remain anonymous, but I hope I return their gift in an expression of appropriate mutuality and desire for communion, and an investment in and hope for the future of religious life for women.

Abbreviations

CCC	Catechism of the Catholic Church
CCL	Code of Canon Law
CICLSAL	Congregation for Institutes of Consecrated Life and Societies of Apostolic Life
CMSWR	Council of Major Superiors of Women Religious
COREW	Conference of Religious of England and Wales
IBVM	Institute of the Blessed Virgin Mary
LCWR	Leadership Conference of Women Religious
PC	*Perfectae Caritatis*
RLI	Religious Life Institute
UISG	Union of International Superiors General
VC	*Vita Consecrata*
VCRM	Voice-Centred Relational Method

CHAPTER 1

Women in Apostolic Religious Life

1.1   Introduction

This book explores the experience and understanding of Roman Catholic sisters[1] of their vocation, or call, to the apostolic form of religious life[2] at a stage in their lives when they are no longer in formal or paid ministry external to their communities. It is based on a series of interviews with a group of British and Irish sisters from five active or apostolic orders founded in England. They were aged between sixty-six and ninety when I first contacted them, an age which mainstream society would consider to be one of retirement, and my research explores to what extent the women would consider themselves as 'retired.' I wanted to understand how these women describe their vocation to service and activity at a time in life when these might be curtailed by physical diminishment and, we might assume, increasingly reduced social interaction and influence.

In this work I am also seeking to hear how the women express themselves theologically. Through listening to and engaging with the sisters' stories, I heard a range of different theologies; their different experiences and truths cannot be expressed in a single theology. Each sister has developed her own theological voice, formed through experience, knowledge, and reflection. I have heard

---

1   'Sisters' belong to apostolic or active orders or congregations, whereas 'nuns' live in monastic or enclosed orders. They live without cloister and have an external ministerial focus such as nursing or education. In this book, I use the terms 'sisters' and 'women religious' interchangeably.

2   Suenens helpfully defines 'apostolic' as bringing "Christ to the world" and "communicating life and grace, in giving Christ to others," reflecting the words of the women in this study. Léon Joseph Suenens, *The Nun in the World: New Dimensions in the Modern Apostolate* (London: Burns and Oates, 1962), 117. A more common usage of 'apostolic' in the Catholic Church is as one of the four marks of the church, professed to be "one, holy, catholic, and apostolic" in the Nicene Creed. The Catechism of the Catholic Church (CCC) explains this apostolic nature as "founded on the apostles … the witnesses chosen and sent on mission by Christ himself," and we are "taught, sanctified, and guided by the apostles until Christ's return, through their successors in pastoral office" (CCC, §857). This final point links to a second common form of usage in the term 'apostolic succession,' or the handing on of authority through an unbroken chain of office. The first of these usages speaks of the mission of the church and the second of the conferring of authority. Both have their roots in the experience and reality of the apostles, initially as Christ's first followers, and second as those who are sent by the apostles in an unbroken chain of succession, in which the sisters in this study would include themselves.

in these voices different experiences of, and perspectives on, apostolic work or ministry[3] which continues to the end of their lives, when physical infirmity and age have stripped them of external ministerial responsibilities. My work both expands on the theology of ministry encountered in the literature on contemporary religious life and points to new theologies of ministry. I draw on concepts such as presence, becoming, and self-gift, unrelated to activity as such, where the self plays a significant role. I have also identified in the sisters' experiences a perspective on apostolic religious life which has ramifications for the identity and theological reality of apostolic religious life for women more broadly.

These women are survivors in many senses, and the religious life they continue to live in the UK finds itself at a very particular point in its history: one of institutional diminishment in terms of visibility, influence, and membership. This issue of declining membership and concern with purpose and identity, particularly but not exclusively in post-institutional congregations, has its roots in the recent history of religious life, particularly since the early part of the twentieth century.

1.2   From Active to Semi-monastic Life: the Historical Context before the Second Vatican Council (1962–65)

From the early days of the Church, women have sought to live a way of life which embraced an external, ministerial, or charitable focus. Medieval historians have established that by the late twelfth century, women were living in community in order to support apostolic works, as part of the Beguine movement of northern Europe, and possibly even a century earlier.[4] Communities of women in simple vows, as opposed to the perpetual vows of established monastic orders, began to be more formally recognized in the fifteenth and sixteenth centuries with the development of the Ursuline order and later, in England and on the Continent, Mary Ward's Institute of the Blessed Virgin Mary (IBVM).[5] However, the idea and reality of women living consecrated lives, unenclosed by convent walls, characterized by some form of common

---

3   Their charitable works were traditionally known as apostolates but now, in Europe, the United States, and much of the Global North, are widely described as ministries.

4   Craig Harline, "Actives and Contemplatives: The Female Religious of the Low Countries Before and After Trent," *The Catholic Historical Review* 81, no. 4 (October 1995): 543.

5   In 2002, the IBVM was renamed the Congregation of Jesus in line with the express wishes of Mary Ward herself to 'take the same as the Society,' with direct reference to the Society of Jesus.

life and working to meet the needs of the poor, has never proved palatable to Church authorities, and the founders of these early congregations had to fight for approval.[6]

Yet this apostolic life form flourished in the late-eighteenth and throughout the nineteenth century in Britain, continental Europe, and the United States so that by the dawning of the twentieth century, there were many hundreds of such congregations unrecognized in the Church. When finally papal recognition and approval came with the Apostolic Constitution *Conditae a Christo* (1900) and its *Normae*, or executive instructions, in 1901, it was something of a mixed blessing.[7] Although this accorded the lifeform validity, with the formal use of the term 'apostolic congregations,' the *Normae* in particular imposed a standardized semi-monastic lifestyle on the women, often taking them away from their original purpose and founding charism. Although many would already have been forced by social norms and pressure from ecclesiastical authorities to live a semi-monastic form of life—for example, the IBVM—the Apostolic Constitution made this a formal legal requirement in Canon Law and part of the price to be paid for the Vatican seal of approval. It had the effect of imposing one uniform model of apostolic religious life upon what had been, to that date, a wide variety of approaches to apostolic work. This led to a curtailing of the women's freedom and of their ability to innovate in apostolic works as these had to fit around a daily *horarium* or rigid timetable of prayer, work, meals, and communal recreation times, and often had to be carried out within the confines of the convent institution.

Thus, this form of apostolic religious life, lived particularly in the UK and the US, was neither apostolic nor monastic, but a 'hybrid' of the two, or what Mangion terms 'the mixed life.'[8] The irony is not only that this was never the form of life that the foundresses of these congregations had intended for their

---

6   Elizabeth Rapley, *The Dévotes: Women and Church in Seventeenth-century France* (Montreal: McGill-Queen's University Press, 1990); James Sweeney, "Religious Life Looks to the Future," in *A Future Full of Hope?*, ed. Gemma Simmonds (Dublin: Columba Press, 2012), chap. 9; Susan O'Brien, "A Note on Apostolic Religious Life," in *The Disciples' Call: Theologies of Vocation from Scripture to the Present Day*, ed. Christopher Jamison (London: Bloomsbury, 2013), 155–66; and O'Brien, "'Yes, But What Do You Do?' What is Distinctive about the Exercise of Ministry by Religious?," paper presented at the Compass Catholic Vocations Projects study day, St. Mary's Church, Moorfields, London, June 6, 2015.

7   D. I. Lanslots, *Handbook of Canon Law for Congregations of Women under Simple Vows* (New York: Fr. Pustet, 1922).

8   Carmen M. Mangion, "The 'Mixed Life': Balancing the Active with the Contemplative," in *Gender, Catholicism and Spirituality: Women and the Roman Catholic Church in Britain and Europe, 1200–1900*, ed. Carmen M. Mangion and Laurence Lux-Sterritt (Basingstoke: Palgrave Macmillan, 2010), 165–79.

membership, but also that, in seeking Vatican approval, they found themselves being further institutionalized under pressure of Canon Law, and societal pressures which preferred not to see women 'abroad.'

O'Brien describes the period between recognition and the years before the Second Vatican Council, held from 1962 to 1965, as one of consolidation of these semi-monastic congregations.[9] Despite the imposed lifestyle, it was, for a period, a very successful model. Services offered by active religious orders at the time met a range of health and educational needs not yet provided for by government and their apostolates, and their commitment to service to the poorest gave them a strong and clear identity which earned them the respect of the Catholic community. Furthermore, their way of life provided opportunities for women in professions otherwise closed to them at the time, as well as the possibility of missionary work for the more adventurous women with plenty of initiative.

Numbers of Catholics both in Britain and the US at the time were at their peak, and the strong support of the Catholic population meant that orders were able to recruit from among people experiencing the insecurity and instability of the impact of two world wars. Thus, the period saw very high numbers of women joining apostolic congregations.[10] It was a time of large novitiates, with groups of women working together in common apostolates, often owned and managed by the congregations themselves. This came to be viewed by religious, the Church, and the Catholic population at large as 'the norm.' It meant that the sudden and quite marked decline in numbers from the late 1950s onwards, and possibly earlier in Britain,[11] was experienced as a serious crisis by both the ordinary Catholic and the hierarchy, especially as the decline in membership has continued to the present day.

1.3 The Second Vatican Council and Apostolic Religious Life

The Second Vatican Council changed the very fabric and understanding of religious life. The two documents dealing specifically with change in apostolic

---

9   Susan O'Brien, "Religious Life for Women," in *From without the Flamian Gate: 150 years of Roman Catholicism in England and Wales, 1850–2000*, ed. V. Alan McClelland and Michael Hodgetts (London: DLT, 1999), chap. 5.
10 Rodney Stark and Roger Finke, *Acts of Faith: Explaining the Human Side of Religion* (Berkeley, CA: University of California Press, 2000).
11 Susan O'Brien, *Leaving God for God: The Daughters of Charity of St. Vincent de Paul in Britain, 1847–2017* (London: DLT, 2017), 280–81.

religious life were *Perfectae Caritatis* (1965) [12] and *Ecclesiae Sanctae* (1966),[13] which set out the approach to the practical implementation of the proposed renewal. However, the documents which pulled the ground out from under the feet of the theological underpinning of apostolic religious life in particular were not necessarily those dealing specifically with religious life. The teaching documents which did this were two of the core documents which articulated the theology and ecclesiology of the Council. The first of these, *Lumen Gentium*, or the *Dogmatic Constitution on the Church* (1964), established the concept of the "universal call to holiness" of each baptized Christian (chapter 5) and, in doing so, blurred the lines between lay and religious vocations.[14] It brought to an end any idea of hierarchies of states in life whereby religious life is a superior or more perfect form of life; as Wittberg claims "In one stroke, it nullified the basic ideological foundation for eighteen centuries of Roman Catholic Religious Life."[15] It left religious as neither fish nor fowl, with sisters and brothers being incorporated into the lay state, and religious priests being drawn further into the category and identity of the ordained. The change contributed to a loss of clarity of the definition and purpose of religious life, its work and identity, particularly in relation to other vocations in the Church, and in terms of ministry and the lay vocation. If religious were no longer special and no longer uniquely called, what was the purpose of religious life?

The second document was *Gaudium et Spes*, or the *Pastoral Constitution on the Church in the Modern World* (1965),[16] which ended the centuries-long hostility of the Catholic Church to the outside and increasingly secular world. This shift in approach heralded an era of *aggiornamento* or opening up to and engagement with the world and its needs, representing an ecclesial 'turn to the world.' This new stance was particularly significant for apostolic women religious as it was instrumental in bringing down the convent walls and grills, as

---

12   Pope Paul VI, *Decree on the Adaptation and Renewal of Religious Life: "Perfectae Caritatis,"* October 28, 1965, accessed April 15, 2012, http://www.vatican.va/archive/hist_councils/ii_vatican_council/documents/vat-ii_decree_19651028_perfectae-caritatis_en.html.
13   Pope Paul VI, *Apostolic Letter: "Ecclesiae Sanctae,"* August 6, 1966, https://www.vatican.va/content/paul-vi/en/motu_proprio/documents/hf_p-vi_motu-proprio_19660806_ecclesiae-sanctae.html.
14   Pope Paul VI, *Dogmatic Constitution on the Church: "Lumen Gentium,"* November 21, 1964, https://www.vatican.va/archive/hist_councils/ii_vatican_council/documents/vat-ii_const_19641121_lumen-gentium_en.html.
15   Patricia Wittberg, *The Rise and Fall of Catholic Religious Orders: A Social Movement Perspective* (Albany, NY: SUNY Press, 1994), 339.
16   Pope Paul VI, *Pastoral Constitution on the Church in the Modern World: "Gaudium et Spes,"* December 7, 1965, https://www.vatican.va/archive/hist_councils/ii_vatican_council/documents/vat-ii_const_19651207_gaudium-et-spes_en.html.

well as the disappearance of habits and structures seen to represent a barrier between apostolic religious and 'ordinary' people.

Many of the depictions of religious life in the years following the Council describe it as something of a roller coaster experience of great excitement, as religious responded vigorously and enthusiastically to the call for renewal,[17] as they were invited to do in *Ecclesiae Sanctae*. Women religious responded to the Council's teachings particularly positively and wholeheartedly, and perhaps more so than any other single group in the Church.[18] The excitement of re-writing constitutions, rediscovering foundresses and charisms, and stripping away the externals that made the 'norms' of twentieth-century religious life so recognizable were, however, replaced by exhaustion and, in many cases, disappointment.[19] Yet many of the changes were ultimately to prove unattractive to both new and large numbers of existing members.

1.4 Implications for the Women in This Study

From this recent historical context, two really significant factors have shaped the religious lives of the women in this book. The first of these, the context of institutional and numerical diminishment, has in turn led to a second: a questioning of both purpose and identity, particularly of apostolic women religious, as they have acquired a new, post-institutional identity.

The upheavals caused by the post-Vatican II re-examination of almost every aspect of religious life provided a significant context to the first factor. The emergence of apostolic or active congregations out of a semi-monastic existence contributed to large numbers of women leaving their congregations.[20] This was followed by a dramatic reduction in the number of new members entering so that there were one million Catholic women religious worldwide in 1960.[21] Yet by 2010, that figure had fallen by almost 30% to 729,371.[22] In the US,

---

17 Vivienne Keely, "Aspects of Mission in Religious Life Since the Second Vatican Council," in *A Future Built on Faith: Religious Life and the Legacy of Vatican II*, ed. Gemma Simmonds (Dublin: Columba Press, 2014), 83.
18 Tony Flannery, *The Death of Religious Life?* (Dublin: Columba Press, 1997).
19 Flannery, *Death of Religious Life?*.
20 Stark and Finke, *Acts of Faith*, 169–70; Diarmuid O'Murchu, *The Seed Must Die* (Dublin: Veritas, 1980); Desmond Murphy, *The Death and Rebirth of Religious Life* (Alexandria, New South Wales: E. J. Dwyer, 1995); and Flannery, *Death of Religious Life?*
21 Stark and Finke, *Acts of Faith*; and Diarmuid O'Murchu, *Religious Life: A Prophetic Vision* (Notre Dame, IN: Ave Maria Press, 1991).
22 *Catholic Herald*, "Number of Catholics in the World Grows by 15m in a Year," February 21, 2011, http://www.catholicherald.co.uk/news/2011/02/21/number-of-catholics-in-the-world-grows-by-15m-in-a-year/.

membership fell 71% between 1966 and 2014,[23] declining from a peak of 181,421 in 1965 to just 39,452 in 2021.[24] Worldwide figures specifically for members of apostolic women's orders reflect a similar trend, falling by 29.3% between 2001 and 2020 to just 417,995, despite the large numbers of women who continue to enter religious orders in the Global South.[25]

In Great Britain, the total number of apostolic women religious declined by 45.5% in the fourteen years between 2006 and 2020, with numbers of novices falling by 38.4%.[26] In 2010, a report for the Compass vocations project found that 49% of sisters in England and Wales were aged over eighty with less than 10% under the age of fifty, and these are also trends which show no indications of change in the medium term.[27] The situation is exemplified in one diocese in northern England where, in the forty-two years between 1980 and 2022, members of congregations of pontifical right declined from 680 to just 90, many of whom are resident in care communities.[28] With the majority of their membership now aged eighty and over,[29] and no entrants for some years, many of these congregations are facing the possibility of disappearing completely from Britain within the next twenty years or so after a presence stretching back two hundred years. The sisters featured in this study all belong to congregations who face such a prospect.

The second factor relevant to the ministerial lives of the women in this study is the development of a post-institutional reality and identity. With a semi-monastic lifestyle imposed upon them through the Apostolic Constitution

---

23 Erick Berrelleza, Mary L. Gautier, and Mark M. Gray, *Population Trends Among Religious Institutes of Women* (Washington, DC: Georgetown University/Center for Applied Research in the Apostolate, 2014).

24 Dan Stockman, "LCWR Leaders Talk about Unprecedented Transformation of Religious Life," *Global Sisters Report*, January 12, 2023, https://www.globalsistersreport.org/news/lcwr-leaders-talk-about-unprecedented-transformation-religious-life.

25 *Annuarium Statisticum Ecclesiae/Statistical Yearbook of the Church* 2006 (Città del Vaticano: Libreria Editrice Vaticana, 2008), 418; and *Annuarium Statisticum Ecclesiae/Statistical Yearbook of the Church* 2020 (Città del Vaticano: Libreria Editrice Vaticana, 2022), 418. Figures are presented according to three classifications: autonomous houses (monastic houses), centralized institutes (apostolic/active congregations), and secular institutes.

26 *Statistical Yearbook of the Church* 2006, 397–98; and *Statistical Yearbook of the Church* 2020, 397–98.

27 National Office of Vocations of the Catholic Bishops Conference of England and Wales and The Compass Project, *Religious Life in England and Wales: Executive Summary* (London: Compass Project, 2010), 7.

28 This is taken from the annual statistics submitted by the Diocese of Leeds to the Vatican, provided by the diocesan archivist in May 2023.

29 National Office of Vocations of the Catholic Bishops Conference of England and Wales and The Compass Project, *Religious Life in England and Wales*.

Conditae a Christo,[30] many apostolic orders developed institution-based corporate apostolates, such as nursing and teaching, which enabled them to live within the confines of a 'total institution.'[31] As they have either chosen or been forced to relinquish these apostolates, many congregations have found themselves engaged instead in a wide range of individualized and sometimes rather disparate ministries. All of the sisters included in this study entered in the period following the Second World War and spent their working lives largely in congregational and/or common apostolates until statutory retirement, and then worked in individualized ministries.

Furthermore, sisters I interviewed in earlier work spoke of how being in 'post-institutional' congregations is affecting their relationship with the hierarchical/institutional Church and local parish as they strive to find a new place for ministry to, and within, the Church.[32] Wittberg describes how, in their former semi-enclosed contexts, women religious experienced influence and power, and the room to grow and develop, living almost beyond the direct control of the institutional Church.[33] Many of these women, who have not traditionally served in parishes, have had to negotiate new roles with priests who are often disinterested, even hostile, or who simply do not understand the potential they may have to offer.

This uncertainty about the role and purpose of religious life in relation to the Church is exacerbated by uncertainty about the identity of religious. Women expressed concerns both about their sense of identity as religious and their lack of visibility.[34] Furthermore, being 'post-institutional,' these religious and their congregations are no longer identified with a clear and well-known 'corporate' ministry, particularly as the majority of apostolic women religious in the UK no longer wear any form of distinctive dress which identifies them as religious. This is something which undermines the potential sign or witness

---

30   Published initially in Latin in 1900, but the Congregation for Bishops and Regulars provided more detailed specifications in the General Norms of 1901. These were made available more widely in Lanslots, *Handbook of Canon Law*.
31   Erving Goffman, "The Characteristics of Total Institutions," in *A Sociological Reader on Complex Organizations*, ed. Amitia Etzioni and Edward Lehman (New York: Holt, Rinehart, and Winston, 1980), 319–39.
32   Catherine Sexton, "Still Life in Us Yet: In Search of a Narrative of Diminishment," paper 2 in partial fulfilment of the Professional Doctorate in Practical Theology (Cambridge Theological Federation and Anglia Ruskin University, 2013).
33   Patricia Wittberg, *From Piety to Professionalism and Back* (Oxford: Lexington, 2006), 89–109.
34   Sexton, "Still Life in Us Yet," 7–8.

value of religious life and thus further serves to weaken the eschatological potential and role of religious.[35]

1.5 The Significance of the United States' Context for the Discourse on Religious Life in the United Kingdom

Post-Second Vatican Council writing in English on religious life is dominated by work originating in the United States, along with a small number of Irish and Australian writers. My concern here is whether the US voices can, and do, apply to the British context, and to ask to what extent those voices have shaped and influenced the British discourse.

Even as I begin to focus more closely on the discourse in the context of the United Kingdom, I still argue that the British discourse cannot be seen in isolation from what has happened in both the Catholic Church as a whole and in religious life in the United States. The US has represented, and continues to represent, a very significant resource for and influence on the British context, and yet the contexts are substantially different.

In the last fifty years, the vibrant North American context has exerted great influence over religious life in Britain, replacing the earlier influence exerted from Ireland and, indeed, France, the birthplace of many congregations now present in Britain. The flourishing theology departments and sabbatical programmes of Catholic universities in the US have attracted many British religious for leadership training and sabbatical programmes. These same universities have trained American women religious theologians and academics who reflect publicly on the state and future of religious life.

Catholic religious life was established in the US at a time when the modern state was in formation, and when Catholicism in America was growing rapidly through mass migration from Europe. Active women religious (more commonly known as 'sisters' in America) supported immigrant communities through large-scale educational, health, and welfare initiatives. The sisters' apostolates were vital from a Catholic perspective, given Protestant hegemony in nineteenth-century America, but in due course their services were also welcomed by the wider society and became socially significant. In this pluralist society with no established religion, the Catholic Church developed a public

---

35   Gemma Simmonds, ed., *A Future Full of Hope?* (Dublin: Columba Press, 2012), 116–28; and Joseph Tobin, "How Did We Get Here? The Renewal of Religious Life in the Church Since Vatican II," in *A Future Built on Faith: Religious Life and the Legacy of Vatican II*, ed. Gemma Simmonds (Dublin: Columba Press, 2014), 36.

presence across all social realms which mass migration from Latin America has sustained in recent decades. As a consequence of this context and history, sisters have enjoyed a high social profile there.

Two investigations into women's religious life in the US, conducted in recent years by the Vatican, have further increased the sisters' profile, establishing them firmly on the moral high ground and winning them significant public support. In 2008, the Vatican's Congregation for the Defence of the Faith, a department with responsibility for overseeing Catholic doctrine, launched a five-year doctrinal evaluation of the Leadership Conference of Women Religious (LCWR). Its membership is highly active in social justice work, of liberal leanings doctrinally, and represents over 80% of American women religious. The Vatican focussed exclusively on the LCWR and not on the smaller, and more traditional, Council of Major Superiors of Women Religious (CMSWR). Thus, it appeared to endorse the traditional congregations while admonishing the LCWR, exacerbating an already highly polarized landscape among American religious and in the US Catholic Church more generally.[36] One year later, in 2009, the Congregation for Institutes of Consecrated Life and Societies of Apostolic Life (CICLSAL)[37] announced a visitation of all congregations of women religious in the United States, overtly driven by concern for the decline in membership.[38] Taken together, these aspects of the North American context may have contributed to a process of radicalization of sisters which has not taken place in Britain. The report produced by the Apostolic Visitation (2014) is largely and unexpectedly (although not unreservedly) positive about the sisters and their commitment to apostolic service. Nonetheless, the Visitation was widely seen and experienced as an attack on sisters, and the sorry episode won them even greater public support.

---

36 John Allen, "Notes on the LCWR Overhaul," *National Catholic Reporter*, April 27, 2012, https://www.ncronline.org/blogs/all-things-catholic/notes-lcwr-overhaul; Phyllis Zagano, "A Very Public Rebuke," *The Tablet*, April 8, 2012, 4–5; Lawrence Freeman, "These are Not Crazy, Dangerous Women. They are Deeply Loved and Respected," *The Tablet*, May 5, 2012, 11–12; and Michelle Bauman, "Vatican Announces Reform of US Women's Religious Conference," CAN/EWTN News, April 18, 2012, https://www.catholicnewsagency.com/news/24757/vatican-announces-reform-of-us-womens-religious-conference.

37 CICLSAL is the Vatican dicastery or department responsible for religious congregations.

38 Thomas C. Fox, "Stonehill Symposium Played a Role in Women Religious Study," *National Catholic Reporter*, November 4, 2009, https://www.ncronline.org/news/stonehill-symposium-played-role-women-religious-study.

1.6 United States Writing: Two Articulations of Apostolic Life for Women

In the decades following the Second Vatican Council, when the first flushes of enthusiasm for the changes had passed and the exhaustion and confusion set in, the focus of writing about religious life, both in the US and in the UK and Ireland, turned to identifying, naming, and analysing what was by then seen as a 'crisis.'[39]

However, looking at the following decades, from the late 1990s onwards, writing began to emerge no longer speaking of crisis, but attempting to provoke sisters into action. It is already looking over the top of the hill and seeing that there is indeed a road ahead. The nature of the road can be seen in at least two articulations of apostolic religious life which appear to be representative of the 'progressive' and 'traditional' perspectives which have emerged in relation to that road ahead. The members of the LCWR and writers such as Joan Chittister, Patricia Wittberg, and Barbara Fiand, all religious sisters themselves, would certainly identify with Sandra Schneiders' more progressive vision of ministerial life (presented below)—and indeed, in places, Schneiders herself positions her model firmly in the LCWR membership.

The more traditional approach to apostolic life was presented at the time in two main sources. The first was in an address by Sr. Sara Butler at the Stonehill Symposium on apostolic religious life in September 2008.[40] In this address, Sr. Sara, Professor of Dogmatic Theology at St. Joseph's Seminary in New York, asked whether the 'essential elements' of religious life had been abandoned by women religious across the US, particularly those influenced by what she terms 'radical feminism,' and particularly the membership of the two leadership conferences, the LCWR, and the men's equivalent, the Conference of Major Superiors of Men (CMSM). Much of her address sought to identify what exactly was the 'treasure' of religious life that needed reclaiming. It can be no

---

39 Helen Rose Fuchs Ebaugh, *Out of the Cloister: A Study of Organizational Dilemmas* (Austin, TX: University of Texas Press, 1977); O'Murchu, *The Seed Must Die*; Flannery, *Death of Religious Life?*; David J. Nygren and Miriam D. Ukeritis, "The Religious Life Futures Project: Executive Summary," *Review for Religious* 52, no. 1 (1993): 6–55; Wittberg, *Rise and Fall*; Murphy, *Death and Rebirth*; and Joan Chittister, *The Fire in these Ashes: A Spirituality of Contemporary Religious Life* (Kansas City, MI: Sheed and Ward, 1995).

40 Sara Butler, "Apostolic Religious Life: A Public, Ecclesial Vocation," address delivered to the "Apostolic Religious Life Since Vatican II: Reclaiming the Treasure; Bishops, Theologians, and Religious in Conversation" symposium, Stonehill College, Easton, MA, September 27, 2008, http://www.zenit.org/en/articles/sister-butler-at-symposium-on-consecrated-life.

coincidence that the first volume of Schneiders' trilogy on ministerial religious life for women used exactly the same biblical imagery.[41]

The second source was a collection of essays by six American religious, predominantly theologians, in a book which constitutes an articulation of the CMSWR's theology of religious life.[42] The main differences between the vision seen in these essays and the work of Schneiders lie in what Butler terms "competing ecclesiologies."[43] A key source for Butler and the CMSWR authors is the teaching document "Essential Elements in the Church's Teaching on Religious Life" (1983),[44] in contrast, as we see below, to the conciliar teaching and theology so central to Schneiders' contrasting vision of ministerial life. Other points of difference can be seen in terminology—for example, in relation to apostolates or ministries, the nature of and locus of the 'apostolate,' the emphasis on a common life, and distinctive dress.

Schneiders claims that member congregations of the LCWR have "birthed a new form of Religious Life," one that embraces a clear preferential option for the poor,[45] which she terms 'ministerial life.'[46] She states that although it is based on the true origins of apostolic religious life modelled on Christ's itinerant ministry, it is also a new form of apostolic life for women. Her ecclesiology is grounded in *Lumen Gentium*, which teaches that while all Christian believers are equally called to minister in the steps of Christ by virtue of their baptism, not all are called to this form of ministerial religious life, which is "a particular

---

41   Sandra Schneiders, *Finding the Treasure: Locating Catholic Religious Life in a New Ecclesial and Cultural Context* (Mahwah, NJ: Paulist Press, 2000).

42   Council of Major Superiors of Women Religious, ed., *The Foundations of Religious Life: Revisiting the Vision* (Notre Dame, IN: Ave Maria Press, 2009).

43   Sara Butler, "Apostolic Religious Life."

44   Sacred Congregation for Religious and for Secular Institutes, "Essential Elements in the Church's Teaching on Religious Life as applied to Institutes Dedicated to Works of the Apostolate," May 31, 1983, https://www.vatican.va/roman_curia/congregations/ccscr life/documents/rc_con_ccscrlife_doc_31051983_magisterium-on-religious-life_en.html. According to the Council of Major Superiors of Women Religious' *Study Guide for the Foundations of Religious Life* (Notre Dame, IN: Ave Maria Press, 2015), 47, the document was apparently written at the request of some US bishops to clarify the guidelines of the Church regarding religious institutes and sets out the Pope's understanding of the ecclesial nature of a religious institute in its origin, mission, and governance.

45   This is a basic principle of Catholic Social Teaching and liberation theology, articulated by the Latin American Bishops Conference at Medellin in 1968.

46   Sandra Schneiders, "We've Given Birth to a New Form of Religious Life," *National Catholic Reporter*, February 27, 2009, accessed November 13, 2012, http://ncronline.org/news/women/weve-given-birth-new-form-religious-life.

assimilation to Jesus's prophetic identity and mission."[47] Schneiders draws on this ecclesiology to differentiate the way she and her LCWR sisters live out ministerial life from the older form of apostolic life in stating that congregations like those of the CMSWR

> read *Perfectae Caritatis* and did what it asked: deepened their spirituality (I hope), and did some updating—shorter habits, a more flexible schedule, dropping customs that were merely weird, etc. We read *Perfectae Caritatis* through the lenses of *Gaudium et Spes* and *Lumen Gentium* and we were called out of the monastic/apostolic mode and into the world that *Gaudium et Spes* declared the Church was embracing after centuries of world rejection.[48]

The two models also differ in their interpretation of the nature of, and emphasis on, community. Unlike the CMSWR writers, Schneiders does not see a life lived physically in common as an essential feature of apostolic/ministerial religious life and believes that community can be achieved through single living, if need be. For her, community must always be driven and shaped by the needs of the itinerant ministerial life.

Schneiders contends that by and large, the old model of apostolic religious life no longer exists.[49] This is not entirely accurate—certainly not in the United States where congregations such as the Nashville Dominicans attract large numbers of young women to a traditional teaching order, and whose website features serried ranks of habited young faces reminiscent of the 1950s. As Stark and Finke show, this model, with what they term high costs and high benefits, is extremely attractive to younger generations.[50] Research conducted by Mahoney found that the majority of women entering religious life in the US want to live in a community located in the same physical location, and not a virtual community.[51] They want to work in traditional apostolates and be

---

[47] Sandra Schneiders, "Religious Life as Prophetic Life Form," pt. 11.6, *National Catholic Reporter*, January 4–8, 2010, accessed November 9, 2011, http://ncronline.org.

[48] Sandra Schneiders, "Discerning Ministerial Religious Life Today," *National Catholic Reporter*, September 11, 2009, accessed November 9, 2012, https://www.ncronline.org/news/discerning-ministerial-religious-life-today.

[49] Sandra Schneiders, *Buying the Field: Religious Life in the New Millennium* (Mahwah, NJ: Paulist Press, 2013).

[50] Stark and Finke, *Acts of Faith*, chaps. 6–7.

[51] Kathleen A. Mahoney, *Catholic Sisters in America: Trends and Opportunities* (Agoura Hills, CA: Conrad N. Hilton Foundation, 2010), 19–20.

externally recognizable by wearing a habit—for example, in direct contradiction to the way of life Schneiders is advocating and, in fact, lives.

There is some anecdotal evidence of a similar trend and views among these groups in Britain.[52] Furthermore, research conducted by Simmonds and Calderón Muñoz with women who were either exploring or had entered religious life since 2000 found a desire for strong community life, lived physically in common, and for some of the external signs such as a religious habit among some of the women they interviewed.[53]

In the years from 2000 to 2020, 277 women entered apostolic institutes in England and Wales, with 190 joining communities of enclosed nuns; so smaller numbers are entering enclosed orders. Nonetheless, the more traditional understanding of apostolic life, lived and worked in common, as articulated by the CMSWR writing, is not being revived in the British context. This may simply be due to insufficient new vocations, or it may be that those of such leaning are drawn to monastic orders, or that they are not staying in religious life. During a symposium with Schneiders in the Religious Life Institute in London in August 2014, the responses from British women religious present clearly indicated that they do not wish to give up community life physically lived in common as easily as she suggests it should be done. Nor do they necessarily feel that 'traditional' apostolates are no longer relevant. Therefore, it would appear that neither of the models established or emerging in the US context are necessarily applicable nor attractive to the British context.

1.7 Discourse on Religious Life in the United Kingdom, 2000–18

In Britain, Catholicism and its women religious have had a very different history to that of their sisters in the United States. Even after the emancipation of Catholics in 1829, with the return from the continent of many exiled congregations and the arrival of newer ones, religious life adopted a low profile in response to a highly charged and negative reaction to the re-introduction of convents and religious life into Britain. There are only a handful of British women religious academics, particularly theologians, and even fewer with a public profile. The only tertiary education managed by sisters was almost

---

[52] Joanna Gilbert, "Young People in Search of Religious Vocation," in Simmonds, *A Future Full of Hope?*, chap. 6; and Cathy Jones, "What is Distinctive about Vocations to Religious Life?," in Jamison, *Disciples' Call*, chap. 8.

[53] Gemma Simmonds and María Calderón Muñoz, *Religious Life: Discerning the Future* (self-pub., 2020).

entirely focussed on teacher education, and there was no Catholic university sector until the twenty-first century. In Britain, there have been no Vatican investigations and public outcry, no lively discussions of obedience or resistance, nor the same level of polarization. Going by the evidence of the extant literature, the culture of women religious in Britain is not as openly assertive. British women religious are not as sure of their identity or place in the hearts of the public or Church as their American sisters.

Perhaps some of this is due to a long-standing atmosphere of anti-Catholicism in Britain, within the political establishment and elite if nowhere else. This meant that few British Catholics paraded their Catholicism publicly. It may also be that just as British religious have responded to, and been influenced by, the situation of religious life in the US, so they have become associated to some extent with aspects of the religious life and the Church in Ireland, portrayed in films such as *The Magdalene Sisters* and *Philomena*. It is hard to draw parallels between the experience of being a religious sister in the UK, where Catholicism has not been mainstream since pre-Reformation times, and those in Ireland, where the Catholic Church is retreating to the margins of society. Nonetheless, religious sisters in contemporary Britain are often either viewed as malicious child molesters[54] or as figures of fun, such as 'Nunzilla.' Over the last three decades or so, the growing awareness of large numbers of incidents of clerical child sexual abuse have forged new stereotypes. These contextual factors would certainly affect the self-image, identity, and confidence of women religious.

This situation has contributed to the dearth of material published in Britain on the present and future of religious life. For many years, almost all of the published material about the theology and practice of religious life read and used by women religious in Britain was written in the US or Ireland. The imbalance in the literature has contributed to the gap in knowledge and discussion in Britain and has also meant that academic research has had to rely heavily upon US sources.

British religious have not responded to the post-conciliar upheaval by publicly critiquing religious life and calling on their fellow religious to respond before it is too late; this has largely been undertaken by the American writers Joan Chittister and Sandra Schneiders on speaking tours to the UK and Ireland, and even more so by the Irish writer Diarmuid O'Murchu. Simmonds notes a certain crisis in identity among British religious, seeing evidence of this in the

---

54 BBC Radio 4, "Where Have All the Good Nuns Gone?," *Woman's Hour*, radio broadcast, November 12, 2013, accessed November 3, 2015, http://www.bbc.co.uk/programmes/b03h2rdn.

lack of information (initially) about religious life and vocations on the website of the Conference of Religious of England and Wales (COREW), whereas information on the social outreach work of religious, particularly in addressing the causes and impact of trafficking, was prominent.[55] Of this, she says, "It is tempting to see the causes as displacement activities, supplying some sort of credentials which the vowed life itself did not." The website was later updated, "but the silence about religious life spoke for itself."[56]

This perhaps contributed to the founding of the Religious Life Institute (RLI) in 2007 at Heythrop College in the University of London.[57] Simmonds writes that it came out of a sense that "the renewal of religious life in Britain and Ireland needed collaborative work towards a renewed theology of the consecrated life."[58] This gap she was identifying was addressed by the RLI, offering courses and seminars on religious life, and a centre for discussion, research, and publications. However, since the establishment of the Independent Inquiry into Child Sexual Abuse (IICSA) in 2015, the work of COREW has been dominated by another issue: the need both to serve the investigations, and to address the issue of safeguarding training needs and procedures among its membership.

Aside from the publications mentioned in this chapter, few books have been published on the theology and development of religious life by British writers in recent years.[59] Individual reflection takes place internally in individual orders—for example, within the Dominicans[60]—but this is often specific to those orders. Of the key books on the future of religious life published in the last decade or so, Simmonds and Jamison do not list or refer to any British writers or works on religious life, nor do they mention any COREW documents or publications.[61]

---

55 Simmonds, *A Future Full of Hope?*, 17.
56 Simmonds, *A Future Full of Hope?*, 17.
57 Since the closure of Heythrop College in 2020, the RLI has been housed at the Margaret Beaufort Institute of Theology in Cambridge.
58 Simmonds, *A Future Full of Hope?*, 18.
59 One exception is a booklet by Ronald J. McAinsh, *Living the Consecrated Life in the Third Millennium* (Chawton, UK: Redemptorist Publications, 2014). There have also been several excellent histories of near-contemporary religious life, including Susan O'Brien's *Leaving God for God*, and Carmen M. Mangion's *Catholic Nuns and Sisters in a Secular Age: Britain 1945–90* (Manchester: Manchester University Press, 2020).
60 Such as Timothy Radcliffe's *Sing a New Song: The Christian Vocation* (Springfield, IL: Templegate, 1999).
61 See Simmonds, *A Future Full of Hope?*; Simmonds, ed., in *A Future Built on Faith: Religious Life and the Legacy of Vatican II* (Dublin: Columba Press, 2014); and Jamison, *Disciples' Call*.

In considering a 'British discourse,' this work focusses on a small number of collections of edited papers presented at symposia and conferences, and on a small number of journal articles. This body of work is largely comprised of papers presented in symposia held with a particular purpose in mind. This means that generally the writers are not responding to, or in dialogue with, each other, but have been invited to address specific aspects of a topic chosen by the host, the RLI, or the Claretian order in hosting the now-annual conference (since 2012) on consecrated life. I am not attempting to define these writers as a group but rather to identify whether they articulate alternative models of apostolic religious life to those coming out of the US which may speak to the context of women religious in Britain today. I also want to clarify the way apostolic religious in the UK understand how they minister, and to whom and why.

1.7.1 Recurring Concerns and Themes

The first striking feature of much of the literature and discourse reviewed here is that although published in the first decades of the twenty-first century, it raises many of the same concerns addressed in the earlier literature of the 1980s and 1990s. This, therefore, suggests that either the situation has not changed, or that it is slightly more difficult in the UK than in the US, where there appears to be more confidence in the future of religious life. First, there is still a sense of religious life being in an ongoing and unresolved crisis.[62] Sweeney refers to "the deep trough in which religious life is currently snared,"[63] noting that the Second Vatican Council led to change which deepened rather than resolved the crises. By 2012, Sweeney had not observed any significant change: "The mood among the established religious orders after all their efforts at renewal is one of puzzled inertia."[64]

Second, these writers are still cautioning religious against denial of the reality of the situation, and against complacency. Collins notes that "some barely surviving forms of religious life are clearly hovering on the verge of extinction,

---

62 James Sweeney, "Prophets and Parables: A Future for Religious Orders," *Informationes Theologiae Europae: Internationales ökumenisches Jahrbuch für Theologie* 4 (2001): 273–92; Sweeney, "Religious Life Looks to the Future," 129–44; Gregory Collins, "Giving Religious Life a Theology Transfusion," in Simmonds, *A Future Full of Hope?*, 23–37; Tony Flannery, "The Death of Religious Life? Seven Years On," *The Furrow* 55, no. 2 (2004): 92–96; Timothy Radcliffe, foreword to Simmonds, *A Future Full of Hope?*, 7–10; and Radcliffe, "Religious Life: Candlemas Time?," in *Envisioning Futures for the Catholic Church*, ed. Staf Hellemans and Peter Jonkers (Washington, DC. Council for Research in Values and Philosophy, 2018), chap. 9.

63 Sweeney, "Prophets and Parables," 278–79.

64 Sweeney, "Religious Life Looks to the Future," 143.

beyond even palliative care"; he further cautions "we do ourselves no favours by choosing to live in a land of denial."[65]

Third, this literature continues to identify the need for a renewed theology of religious life, a need first identified in the early 1980s,[66] and this has continued.[67] This desire to explore more deeply the theological nature of religious and particularly apostolic life is driven by several factors. Schneiders' own theological reflection was shaped by the loss of certainty of purpose and previously unexamined superiority of religious life over the lay state resulting from *Lumen Gentium*'s "universal call to holiness."[68] There is also clear recognition among North American writers that apostolic sisters can no longer be viewed as the workforce of the Church, supplying labour to congregation, Church, and parish apostolates.[69] This conclusion leads them to address the particular purpose of religious life at this time. Although individual religious in Britain may hold this view, it is not being expressed in the current literature.

For Sweeney, theological reflection ought now to focus on what he calls "the fundamental impulse of the apostolic religious life."[70] Despite the years of reworking and revisioning, he sees apostolic orders in particular continuing to find themselves in difficulty. In part he ascribes this to the move away from the 'religious' towards the 'ordinary' within apostolic congregations, and therefore, "while some stabilisation of religious life is now discernible in at least some of the monastic-mendicant inspired orders, for religious life to be fully fit for the future depends ultimately on a renewal within the apostolic paradigm."[71] However, he sees the reasons behind the continuing difficulties in the "apostolic paradigm" as fundamentally historical, relating back to the difficulties religious faced in earning recognition from the Church authorities; "this was especially true of orders of women which were put under pressure, even into the late nineteenth century, to adopt monastic enclosure."[72] Despite

---

65   Collins, "Giving Religious Life a Theology Transfusion," 25.
66   O'Murchu, *The Seed Must Die*; and Sandra Schneiders, *New Wineskins: Re-imagining Religious Life Today* (Mahwah, NJ: Paulist Press, 1986).
67   O'Murchu, *Religious Life*; O'Murchu, *Consecrated Religious Life: The Changing Paradigms* (Manila: Orbis, 2005); Sweeney, "Prophets and Parables"; Sweeney, "Religious Life Looks to the Future"; Collins, "Giving Religious Life a Theology Transfusion"; Simmonds, *A Future Full of Hope?*; and Radcliffe, "Religious Life: Candlemas Time?".
68   Schneiders, *Finding the Treasure*, 124–27.
69   Wittberg, *Rise and Fall*; Schneiders, *Finding the Treasure*; and Schneiders, *Selling All: Commitment, Consecrated Celibacy, and Community in Catholic Religious Life* (Mahwah, NJ: Paulist Press, 2001).
70   Sweeney, "Religious Life Looks to the Future," 139.
71   Sweeney, "Religious Life Looks to the Future," 139.
72   Sweeney, "Religious Life Looks to the Future," 142.

the changes and the efforts to revisit and recapture their founding inspiration, "this apostolic religious life charisma is a difficult 'fit' with the predominant patterns of the institutional church. It was ever so."[73]

So, while some form of crisis is widely acknowledged, few of these writers counsel despair. Sweeney also draws our attention away from an obsession with numbers and other outward signs: "Decline in numbers, institutions, works and influence does not touch the heart of what the religious life tradition has been in and to the church."[74] Radcliffe urges religious to look outward, beyond their own survival, at the crisis of meaning in society.[75] In a 2018 piece,[76] Radcliffe threads his way along a delicate path between hope and the reality of the decline, between light and dark, locating religious life in Candlemas time, half way between the darkness of mid-winter and the spring equinox. He urges religious to accept the fact of the imminent death of many religious congregations, recognizing that for many communities, seeking new members is irresponsible; it is simply not fair to the younger generations. However, he sees a future for religious life in the continuing interest expressed by many younger people, in their desire to commit themselves to Christ, to community, and to others. His hope is rooted in the theological rather than a simply sociological or organizational nature of religious life, and in a theological stance of not knowing but trusting in God that the life will re-emerge in new and still unknown forms.

This British discourse seems to seek both a path which avoids the polemics of the US situation and a form of apostolic or active religious life in between the two 'models'—ministerial or 'progressive' and traditional—articulated in the US writing. This may explain the emphasis on dialogue and a sense of a 'middle way' being forged through the various dualisms which have characterized attempts to describe religious life, particularly since the Second Vatican Council. There appears to be either a conscious or unconscious concern to eschew dichotomies, to move beyond what are identified as two (generally) opposing images or models, and to envisage a more unified religious life.[77]

There also appears to be a concern in the UK to avoid the kind of open conflict between women religious and the Church hierarchy as seen in the US over the last several years: rather to be a bridge or "experts in communion"

---

73 Sweeney, "Religious Life Looks to the Future," 142.
74 Sweeney, "Prophets and Parables," 275.
75 Radcliffe, foreword, 7–10.
76 Radcliffe, "Religious Life: Candlemas Time?".
77 For more on these dualisms, see Kate Stogdon, "'Nothing Was Taken From Me: Everything Was Given': Religious Life and Second Wave Feminism," in Simmonds, *A Future Full of Hope?*, chap. 4.

(*VC*, 1996).[78] This is evidenced by the interest over this period at the RLI in the updating of *Mutuae Relationes* (1978), the Vatican Directive on relationships between religious and bishops, in the wake of the report of the Apostolic Visitation in 2014.[79]

There are two writers in particular who seek to move beyond dualisms. The first is Martin Poulsom, a Salesian priest, who presents two images of religious life.[80] The first are 'Mystics,' for whom the emphasis is on being rather than doing and is identified with the concept of *ressourcement*,[81] and secondly, 'Prophets,' who responded to the call of Vatican II to *aggiornamento*[82] by taking "religious life to the margins of society and church."[83] His call, rooted in the Transfiguration theology of *Vita Consecrata* (§§14–16) is for his own generation of religious to find a way of creating a new language to describe and hold together the contemplative and active dimensions within and across religious life. Poulsom seeks to move beyond the dualism by identifying God's presence in the interaction between these two modes so that "our being and doing are dynamically interlinked" in a reflection of the image of God.[84]

The second writer is James Sweeney, a British sociologist and member of the Passionist order, who also identifies two models: the prophetic and the observant, based on Weber's distinction between the roles of priest and prophet.[85] Sweeney views them as two different articulations of ecclesiology: the prophetic model wishes to transform the Church itself, whereas the observant model stays within the nineteenth-century framework and bolsters the institutional Church.[86] He believes, however, that without dialogue between the

---

78 Pope John Paul II, *Post-synodal Apostolic Exhortation: "Vita Consecrata,"* March 25, 1996, accessed November 23, 2015, http://w2.vatican.va/content/john-paul-ii/en/apost_exhor tations/documents/hf_jp-ii_exh_25031996_vita-consecrata.html.

79 Sacred Congregation for Religious and for Secular Institutes, "Directives for the Mutual Relations between Bishops and Religious in the Church," May 14, 1978, http://www.vatican .va/roman_curia/congregations/ccscrlife/documents/rc_con_ccscrlife_doc_14051978 _mutuae-relationes_en.html.

80 Martin Poulsom, "Sustaining Presence: Religious Life in the Midst of Creation," in Simmonds, *A Future Full of Hope?*, chap. 3.

81 *Ressourcement*: a return to the earlier sources, symbols, and traditions of the Catholic Church, or in this case, the original charism received by the founder of the religious order itself.

82 *Aggiornamento*: the Italian term used during the Second Vatican Council to denote the need for religious life to open up to the world. See also page 5 above.

83 Poulsom, "Sustaining Presence," 56.

84 Poulsom, "Sustaining Presence," 62.

85 Max Weber, *The Sociology of Religion*, trans. and ed. Ephraim Fischoff (Boston, MA: Beacon Press, 1963).

86 Sweeney, "Prophets and Parables," 289.

two models, one will emerge as the dominant model by default: that religious life will be observant unless it is prophetic.

Sweeney turns to the past in order to see the future of religious life— "Religious life has maintained the basic apostolic form inherited from the sixteenth century and relied upon building up its institutional strength … [by way of] adaptive re-institutionalisation"—and asks whether this "received form of religious life" is adequate.[87] He questions the validity of the former, but still extant, form of apostolic life and, in a direct reference to the 2014 decision to 'reform' the LCWR, acknowledges that a completely new paradigm in apostolic religious life may not be possible for fear of taking congregations beyond canonical jurisdiction.[88] Both he and Simmonds[89] note the irony that some women's congregations, in striving for ministerial and charismatic authenticity, may in fact move beyond canonical jurisdiction and be forced to abandon their efforts. Again, the discussion of future forms of religious life comes back to ecclesiology. Sweeney questions whether the institutional Church is ready to face the implications of a fully 'prophetic' model of religious life.[90]

1.8 Rationale for This Study

I undertook this work partly in response to calls for a renewed understanding of the theological nature and purpose of apostolic religious life at a time when many apostolic congregations continue to question their identity and discuss the theological meaning and place of the 'apostolic impulse' in religious life.[91] Most women's congregations have, in the post-conciliar period, made great efforts to live out of a renewed and shared understanding of their founding charism and its relevance for today.

---

87   Sweeney, "Prophets and Parables," 284.
88   Sweeney, "Religious Life Looks to the Future," 142.
89   Gemma Simmonds, "Religious Life: A Question of Visibility," in Simmonds, *A Future Full of Hope?*, chap. 8.
90   Sweeney, "Prophets and Parables," 289.
91   O'Murchu, *The Seed Must Die*; O'Murchu, *Consecrated Religious Life*; Schneiders, *Finding the Treasure*; Schneiders, "Religious Life as Prophetic Life Form," pts. 1–5, *National Catholic Reporter*, January 4–8, 2010, accessed November 9, 2011, http://ncronline.org; Collins, "Giving Religious Life a Theology Transfusion," 23–37; and Sweeney, "Religious Life Looks to the Future," 129–44. The phrase 'apostolic impulse' comes from Sweeney, "Religious Life Looks to the Future," 139.

Arbuckle observed that many religious congregations

> are not sure about the meaning, contemporary relevance or mission of religious life and ... find it difficult to cope with often rapidly declining numbers, few or no vocations, and the rising average ages of membership.[92]

Although that observation was made over thirty years ago, the latter part of the statement continues to be a reasonably accurate representation of the situation of the majority of women religious in Britain today. Nevertheless, I found a slightly different, more positive response to this situation when I investigated the language of diminishment widely used as a descriptor of the current state of religious life.

Some twenty years ago, I undertook consultancy work with a congregation of apostolic or active sisters. Their congregation was founded to minister to young people, something the sisters had done faithfully for many years. Now, however, with an average age of seventy-three and few younger women entering, the sisters seemed conflicted about how to continue to live their vocation to active ministry in later life, and, indeed, about what ministry itself means in old age.

Although the word 'diminishment' is often used in connection with women's religious life, and sisters themselves are only too aware of the absence of newer members coming behind them, it was not a word which the sisters easily embraced. I noted they often preferred the language of 'there's still life in us yet' and 'we need to keep going until the end.' I interpreted this as a form of resistance to being defined by others, but also considered whether it reflected a fear of a loss of purpose entangled with a sense of grief for the numerical diminishment of their own congregations, and for their own increasing physical or mental frailty. I was also left with questions about sisters' attitudes towards diminishment and their reception of this as a descriptor of their religious life at this point in its history. Listening to these rather unexpected responses led me to reframe my questions away from exploring the specific experience of diminishment to considering how older and more infirm sisters continue to live apostolic life. I wanted to understand how sisters make meaning and sense of their apostolic vocation in old age, and how this contributes to the evolving theology and identity of apostolic religious life for women.

Schneiders stated that in writing *New Wineskins* she was addressing a gap left by the fact that none of the (then) contemporary theologies of religious

---

[92] Gerald Arbuckle, *Out of Chaos: Refounding Religious Life* (London: Geoffrey Chapman, 1987), 1.

life had been written by women. She argued that theological reflection undertaken by religious women tends to be rooted in their everyday experience of religious life, and for this they do not need to be trained in systematic theology. I am not challenging her observation, but the point here is that even without the training in theology, this theological reflection either has not taken place in the UK or has not found its way to publication. There may yet be a very small window of opportunity for religious women to rediscover and articulate the meaning of their apostolic vocation as they have emerged from semi-monastic enclosure and engage with the contemporary world, and before many of their congregations cease to exist in the UK. However, British publications on religious life reviewed in this work have resulted in three books comprising a total of thirty-one essays, plus introductions, in addition to a number of independent articles.[93] Of these, nine are contributions from seven individual women religious. A new annual conference on consecrated life inaugurated in 2012 by the Claretians was initially widely criticized for putting forward an all-male line-up of speakers to address a majority ageing female audience. This was later addressed, and recent speakers have included both apostolic and monastic women religious.

The British discourse offers a number of theological concepts which are of use in describing and underpinning the apostolic impulse, and from a range of perspectives. However, the fact remains that, first, none of these give voice to a comprehensive interpretation of, or model for, emerging apostolic religious life, and particularly not for women, which could sit alongside those coming from the US; and second, they are ordained men who do have the theological education. If, as Schneiders proposes, women do not need a formal theological education to reflect theologically on their lives, then there is an opportunity and a need for these voices to be heard. This is particularly so for those women who are least represented but now form the majority: those over the age of 75, who through their lived commitment have forged an apostolic practice on which to reflect.

1.9 Structure of This Book

In this first chapter, I have offered an introduction to the recent historical context of apostolic religious life for women and an overview of relevant literature from the English-speaking world. In doing so, I identify the gap in which

---

[93] For example, Radcliffe, "Religious Life: Candlemas Time?," and Gemma Simmonds, "Professed Religious Life," in *The Cambridge Companion to Vatican II*, ed. Richard R. Gaillardetz (Cambridge: Cambridge University Press, 2020), 266–81.

I will present the voices of older women religious and explore their theological understanding of ministry in later life.

However, in chapter 2, I take a slight detour to present the method I devised to enable me to hear those women's voices, and to address the increasing reliance of the field of practice-engaged theology[94] on social science research methods. Drawing on a novel combination of holy listening, the Voice-Centred Relational Method (VCRM) and *Lectio Divina* allowed me to listen attentively to the voices of the individual women as they begin to emerge from the interview texts, which I identify as constituting suitable material for *Lectio*. Thus, I approach method as a theological enterprise, making the work 'theological all the way through.' Readers with limited interest in research methods, even ones with theology in their hearts, may choose to move swiftly on to the later chapters; but I argue that it was this method that enabled me to enter into the lived experiences of the women I interviewed.

Chapter 3 demonstrates how the sisters' understanding of 'apostolic' changed over their lives. I find the sisters hesitant to describe themselves as either apostolic or ministerial, which leads to a discussion of the language sisters use or claim in order to describe or name themselves and how they are apostolic. I identify the importance of their process of narrative becoming. The sisters' growing concern for self is partly based on challenges faced in being able to develop as themselves, in a context where their gifts and interests have often been subverted to the needs of their institutions. Therefore, their sense of self is shaped in the interplay between self, other, and their communities.

In chapter 4, I name the sisters' apostolic identity in terms of being with and being for. This takes their self-understanding beyond one defined by employment or a specific task, so that the nature of apostolic religious life becomes recognized as comprising not what sisters do or what they are, but who they are. The integration of self and apostolic is taken one step further as the centrality of the narrated self to their understanding of being apostolic until the end of their lives becomes clear. This is the self each sister has become through her openness to conversion by the God "who participates in our personal becoming and makes us more rather than less the selves we seek to be."[95]

---

[94] I acknowledge Clare Watkins' use of the term 'practice-engaged theology,' as found particularly in her most recent book *Disclosing Church: An Ecclesiology Learned from Conversations in Practice* (London: Routledge, 2020). I find 'practice-engaged theology' a helpful place in which to locate this work, which is neither systematic theology nor sociology, but which also does not fit in with many of the models in or approaches to the field of practical theology.

[95] Stogdon, "'Nothing Was Taken From Me,'" 73.

I then frame the sisters' experience of being apostolic until the end of their lives in terms of three emerging forms of ministry: a ministry of presence, an explicit form of ministering to each other in a new context when the majority of their Province[96] or congregation is of a similar demographic, and aging together and ministering to their carers. I argue that these forms of ministry contribute to a new self-understanding of apostolic or active religious life, both in old age and more broadly. I recognize the sisters' form of being apostolic as both incarnational and sacramental in making God's presence a reality, through their ministry to others and their relationships, as the sisters constitute signs for others to help them in their own journeys to God.

Throughout chapters 5 and 6, I identify and work with the concept of self-gift as a unifying feature of the theological concepts operant in the data gathered: availability, and gift as reciprocity and mutuality. In recognizing that these concepts underpin the three emerging forms of ministry, the chapters present a theology which gives expression to the lived experience of the sisters in a context of increasing physical constraints. Through the emergence of these forms of ministry, the sisters can be obedient to their context of physical limitations and resulting social diminishment in a way which contributes to service and continues to be dialogical and relational. Bringing Schneiders' theology of ministry as gift into conversation with the sisters' experiences of a ministry of presence, to each other and to and with their carers, suggests a different theology of ministry unrelated to activity.

---

96   Province: a geographical area used as an administrative or governing unit for many congregations—for example, the English Province.

CHAPTER 2

Treading on Holy Ground: Listening for Absent Voices

2.1 Introduction

My starting point for this work was an observation that the voices of older British women religious in particular are minimally represented in the literature in this field available in English. In seeking to address this lack, I drew on three distinct but related bodies of theory to inform how I listened to and heard these voices: an epistemology of hermeneutical phenomenology, a feminist research approach, and reflexivity. Together they represent a means of addressing the conceptual issues arising from my central concern to hear and interpret the experiences of religious women in living their vocation to apostolic religious life. Although reflexivity is usually considered an intrinsic element of feminist research methodology, I claimed it as a separate tool in recognition of what I think is prefigurative for me in terms of my previous experiences of religious life. I would like to offer a brief rationale for the choice of these theoretical bases, which formed the basis of a concrete research design, and informed my choice of specific methods of data collection and analysis, before then moving on to explore those specific methods.

2.2 Theoretical Basis for Research Design

2.2.1 *An Approach to Interpretation: Hermeneutical Phenomenology*

The first of the critical or theoretical tools upon which I drew is phenomenology, as my aim was to observe, be attentive to how the situation appeared, and allow the sisters to speak for themselves. Collinson describes 'pure' phenomenology as a method of observing and describing objects or phenomena, with a focus on observing its intentionality or a recognition that what is being observed includes "an object intentionally within themselves."[1] It is achieved through paying attention to the object's own intentionality or its interiority and experience of being aware of a particular thing. Phenomenology "seeks to begin by not making assumptions about whether the things described really

---

1 Diané Collinson, *Fifty Major Philosophers: A Reference Guide* (New York: Routledge, 1987), 128.

exist or not,"[2] adopting the position that an object is only 'real' in our perceptions of it. This is why Knott considers a phenomenological approach appropriate in the study of religion, in order to understand "the 'insider' position while refraining from forming a judgement as to its truth or falsity."[3]

Furthermore, I was concerned with how I might interpret and make my own meaning from that data, in that I was also seeking an interpretation or hermeneutic of participants' actual experience and articulation of that experience. In this case, the methodology is, therefore, necessarily interpretivist. It begins with our lived experience of a situation and "seeks to explore the complex dynamics of particular situations in order to enable the development of a transformative and illuminating understanding of what is going on within these situations."[4]

This interpretivist approach means that a 'pure' or even a descriptive phenomenological approach is not appropriate or possible here. A key element of Husserl's phenomenology is the idea of reduction or bracketing off not only of the question of existence of the 'phenomena,' but also of the preconceptions and assumptions which the observer might bring into the process, and describing what remains after the 'bracketing.'[5] Husserl's concept of 'bracketing' contrasts with my own approach of acknowledging the experience and perspectives I, as researcher, bring to the research process. While I accept the usefulness of observation and description in the phenomenological approach, my own position is influenced by Ricoeur's understanding of phenomenology as a hermeneutical task. Hermeneutical phenomenology seeks both to understand and explain, emphasizing the relationship between these acts, and the subject-object relationship.[6] I believe that I cannot and do not wish to bracket off my experience, responses, and assumptions, and that these responses and my interpretation as the reader of the text to be a necessary part of the process, valid in itself. I am not aiming for a pure, objective description or for a "transcendental phenomenology,"[7] and I am not pursuing this ideal of purity of

---

2 David Pellauer, *Ricoeur: A Guide For the Perplexed* (London: Continuum, 2007), 11.
3 Kim Knott, "Insider/outsider Perspectives," in *The Routledge Companion to the Study of Religion*, ed. John R. Hinnells (London: Routledge, 2005), chap. 13.
4 John Swinton and Harriet Mowat, *Practical Theology and Qualitative Research* (Canterbury: SCM Press, 2006), xvii.
5 Collinson, *Fifty Major Philosophers*, 129; Swinton and Mowat, *Practical Theology and Qualitative Research*, 111; and Paul Bazeley, *Qualitative Data Analysis: Practical Strategies* (London: Sage, 2013), 9.
6 Paul Ricoeur, *Hermeneutics and the Human Sciences*, trans. and ed. John B. Thompson (New York: Cambridge University Press, 1981), 105.
7 Pellauer, *Ricoeur*, 64.

intention towards what I am observing as a "pure knower" coming to this work with a "view from nowhere."[8]

Swinton develops Gadamer's notion of the 'fusion of horizons' to propose that the interpreter cannot be removed from the research process, arguing that the researcher bringing her own meaning into the research is not only useful, but necessary in the interpretive endeavour.[9] My own perspective recognizes that the voices of the participants are not the only source of data. As researcher and participant, I and the women interviewed are bound together and engaged in a task of joint sense-making. I believe that knowledge as to how the sisters continue to be, or understand themselves to be, apostolic when no longer in formal employment is constructed both through the conversation taking place as part of this study, and also through my hearing and interpretation of their words.

2.2.2   A Feminist Approach

The second critical tool I drew on is a feminist approach. I say 'approach,' as there is little if any consensus among feminist writers on a distinct form of feminist methodology.[10] Some writers reject the notion altogether.[11] The lack of a common understanding of a feminist research methodology largely results from the wide range of ontologies and epistemologies employed by feminist researchers. However, most see feminist methodology comprising the following elements: the provision of insights into the lives of women which we would not otherwise access;[12] the recognition of the value and worth of those voices; and making a difference to those lives on a personal and/or political level.[13] It is essentially a 'view from somewhere' in the emphasis it places

---

8   Pellauer, *Ricoeur*, 65.
9   John Swinton, "'Who is the God We Worship?' Theologies of Disability; Challenges and New Possibilities," *International Journal of Practical Theology* 14, no. 2 (2011): 286.
10 Liz Stanley and Sue Wise, *Breaking Out Again: Feminist Ontology and Epistemology* (London: Routledge, 1993); Mary Maynard, "Methods, Practice and Epistemology," in *Researching Women's Lives from a Feminist Perspective*, ed. Mary Maynard and June Purvis (London: Taylor and Francis, 1994), chap. 1; and Maithree Wickramasinghe, *Feminist Research Methodology: Making Meanings of Meaning-making* (New York: Routledge, 2010).
11 Shulamit Reinharz, *Feminist Methods in Social Research* (Oxford: Oxford University Press, 1992); Stanley and Wise, *Breaking Out Again*, 188; and Nicola Slee, *Women's Faith Development: Patterns and Processes* (Guildford: Ashgate, 2004).
12 Caroline Ramazanoglu and Janet Holland, *Feminist Methodology: Challenges and Choices* (London: Sage, 2002), 147.
13 Maynard, "Methods, Practice and Epistemology"; Ramazanoglu and Holland, *Feminist Methodology*; and Wickramasinghe, *Feminist Research Methodology*.

on the importance of the context and position of the researcher, and on the social-cultural context and experience of the research participants. For Slee, the key is to ground the methodology in "feminist principles of research."[14] She understands that the fundamental principle is to "deliberately privilege women and girls as the focus of our study."[15] This is a particularly appropriate principle to apply in research which seeks to privilege the unheard voices of British women religious speaking about their own context and experience.

A hermeneutical phenomenology in this instance is strengthened by an epistemological framework which not only privileges the women's voices and experience, but values them as a contribution to producing knowledge about this topic. It allows the privileging of the women's own voices in developing an understanding of the 'apostolic impulse' to which Sweeney alludes.[16] A feminist approach connects its epistemology to the realities of the women's situation. It favours a strong and symbiotic relationship between ontology and epistemology.[17] Although the women participants have lived their lives within autonomous religious congregations, these are 'nested' within, and regulated by, a highly patriarchal institution which regards its received teaching as the transmission of a body of truth and rarely concedes that the women themselves and their experience have a contribution to make. Moreover, for many religious orders, the highest authority has to be a male cleric such as the relevant bishop, the Pope, or in some congregations with male and female members, a male general superior. The women's autonomy is circumscribed by this reality as the investigation into the Leadership Conference of Women Religious (LCWR) showed. This, in turn, is recognized by feminist theology, which views Church institutions as sexist. "Feminist theology is first and foremost a critical comment on the sexist, exclusive character of theological reflection and church practice," states Hogan,[18] who also claims that "the dominant

---

14   Slee, *Women's Faith Development*, 43.
15   Nicola Slee, "Feminist Qualitative Research as Spiritual Practice: Reflections on the Process of Doing Qualitative Research," in *The Faith Lives of Women and Girls: Qualitative Research Perspectives*, ed. Nicola Slee, Fran Porter, and Anne Phillips (Farnham: Ashgate, 2013), 17.
16   James Sweeney, "Religious Life Looks to the Future," in *A Future Full of Hope?*, ed. Gemma Simmonds (Dublin: Columba Press, 2012), 139.
17   Stanley and Wise, *Breaking Out Again*; and Wickramasinghe, *Feminist Research Methodology*.
18   Linda Hogan, private correspondence, cited in Janet Eldred, "Community, Connection and Caring: Towards a Christian Feminist Practical Theology of Older Women" (PhD diss., University of Leeds, 2002), 16, accessed June 24, 2015, http://etheses.whiterose.ac.uk/642/.

experiences of women in the Christian tradition have been of exclusion and marginality."[19]

The extent to which this applies to women religious may be further evidenced by their lack of participation in the formulation of papal teaching on religious life. Examples of this include the experience during the 1994 *Lineamenta* preparation,[20] and in the recent history of women religious in the United States who have only been able to articulate publicly in the Church context their lived understanding of apostolic religious life through a prolonged battle with the Vatican involving two formal investigative processes. Therefore, in adopting this feminist (and feminist-theological) approach I am expressing my own position of belief in the validity of the women's experiences, voices, and opinions as a source of knowledge.

2.3 The Centrality of Women's Experience and Attendant Challenges

Women's experience is central to feminist research methodology. It is also the starting point and the primary resource for reflection in Christian feminist theology.[21] However, both fields recognize that this centrality can present methodological problems. Experiences tend to be articulated as individual rather than collective and can lead to fractured findings and analysis, presenting challenges to developing unified or universalized perspectives. This is particularly the case in feminist theology, where grounding theological reflection in individual women's experiences (both negative and positive) has the potential to undermine some of Christianity's core teachings, as well as the Christian identity claims of the researcher.[22]

Over-reliance on experience as the sole source for research is thought to be insufficient to demonstrate validity claims.[23] The "unmediated subjectivity" of experience demands "interpretation, evaluation and critique," and needs to be taken beyond the individual in order to make wider connections,[24] although

---

19 Linda Hogan, *From Women's Experience to Feminist Theology* (London: Sheffield Academic Press, 1997), 104.
20 See Vivienne Keely, "Aspects of Mission in Religious Life Since the Second Vatican Council," in *A Future Built on Faith: Religious Life and the Legacy of Vatican II*, ed. Gemma Simmonds (Dublin: Columba Press, 2014), 81–102.
21 As exemplified by works such as Rosemary Radford Ruether, *Sexism and God Talk* (London: SCM Press, 1983), and Hogan, *From Women's Experience to Feminist Theology*. See also page 31 below.
22 Hogan, *From Women's Experience to Feminist Theology*.
23 Maynard and Purvis, *Researching Women's Lives*, 6.
24 Hogan, *From Women's Experience to Feminist Theology*, 17.

TREADING ON HOLY GROUND: LISTENING FOR ABSENT VOICES   31

as we have seen, subjectivity still plays a role—and often a welcome one. The impact of postmodernism on feminist methodology is seen in its questioning of the previously assumed direct link between experience, knowledge, and reality.[25] Its opposition to metanarratives or grand narratives,[26] which might seek to 'explain' or underpin an analysis such as the patriarchal nature of the Church, has also had an impact. Nevertheless, none of these writers abandons their emphasis on the importance of grounding feminist theory and theological reflection in experience. Instead, Radford Ruether answers these concerns by recognizing the bias inherent in all research; Hogan calls for the recognition of difference and diversity to be central to feminist theological methodology; and Maynard re-emphasizes the role of the researcher in the interpretation and representation of texts, complementing Ricoeur's theory of the interpretation of the text. Ramazanoglu and Holland, after full consideration of the reasons for and against considering experience as a source of knowledge, conclude that "there is a case for grounding feminist knowledge in experience," but maintain that there is a continuing role for interpretation.[27]

I acknowledge the potential limitations of grounding my research in women's experience and voices. However, this approach continues to be the best means of accessing 'knowledge' held by the participants. Their experiences and my interpretation will be necessarily individualistic and subjective, and I value the women's experience as 'holy ground' which includes "experience of the divine, experience of oneself and experience of the community and the world, in an interacting dialectic."[28] It is a source of revelatory experience and theology which Radford Ruether claims begins with the individual.[29] I also value the sisters' encounters with me in this research process, and acknowledge the validity of the experience I bring to the interpretive process.

2.4   Reflexivity

The third aspect of my conceptual approaching to interpreting my data is reflexivity. A feminist approach also allows for the researcher to 'write herself into'

---

25   Maynard, "Methods, Practice and Epistemology", 18–23; and Ramazanoglu and Holland, *Feminist Methodology*, chap. 5.
26   Jean-François Lyotard, *The Postmodern Condition: A Report on Knowledge* (Manchester: Manchester University Press, 1984; first pub. 1979), cited in Ramazanoglu and Holland, *Feminist Methodology*, 93–94.
27   Ramazanoglu and Holland, *Feminist Methodology*, 127.
28   Radford Ruether, *Sexism and God Talk*, 12.
29   Radford Ruether, *Sexism and God Talk*, 13.

the process. Having been brought up as a lay woman in the Roman Catholic Church, I have, to a large extent, been shaped by the institutional experience of not having a voice or role in shaping theological knowledge. Reinharz recognizes that for many feminist researchers 'finding a voice' is a central part or even aim of the research process.[30] A feminist-influenced methodology also recognizes that the researcher herself will bring valid perspectives to the process. Swinton names this specifically in recognizing the researcher herself as "the research tool."[31] This recognition, particularly from a feminist perspective, demands that the researcher embraces both self-disclosure and reflexivity in her work.

According to McCutcheon, adopting a "reflexive stance" entails adopting "a position which addresses the manner in which all observations are inextricably linked with the self-referential statements of the observer."[32] Such a stance attempts to note the feelings, responses, experience, and thoughts of the researcher, and to be aware of how these might affect and shape the research process and findings. It forms a research practice which thereby enables the researcher to "[examine] his or her personal impressions and responses to experiential encounters and record these reflections."[33]

The complexities of my relationship and connections with my research participants made it important to state my location in relation to them. Pillow proposes that "a reflexive focus requires the researcher to be critically conscious through personal accounting of how his/her self-location, position and interests influence all stages of the research process."[34] Pillow also sees several benefits of working reflexively in that it "assists in understanding and gaining insight into the workings of the social world, but also ... how that knowledge is produced";[35] and to this end, "remaining critically reflective in this context is

---

[30] Reinharz, *Feminist Methods*, 16.
[31] John Swinton, "Where is your Church? Moving Toward a Hospitable and Sanctified Ethnography," in *Perspectives on Ecclesiology and Ethnography*, ed. Pete Ward (Cambridge: Eerdmans, 2012), 81.
[32] Russell T. McCutcheon, ed., *The Insider/Outside Problem in the Study of Religion* (London: Cassell, 1999), 9, cited in Helen Meads, "Insider Research into 'Experiment with Light': Uncomfortable Reflexivity in a Different Field," *Quaker Studies* 11, no. 2 (2007): 285, accessed June 9, 2015, http://www.academia.edu/152231/Meads_Helen._Insider_Research_into_Experiment_with_Light_Uncomfortable_Reflexivity_in_a_Different_Field.
[33] Mary Clark Moschella, "Ethnography," in *The Wiley-Blackwell Companion to Practical Theology*, ed. Bonnie J. Miller-McLemore (Chichester: Wiley-Blackwell, 2012), 225.
[34] Meads, "Insider Research," 285–86, referring to Wanda Pillow, "Confession, Catharsis, or Cure? Rethinking the Uses of Reflexivity as Methodological Power in Qualitative Research," *International Journal of Qualitative Studies in Education* 16, no. 2 (2003): 178.
[35] Meads, "Insider Research," 285–86, referring to Pillow, "Confession, Catharsis, or Cure?," 178.

vital,"[36] thus linking the issue of insider/outsider stance with that of reflexivity. There were two specific reasons why it seemed important for me to embrace reflexivity as a research practice: first is that I have had a long and multi-faceted engagement with religious life and an initially assumed position of being an 'insider'; and second is in recognition of my 'insider' status as a Catholic.

2.5 My Engagement with Religious Life

My engagement with religious life has been almost lifelong. My awareness of an interest in or call to religious life began in my late teens, and time spent living in religious communities discerning a vocation has given me some 'insider' knowledge of both apostolic and monastic religious life. I have also had professional experience of working with women's apostolic congregations, first as a facilitator and accompanier of change processes which led to my being exposed to a deeper engagement with the issues of diminishment and apostolic women's ministerial focus; and second as a researcher on the Religious Life Vitality Project, work which has brought me into contact with a wide range of sisters and congregations.

My experience of the context of diminishment in congregations inspired my original interest in this topic and my curiosity as to what motivates apostolic religious women to be so driven in ministerial terms, and to be so driven to the end of their lives. However, I realized that my approach was also coloured by that very personal experience of discerning a vocation to religious life, which has at its heart a vocational and spiritual search which is lifelong. Furthermore, the personal nature of my own previous encounters with religious life highlighted the need for me to cultivate an awareness of my own stance in relation to women religious.

2.6 Insider/Outsider Stance

One of the primary ways in which I have used reflexivity is to attempt to clarify my insider/outsider stance in relation to the women participants. This question of where the researcher stands in relation to those being researched is increasingly relevant in practice-engaged theology where theologians as researchers draw on empirical and social science research methods. In such

---

36   Helen Cameron and Catherine Duce, *Researching Practice in Ministry and Mission: A Companion* (London: SCM Press, 2013), 91.

settings, researchers are often internal to their own faith context,[37] and this near assumption that our position is straightforwardly one of an insider adds to the necessity of a fuller examination of this in my case.

Some of the comments of the women I was researching made me realize that I considered myself to be more of an insider to religious life than the participants did, even after my 'disclosing' that I had discerned my own religious vocation with two different religious orders. Nonetheless, this 'outsider' stance still has value and validity in terms of offering perspectives those 'inside' may not be aware of.

The second rationale for embracing reflexivity concerns my own identity as a Roman Catholic. In terms of my faith identity, I consider myself an 'insider,' at least through upbringing and cultural contexts. Orsi reflects on the experience of being neither insider nor outsider and attempting to work in this context with integrity. His "complex autobiographical relationship" with the Roman Catholic community he was researching results from his discovery that, having distanced himself from Catholicism, his one remaining link was a cultural one, which he felt did not afford him the intuition and insight he had believed he had[38]—a situation not unlike my experience with religious life.

Knott offers a continuum of positions,[39] from observer to participant, but I am certainly neither of these, and perhaps the closest—"the participant-observer"[40]—does not particularly address my stance either in relation to Roman Catholicism or religious life as I am not fully either, and neither am I attempting to act as an interpreter for either context to the outside world. Labaree also rejects the insider/outsider binary, seeing it instead as a "continual process of introspective enquiry which researchers can use to monitor their position, view and conclusions."[41] Collins is helpful in that he moves beyond both dichotomy and typology, making them largely redundant, and offers a postmodernist view of "a more processual society and a more dynamic self, in which worlds are overlapping and interactive rather than isolated and separate."[42] He understands all research participants to be creating "social

---

37   Cameron and Duce, *Researching Practice in Ministry and Mission*, 91.
38   Robert Orsi, *Between Heaven and Earth: The Religious Worlds People Make and the Scholars Who Study Them* (Oxford: Princeton University Press, 2005), 149.
39   Knott, "Insider/outsider Perspectives," 246.
40   Knott, "Insider/outsider Perspectives," 252.
41   Meads, "Insider Research," 282, referring to R. V. Labaree, "The Risk of 'Going Observationalist': Negotiating the Hidden Dilemmas of Being an Insider Participant Observer," *Qualitative Research* 2, no. 1 (2002): 97–122.
42   Knott, "Insider/outsider Perspectives," 269, referring to Peter J. Collins, "Connecting Anthropology and Quakerism: Transcending the Insider/Outsider Dichotomy," in

meaning through the common practice of story telling,"[43] which breaks down insider/outsider boundaries and allows for in-out movement.

The positions taken by Labaree and Collins complement those of Ganiel and Mitchell, who conclude that "most people occupy some place in-between" the insider/outsider binary.[44] Like Collins, they challenge the dominance of this particular binary in consideration of researcher and participant relations. They contend that this is only one lens through which to view that relationship, and that not only is it not fixed, but it "can be changed through the research process itself."[45] Of the writers cited above, they alone ask whether this religious identity, however flexible and permeable, is really the basis for our relationship with research participants, as it will comprise a range of multiple identities (such as role in academia, nationality, and reputation) which will shape our response. Ultimately, they found that they identified with their respondents on spiritual and emotional levels in ways which overcame doctrinal positions, issues of insider/outsider binaries, "and often mediated social categories,"[46] concluding that "emotional engagement between researcher and respondent ... becomes more significant than their initial social assumptions about one another."[47] This conclusion challenged my own concern with my insider/outsider status in relation to both Catholicism and religious life, and places a new emphasis on the actual nature and quality of the relationship in both spiritual and emotional terms, offering a new way of viewing the focus on insider/outsider.

In this section, I have presented the complexities of my insider/outsider experience and relationship with my research participants, and therefore my reasons for taking a reflexive approach to my research. Following this exploration, I found myself asking whether this was a critical tool or simply a method and, regardless, how I was going to use it—and more importantly, whether it would add anything to the quality of this work: "Does all this self-reflexivity produce better research?"[48] In the following section, I hope to show that the answer was positive.

Theorising Faith: The Insider/Outsider Problem in the Study of Ritual, ed. Elisabeth Arweck and Martin D. Stringer (Birmingham: Birmingham University Press, 2002), chap. 5.

43   Knott, "Insider/outsider Perspectives," 269.
44   Gladys Ganiel and Claire Mitchell, "Turning the Categories Inside-out: Complex Identifications and Multiple Interactions in Religious Ethnography," *Sociology of Religion* 67, no. 1 (2006): 17.
45   Ganiel and Mitchell, "Turning the Categories Inside-out," 17.
46   Ganiel and Mitchell, "Turning the Categories Inside-out," 18.
47   Ganiel and Mitchell, "Turning the Categories Inside-out," 16.
48   Daphne Patai, "When Method Becomes Power," in *Power and method: Political Activism and Educational Research*, ed. Andrew Gitlen (New York: Routledge, 1994), 69.

Method as Holy Listening and Sacred Reading

2.7.1 *Introduction*

My aim in taking some time to set out my approach to data analysis in particular here is twofold. First, it begins with what I see as problematic. Much of the research taking place in practice-engaged theology is empirical and therefore continues to be largely reliant on methods of data collection and analysis drawn from the social sciences[49] so that revealing or articulating the theological character of empirical research, making a thesis 'theological all the way through,'[50] can be a challenge. I wanted the design of my research to reflect the depth of the theological encounter—the 'holy listening'[51] at the heart of research interviews—and to carry that through into reflective data analysis by means of 'sacred reading.'

Second, I want to show how my approach to method constitutes a form of research as contemplative enquiry which is theological in nature and acknowledges the theological character of this work. My combining the analytical rigour of a method from the social sciences—the Voice-Centred Relational Method (VCRM)[52] and thematic content analysis (TCA)—with a theological 'tool,' *Lectio Divina*, converted empirical research methods into 'an act of primary theology'[53] which can be theologically formative for all those involved in the research. In this, I draw attention to the theological character of this work, and that empirical research, in the widest sense, can be 'an act of primary theology' and theologically formative when we are engaging in God-talk with participants. I conclude that the approaches to participants and the texts constitute more than simply method but rather "holy listening" and "sacred reading" and are, therefore, strongly theological. Based on the quality of my encounters with

---

49   One notable exception would be Theological Action Research. For an explanation of this approach, see Helen Cameron, Deborah Bhatti, Catherine Duce, James Sweeney, and Clare Watkins, *Talking about God in Practice* (London: SCM Press, 2010).
50   Cameron et al., *Talking about God in Practice*, 51.
51   Margaret Guenther, *Holy Listening: The Art of Spiritual Direction* (London: DLT, 1993). Guenther uses this term to refer to the practice of spiritual direction, but I apply it more widely to my practice as a researcher.
52   Natasha Mauthner and Andrea Doucet, "Reflections on a Voice-centred Relational Method: Analysing Maternal and Domestic Voices," in *Feminist Dilemmas in Qualitative Research: Public Knowledge and Private Lives*, ed. Jane Ribbens and Rosalind Edwards (London: Sage, 1998), chap. 8.
53   David M. Mellott, *I Was and I Am Dust: Penitente Practices as a Way of Knowing* (Collegeville, MN: Liturgical Press, 2009), 91.

the research participants, themselves arguably 'living gospels,'[54] and the depth of wisdom found therein, I propose that the women's voices constitute material suitable for engagement through the practice of *Lectio Divina*.

2.7.2 *Laying the Groundwork for Listening*
2.7.2.1   Choice of Research Methods
Based on the theoretical and critical principles I set out in the previous section, I drew on qualitative methods of data collection as these value and celebrate "the richness, depth, nuance, context, multi-dimensionality and complexity" of the social world.[55] This form of exploratory approach through open-ended questioning rather than a fixed-question survey allows the researcher to dig deeper into individual responses.

My interview strategy consisted of two rounds of interviews. In the first, I explored the women's apostolic activities and what these had meant to them and their understanding of who they are as religious. After completing the initial analysis of the first-round data, I then conducted a second round of interviews with the aim of hearing the sisters' responses to these first findings, and eliciting any further thoughts or comments. This second round acted as a form of 'participant validation' and served to deepen the conversation.

Member-checking or participant validation is widely viewed by feminists and others as an opportunity to address participants' lack of power in the research process.[56] I followed the method of analysis I used for the first round. I had also posed four particular questions to the sisters, asking them to reflect a little on the process, and to engage with two new questions which had emerged for me.

Such interviewing can produce a rich and 'thick description' of Christian life and practices which lends itself to the theological reflection that is identified as a primary element of practical or practice-engaged theology.[57] The format of semi-structured interviews allows the researcher to be more adaptable in her approach, and freer to probe, following up ideas as they arise.

---

54   Michael Casey, *Sacred Reading: The Ancient Art of Lectio Divina* (Liguori, MI: Liguori Publications, 1996), 104.
55   Jennifer Mason, *Qualitative Researching* (London: Sage, 2002), 1.
56   Sharlene Hesse-Biber, "The Practice of Feminist In-depth Interviewing," in *Feminist Research Practice: A Primer*, ed. Sharlene Hesse-Biber and Patricia Leavy (Thousand Oaks, CA: Sage, 2007), 113–47; Swinton and Mowat, *Practical Theology and Qualitative Research*; and David Silverman, *Interpreting Qualitative Data*, 4th ed. (London: Sage, 2014).
57   Swinton and Mowat, *Practical Theology and Qualitative Research*; and Julie Lunn, "Paying Attention: The Task of Attending in Spiritual Direction and Practical Theology," *Practical Theology* 2, no. 2 (2009): 219–22.

2.7.2.2 Criteria for Selection of Congregations

I adopted a purposive sampling strategy.[58] Within this, I considered three factors: the nature of the congregation to which the sisters belonged, the age of the sisters, and the extent to which they were still in formal or paid external ministry. I contacted participants from active or apostolic congregations. One of the five congregations is slightly different in that the sisters live a form of life which is canonical: apostolic, but lived in a stable contemplative community with external ministries, as opposed to the mobile form of life lived in fully apostolic congregations. The Code of Canon Law of 1917 makes no distinction between this form of congregation and an apostolic one, but only between apostolic and monastic congregations.[59]

I decided to restrict my sampling frame to English foundations of women religious. This was for two reasons. First, my sample was likely to be necessarily limited in scope, with small numbers of likely and eligible participants from a small number of congregations. It was clear I would not be able to claim that this would be representative of British apostolic women religious. Therefore, I decided to limit the size of the wider population and recruit only from English foundations.

A second reason to focus on English congregations was to attempt to limit the cultural influences exerted on the sisters being studied and, therefore, the findings. Many congregations present in the UK were founded in France, Italy, or Ireland, where the cultural and ecclesial contexts are very different. O'Brien, in her study of the Daughters of Charity, found that the culture of their founding country, France, was deeply embedded in their life in Britain, and this would equally be the case with other international foundations.[60] My study focusses on the voices of British women and draws on literature written in English. I attempted, therefore, to identify a group of congregations which were English foundations so that there might be minimal Italian, French, or other external cultural influence on the sisters' understanding of religious life.

There was a different and specific reason to limit the involvement of Irish foundations, in that many were initially diocesan foundations established by a bishop and not of pontifical right, which entails being approved by, and under

---

58   Alan Bryman, *Social Science Research Methods* (Oxford: Oxford University Press, 2004), 33.
59   D. I. Lanslots, *Handbook of Canon Law for Congregations of Women under Simple Vows* (New York: Fr. Pustet, 1922), chap. 1.
60   Susan O'Brien, *Leaving God for God: The Daughters of Charity of St. Vincent de Paul in Britain, 1847–2017* (London: DLT, 2017).

the protection of, the Vatican.[61] Therefore, their understanding and explorations of 'apostolic' in relation both to their identity and to ministry would have been constrained by this history and patrimony. However, religious congregations are increasingly recognized by historians and sociologists as transnational in character,[62] and in practice, even English foundations present in the UK comprise members of varied cultural and ethnic backgrounds, often with Irish sisters representing a significant percentage of the membership. This was reflected in the profile of the participants, whereby six were English, five were Irish, and one Scottish.

O'Brien identified up to eighteen English foundations in the UK,[63] but it was difficult to establish their continued existence or to find personal contacts within many of them. I identified five congregations who might be willing to participate and had sufficient sisters remaining to be considered still viable.

2.7.2.3 Profile of Interview Participants

All prospective participants were 'recruited' through contact with the relevant superior, generally the Prioress or Provincial Superior. The twelve sisters interviewed were all formally retired from paid ministry external to their communities. Ten had been teachers who had later taken up pastoral work; one was a retired probation worker; and one had worked in domestic duties in her own congregation's houses, originally as a lay sister.[64] Two sisters had internal roles

---

61 The distinction between the legal character of diocesan and pontifical right was formally established in *Conditae a Christo* (1900). For a fuller explanation of this, see Carmen M. Mangion, "The 'Mixed Life': Balancing the Active with the Contemplative," in *Gender, Catholicism and Spirituality: Women and the Roman Catholic Church in Britain and Europe, 1200–1900*, ed. Carmen M. Mangion and Laurence Lux-Sterritt (Basingstoke: Palgrave Macmillan, 2010), 165–79.
62 Robert Wuthnow and Stephen Offutt, "Transnational Religious Connections," *Sociology of Religion* 69, no. 2 (2008): 209–32; Helen Rose Fuchs Ebaugh, "Transnationality and Religion in Immigrant Congregations: The Global Impact," *Nordic Journal of Religion and Society* 23, no. 2 (2010): 105–19; Deirdre Raftery, "Teaching Sisters and Transnational Networks: Recruitment and Education Expansion in the Long Nineteenth Century," *History of Education* 44, no. 6 (2015): 717–28, accessed August 7, 2017, https://www.researchgate.net/publication/283116476_Teaching_Sisters_and_transnational_networks_recruitment_and_education_expansion_in_the_long_nineteenth_century; and Anne O'Brien, "Catholic Nuns in Transnational Mission, 1528–2015," *Journal of Global History* 11 (2016): 387–408, https://doi:10.1017/S1740022816000206.
63 Susan O'Brien, "Religious Life for Women," in *From without the Flaminian Gate: 150 years of Roman Catholicism in England and Wales, 1850–2000*, ed. V. Alan McClelland and Michael Hodgetts (London: DLT, 1999), chap. 5.
64 Up until the 1950s and later, many congregations maintained a two-tier system, usually class-based, of choir and lay sisters. Lay sisters generally worked as domestic servants in their congregations' houses. Many Irish sisters who entered teaching orders in the

in their own congregation's retreat houses; five were retired but still involved in voluntary ministries outside their communities, largely in parishes; four were largely limited to ministry within their home community. Three sisters lived alone; two lived with just one other member of their congregation; five lived in communities of four or more sisters; and one was resident in a care community.[65]

2.8 Holy Listening: Encounters with Religious Women

In reflecting on how I related to the women in these interview encounters, I was aware that my attitude towards them was shaped by the very fact of their being religious. Although I just narrowly fit into the category of the 'post-Vatican II generation,' I was brought up in a time when women religious were still very visible in the Church, and my encounters with them then, and later in life, engendered a sense of respect for this 'superior' form of life. Consequently, while I recognize that they as individuals have probably had a lifetime of struggling with commitment on a daily basis, I am aware of viewing them as "religious virtuosi."[66]

Furthermore, my own experience of discerning a vocation to religious life shaped my view of women religious. During the interviews, I observed for myself that I saw them, by and large, as women who were living a life that I had at one time thought I was called to. Although clear I had not wanted to stay in religious life, working with these women awoke in me some residual questioning of whether that sense of vocation had been fully laid to rest. This may have been compounded by the fact that all the interviews were held on the sisters' home ground, in religious communities. The hospitality offered by the sisters, and the food, prayer, and chatting both before and after the interviews, often centred on my own vocation and relationship with religious life. One sister even assured me that I was not yet too old for religious life, commenting, "I'm sure someone will still have you."

Consequently, instead of being easily able to embrace the feminist recognition of the power all being in the possession of the researcher, I actually

---

UK became lay sisters. See Barbara Walsh, *Roman Catholic Nuns in England and Wales, 1800–1937: A Social History* (Dublin: Irish Academic Press, 2002), 125, 142, 197.

65 During the course of the study, another research participant moved to her congregation's care community.

66 Patricia Wittberg, *The Rise and Fall of Catholic Religious Orders: A Social Movement Perspective* (Albany, NY: SUNY Press, 1994), 13–22, following Max Weber.

often felt, like others before me,[67] rather exposed and vulnerable. However, I do believe that this choice to self-disclose aided a sense of mutuality and trust. The women could at least be certain that they were telling their stories to someone who valued religious life and was likely to honour their lived experience.

2.8.1   The Interviews: a Third Presence in the Space in Between

I conducted all the first interviews over a period of six months. Increasingly within the actual interviews, I began to experience a sense of something else happening on a level deeper than simple conversation or information gathering: almost an enriched sense of my being and presence through my encounters with the women themselves. I felt somehow more fully myself. I identified this in Merton's terms as "that *scintilla animae*, that 'apex' or 'spark' which is freedom beyond freedom, an identity beyond essence, self beyond ego, a being beyond the created realm and a consciousness that transcends all division, all separation," as I saw that my research might actually take the form of contemplative inquiry.[68]

After carrying out the second interviews, I wrote in my research journal that it had felt oddly reminiscent of some of the practice sessions conducted in my earlier training as a spiritual director. I was reminded of that sense of God being present in the space in between the director and directee. In the "concentrated human encounters" that are research interviews,[69] when the talk is of God and, therefore, theological, it is surely unsurprising for those involved to experience the presence of God. Conroy, in reference to the supervision of spiritual directors, writes that "awareness of God's presence in spiritual direction and supervision sessions is essential, resulting in spiritual directors becoming interiorly freer to linger more deeply with directees' experiences."[70] She notes that this is the case because "spiritual directors are in relationship with God and have a desire to help others find God." The three-way encounter

---

67   Ann Oakley, cited in Andrea Fontana and James H. Frey, "The Interview: From Structured Questions to Negotiated Text," in *Collecting and Interpreting Qualitative Materials*, 2nd ed., ed. Norman J. Denzin and Yvonna S. Lincoln (London: Sage, 2003), 83; and Dawn Llewellyn, "Maternality Matters: Self-disclosure, Reflexivity, Participant Relationships and Researching Motherhood," paper presented at "The Faith Lives of Women and Girls" symposium, The Queen's Foundation, University of Birmingham, October 25, 2014.
68   Thomas Merton, *Love and Living*, ed. Naomi Burton Stone and Patrick Hart (New York: Farrar, Straus, and Giroux, 1979), 9, cited in Bernadette Flanagan, "*Quaestio Divina*: Research as Spiritual Practice," *The Way* 53, no. 4 (2014): 128.
69   Swinton and Mowat, *Practical Theology and Qualitative Research*, 63.
70   Maureen Conroy, *Looking into the Well: Supervision of Spiritual Directors* (Chicago, IL: Loyola University Press, 1996), 5.

is described as "the threefold communication of the spiritual director, directee and God," and, indeed, as explicitly Trinitarian.[71]

This analogy is helpful in several ways. First, the idea of "becoming interiorly freer to linger more deeply" with the heard experiences points to the possibility and necessity of a practice of attentive listening, which allowed me to develop a view of contemplative engagement with the text as a form of *Lectio Divina*, which I explore later in this chapter. Second, the analogy reflects my experience of being, in this context, not only 'director' but also 'directee,' as one engaged in spiritual conversation and 'talk about God' with a director or accompanier, and in receipt of the gift of their wisdom. And so, at times, the power imbalance leads to role reversal in an unexpected direction.

Continuing with the analogy of spiritual direction, Conroy notes that although accompanying another, the spiritual director nevertheless experiences "a variety of interior reactions, such as *consolation or movement toward God*, ... [and is] drawn into the experience—attracted, engaged, and resonating with [its] sharing."[72] This she attributes to the director herself being a "prayerful" person "drinking regularly from the living waters of God's loving presence."[73] The participants in this study were most certainly "prayerful" people, and yet I felt that I, as researcher, was also accompanying them, and in this also as attentive to God's presence as a theologian operating as researcher strives to be.

Conroy works within the tradition of Ignatian spirituality, and so draws on the concept of the discernment of the movement of spirits introduced by St. Ignatius Loyola in the Rules for Discernment of the first week of his *Spiritual Exercises*.[74] In these Rules, Ignatius identified movements of the spirit which affect our interior lives, and which might drive us to action. He saw the need for discernment of the sources of the movement, whether from a good spirit, which he called a sense of consolation or a movement towards God, or of the Spirit, or from the evil spirit, or a counter-movement, known as desolation. Conroy notes that a director may experience both consolation and desolation, becoming bored, feeling restless, distracted and "move away from a contemplative stance to a problem-solving, preaching and advice-giving stance."[75] I recognized this ebb and flow in several ways, and when I reflected on this later in my research journal, it actually resonated with that Ignatian sense of movement

---

71 Conroy, *Looking into the Well*, 8.
72 Conroy, *Looking into the Well*, 7, emphasis original.
73 Conroy, *Looking into the Well*, 8.
74 David Fleming, *Draw Me into your Friendship: A Literal Translation and a Contemporary Reading of the Spiritual Exercises* (Saint Louis, MO: Institute of Jesuit Sources, 1996).
75 Conroy, *Looking into the Well*, 8.

of the spirits: a flowing between desolation and consolation. Initially it was in recognition and awareness of the presence, influence, and actions of God in the present and in our lives. Sr. Collette, in her interview, spoke at length about seeking to work out of a 'contemplative stance' rooted in the present moment. She undoubtedly influenced the way I thought about a more explicit practice of working contemplatively in that awareness of the presence.

This most open and energizing listening felt holy and "care-full."[76] Reflecting back now, the sense of consolation seems to have been a confirmation of a vocation to research, and to 'talk about God.' That is what we were engaged in: 'talk about God,' or faith seeking understanding. Together in this context, we were engaged in meaning-making, and we were doing theology.

Reflecting on the interview as a theological encounter puts the focus back on me and what I took away from it as a researcher, reinforcing the idea that I had the power in this process. Slee notes that feminist practical theologians must embrace "the conviction that our work is not just for us, but for others: first and foremost, our research participants."[77] I would concur with this, although it is difficult to know how or whether my work impacted upon the participants, or what ramifications it may have beyond this small group. I can, however, observe and record that it appears to have had a lasting impact on me. I finish this section with a final reference to Slee, who refers to researchers participating in "a kind of paschal process ... a sharing in the passion of God to make and remake the world" where I was formed and transformed as a researcher.[78]

2.8.2   *After the Interviews: the Process of Data Analysis*
2.8.2.1   The First Component of Method: Choosing the Voice-Centred Relational Method (VCRM)

I had intended to approach data analysis through use of thematic coding. However, early on in the process, I noted that the women all used story as a way of reflecting on their coming to understand their apostolic vocation: "Story represents the mode nearest to experience, most concrete and accessible, and yet ... [remains] most capable of capturing the complexity, dynamism and nuanced nature of lived experience."[79] I realized I was hearing narratives that

---

76   Mary Clark Moschella, *Ethnography as a Pastoral Practice: An Introduction* (Cleveland, OH: Pilgrim Press, 2008), 141.
77   Slee, "Feminist Qualitative Research," 22.
78   Slee, "Feminist Qualitative Research," 24.
79   Slee, *Women's Faith Development*, 68.

deserved careful and attentive listening. I began to view each transcribed text as "a subjective document worthy of attention and study in its own right."[80]

This made me wary of moving too quickly into thematic coding. I was struck by the language associated with coding: a language of 'breaking open' the data; chunking; splitting; lumping; dissecting; breaking down; distilling, cutting up, reducing and "fracturing."[81] I realized these terms jarred with me and my experience of the women as individuals. Furthermore, I feared this might contradict the approach of seeing each transcript as a complete text in itself.[82] Like Slee, I found that "narrative emerged from the women's interviews as a primary and fundamental mode of patterning experience."[83] I wanted an approach that would allow me to listen attentively, present to the women's telling of themselves.

The process of data analysis had really begun in the interviews. Consequently, I was already recognizing the extent to which my research participants saw themselves as relational. I was, therefore, open to an interpretation of their spirituality being highly relational.[84] In my search for a method, I encountered the Voice-Centred Relational Method (VCRM).[85] VCRM is rooted in the work of Gilligan and the Listening Method developed by Brown and Gilligan.[86] VCRM has at its heart a relational ontology or "selves-in-relation"[87] and places particular emphasis on three principles: first, spending as much time as possible hearing the 'I' voice and perspective of research participants;[88] second, acknowledging fully and making room and time to explore the influence of the researcher in shaping and determining the analysis; and third, emphasizing the relationship between the researcher and the participants, and relationality more broadly.

---

80   Mauthner and Doucet, "Reflections on a Voice-centred Relational Method," 136.
81   A. L. Strauss, *Qualitative Analysis for Social Scientists* (Cambridge: Cambridge University Press, 1987), cited in Bazeley, *Qualitative Data Analysis*, 144; Mauthner and Doucet, "Reflections on a Voice-centred Relational Method," 138; and Virginia Braun and Victoria Clarke, "Using Thematic Analysis in Psychology," *Qualitative Research in Psychology* 3, no. 2 (2006): 77–101, http://dx.doi.org/10.1191/1478088706qp063oa.
82   Sharon Kaufman, "In-depth Interviewing," in *Qualitative Methods in Aging Research*, ed. Jaber F. Gubrium and Andrea Sankar (Thousand Oaks, CA: Sage, 1994), 136.
83   Slee, *Women's Faith Development*, 68.
84   Carol Gilligan, *In a Different Voice: Psychological Theory and Women's Development* (London: Harvard University Press, 1982); and Slee, *Women's Faith Development*.
85   Mauthner and Doucet, "Reflections on a Voice-centred Relational Method."
86   Gilligan, *In a Different Voice*; and Lyn Mikel Brown and Carol Gilligan, eds., *Meeting at the Crossroads: Women's Psychology and Girls' Development* (Harvard: Harvard University Press, 1992).
87   Mauthner and Doucet, "Reflections on a Voice-centred Relational Method," 125.
88   Mauthner and Doucet, "Reflections on a Voice-centred Relational Method," 119.

The method's recognition of the importance of reflexivity in the researcher echoes my own concern with representing and respecting what I heard from the women in a way that "embodies respect for individual respondents."[89] I concluded that this method would also enable me to remain with and among the voices in the deeply contemplative way of working I was already developing.

2.8.2.2 The Four Readings of the VCRM

The method comprises up to four structured and intentional readings of transcripts. There are two aspects to the first reading. The first is to identify the overall story being told by the participant through the main events, subplots, and characters. The researcher listens for "recurrent images, words, metaphors and contradictions in the narrative"[90] so as to "follow the unfolding of events ... (the who, what, when, where, and why of the narrative)."[91] As I worked through the first reading and took notes which I formed into a short narrative report on the interview, noting each of the elements above.

In the second 'reader-response' part of the first reading,[92] I read to listen to how I responded to the text, attempting to hold an awareness of my own thoughts and feelings in response to both text and participant. As I read the text, I 'wrote myself in' to my analysis by noting my own responses and recording them in the short report I was producing on each transcript, using a different coloured font.

The purpose of the second reading is to read for the 'I' voice of the participant: listening for "how she speaks of herself before we speak of her."[93] VCRM encourages and enables the researcher to stay with the participants' voices for as long as possible before trying to fit what she hears into her own categories.[94] In practice, this was difficult, as I noticed that I was now again identifying sub-themes and codes, having begun this to a limited extent before settling on the VCRM as a method for analysis. In effect, I found myself coding in something of an ad hoc way, and, therefore, I decided simply to note potential

---

89 Mauthner and Doucet, "Reflections on a Voice-centred Relational Method," 135.
90 Mauthner and Doucet, "Reflections on a Voice-centred Relational Method," 126.
91 Brown and Gilligan, *Meeting at the Crossroads*, 27.
92 Mauthner and Doucet, "Reflections on a Voice-centred Relational Method," 127.
93 Brown and Gilligan, *Meeting at the Crossroads*, 27–28.
94 Carol Gilligan, Renee Spencer, Katherine Weinberg, and Tatiana Bertsch, "On the Listening Guide: A Voice-centred Relational Model," in *Qualitative Research in Psychology: Expanding Perspectives in Methodology and Design*, ed. Paul M. Camic, Jean E. Rhodes, and Lucy Yardley (Washington, DC: American Psychological Association, 2003), 169.

themes within the short report, and to return to a more formal thematic coding after I had finished the four readings.

The process of working with VCRM and the thematic coding thus became intertwined and iterative. Initially it felt overwhelming to work with two such different processes, one feeling very vertical, and the other horizontal, almost forming a matrix through which I was viewing the text. However, using the two different tools brought both the narratives and the themes to life, and ultimately the findings of both became mutually reinforcing, as the coding later reinforced the narratives that emerged.

I took notes on the second reading and wrote up a second short report, commenting on the use of 'I.' I began to pay more attention to narratives and how independent self-contained or nested narratives are used to illustrate a point. I then incorporated these notes into the initial reports, either strengthening the 'subplots' identified in the first reading and naming these as narratives, or noting new narratives.

In an effort to identify the plot(s) in each text, I wrote a short two-to-three-page summary of the chronological or important events, as the chronological sequence of events itself seemed initially to present the main story and the way of making meaning of their lives and ideas. I was also trying to identify patterns across the participants, so I began to work more horizontally. Moreover, I wanted to see if there was any connection between particular events and a changed understanding of what it means to be apostolic.

Mauthner and Doucet recommend selecting smaller sub-sets for the later readings.[95] For this third reading, focussing on relationship, I selected four participants whose talk of relationship seemed particularly rich. I printed out another set of transcripts, and using coloured pens I highlighted all discussion of, and reference to, relationship and noted how this covered the vast majority of the text. I focussed on each sister's relationships with their community and congregation, as an institution and with individuals; friends; family; the neighbourhood; God; her relationship with herself; and general theorizing about relationship, or presenting canonical narratives about relationship.[96] These categories were inductive in that they emerged from the first and second readings of each text. At the end of each third reading, I wrote another short report drawing together comments on relationship in the above categories, highlighting significant quotations as instances, and making observations as to how these categories were developed and addressed in the text.

---

95 Mauthner and Doucet, "Reflections on a Voice-centred Relational Method."
96 Ann Phoenix, "Analysing Narrative Contexts," in *Doing Narrative Research*, 2nd ed., ed. Molly Andrews, Corinne Squire, and Maria Tamboukou (London: Sage, 2013), chap. 3.

I then selected a different set of four participants for the fourth reading so that I conducted at least three readings of as many of the participants' texts as possible. I read to listen for the interplay between the participants' narratives and voices and their environment in terms of organizations and institutions, cultures and contexts, "placing it within broader social, political, cultural and structural contexts."[97] Some participants I selected for this reading had either particularly complex relationships with their congregations, or striking attitudes towards the institution of the Church. I selected others for whom the socio-cultural or historical context had been significant. I wrote another short report on my reading of each of the four texts and noted significant contextual or institutional factors that arose, and how the participant had spoken of these in her interview.

The VCRM is not prescriptive or directive and, therefore, is very adaptable. However, the concomitant disadvantage is that it does not always provide enough guidance on how to use the material gathered. The method generates a great deal of data extra to the actual transcripts in the form of analytical reports on the original texts. I was uncertain how to use these separate reports and whether or not to bring them together. What I did note, even when I worked on the second readings, was that little new emerged from the further readings. For Mauthner and Doucet, one of the advantages of the method is that of "tuning our ear" to the data and voice and story of each participant, allowing them to be more fully heard.[98] I experienced this to be very true, and the purpose of the further readings seem to be fine-tuning and deepening rather than encountering new elements.

If the actual interview and then the transcribing are processes where researcher power becomes an operant issue, then this is even more so at the stage of data analysis, which can be "a deeply disempowering stage"[99] for participants as they have no control over their representation, underlining the need for researcher reflexivity. Mauthner and Doucet call this stage "the moment when we are most powerful and voices can be lost,"[100] concluding that "data analysis is our most vulnerable spot."[101]

At the end of the process, I had a 'main' report on each interview, incorporating the first and second readings. This focussed on drawing out and substantiating (with quotations, line references, and some analysis) the main narratives

---

97   Mauthner and Doucet, "Reflections on a Voice-centred Relational Method," 132.
98   Mauthner and Doucet, "Reflections on a Voice-centred Relational Method," 134.
99   Mauthner and Doucet, "Reflections on a Voice-centred Relational Method," 138.
100 Mauthner and Doucet, "Reflections on a Voice-centred Relational Method," 138.
101 Mauthner and Doucet, "Reflections on a Voice-centred Relational Method," 123.

I had identified, as well as some initial highlighting of sub-themes. I also had a further report from a third or fourth reading on each participant. Although time consuming, this method means that those transcripts read formally for the third and fourth times are necessarily engaged with at a deeper level.

VCRM claims to promote a highly reflexive stance and an inductive approach: "bringing the listener into responsive relationship with" participants.[102] I did find myself very immersed in the world of each participant, and throughout this period I felt I was going quite deeply down, vertically, into each person's voice and stories such that at one stage I had the image of being among a wood of twelve straight tree trunks, moving among them and almost embracing each one in turn. I felt I was physically sitting among these women, in what Slee calls "an intermingling of lives that leaves us profoundly changed by the process."[103]

Mauthner and Doucet claim that working vertically as opposed to linking themes immediately "helps maintain differences between respondents," and the method does indeed serve to emphasize their individuality.[104] Perhaps because I was so deeply immersed in each personality, I then found it difficult to 'extract' myself from what, by this stage, was the privilege of a close-up, 'holy' encounter with a group of individuals rather than 'data.' I feared that I would overlook an element or "lose the complexity" of each woman's voice and story.[105] However, I recognized the necessity of this next step of identifying commonalities across the data. This was then the point to move to thematic analysis and try to connect the branches and start seeing the wood as well as the trees.

2.9 The Second Component of the Method: Listening for the Voice through Sacred Reading

So far, I have been describing and reflecting on the first of the two social science methods of data analysis I used to work with the data. It would make sense in logical terms for me to proceed to the second of those methods, which was the thematic coding. However, this would not reflect the chronological story of my own engagement with the women's voices. In order to do that, I will again adopt the attitude of 'holy listening' to consider how I read and engaged with the transcripts as texts through Sacred Reading, within and across the VCRM.

---

102 Mauthner and Doucet, "Reflections on a Voice-centred Relational Method," 135.
103 Slee, "Feminist Qualitative Research," 20.
104 Mauthner and Doucet, "Reflections on a Voice-centred Relational Method," 135.
105 Mauthner and Doucet, "Reflections on a Voice-centred Relational Method," 135.

I was taught the 'art' of *Lectio Divina* as an approach to contemplative reading and prayer through contact with communities of Benedictine and Cistercian nuns, and I have continued with a daily practice. This has had a significant influence on how I read in general and, in particular, on how I engaged with the texts. Casey speaks of the deep sense of respect and of reverence for the text with which early monks came to *Lectio Divina* or Sacred Reading.[106] Like Slee,[107] I found myself standing on holy ground, whereby reading for the 'I' voice felt a particular act of reverence. I decided, therefore, to explore whether I could bring anything of my own daily practice of *Lectio* into conversation with a method of reading the transcripts. In reality, it happened the other way around.

Lectio Divina is an ancient monastic practice whose four stages of *lectio* (reading), *meditatio* (meditation), *oratio* (prayer), and *contemplatio* (contemplation) were set out by the twelfth-century Carthusian monk Guigo II, literally as four rungs on the ladder of ascent towards Christ.[108] It enabled monastics to use Scripture as a source of prayer, but sought to minimize or contain subjectivity in prayer, while also allowing deep engagement with a particular word or passage which caught the reader's attention.

It is tempting to draw parallels between *Lectio Divina* and the VCRM. Both have 'stages.' Casey likens the process to painting a wall, whereby "two or three coats of paint" are necessary.[109] The process is circular rather than linear, much like the hermeneutical process itself, as we visit and revisit, deepen and move from top to bottom and from bottom to top in search of understanding and meaning. As I read, I chewed over the words and ruminated, stayed with particular sections that caught my attention, and then continued. I read difficult sections out loud, often later returning to the actual tape to listen again more attentively. Both methods are forms of listening actively and attentively to the words.

The purposes of both processes also have much in common. Like Moschella, I recognize that the act of listening, in the context of theological work, is "an act of love."[110] Like Slee, I experience the faith lives of the women with whom I work as "a place where we expect to discern the presence and activity of the divine."[111] The purpose and underpinning theology of *Lectio Divina* more

---

106   Casey, *Sacred Reading*, 4.
107   Slee, "Feminist Qualitative Research," 17.
108   Guigo II, *The Ladder of Monks and Twelve Meditations*, trans. Edmund Colledge and James Walsh (Kalamazoo, MI: Cistercian Publications, 1978).
109   Casey, *Sacred Reading*, 24–25.
110   Moschella, *Ethnography as a Pastoral Practice*, 254.
111   Slee, "Feminist Qualitative Research," 17.

explicitly and single-mindedly focusses on the search for God in "the forming of our heart and minds according to Christ" so that "our actions can be vehicles of grace to others ... it is a school in which we learn Christ."[112] Viewing or experiencing qualitative research as spiritual practice, and using VCRM in this way, can lead to an inhabiting of the voices of those with whom we work, and "an intermingling of lives."[113] Moreover, it has more been my experience of the participants' own presence as a "vehicle of grace to others" in understanding and witnessing their apostolic purpose that has highlighted the final commonality between both processes that those who participate in either bring a willingness to be changed.

However, the analogy is limited, and drawing it any further may undermine the value of this ancient monastic practice. Nonetheless, I would say that I read and listened to the texts with the attitude of *lectio* (as in the first stage of *Lectio Divina*). I would also claim that I moved from this reading into the second stage of *Lectio Divina*, the phase of *meditatio*, through my engaged and embodied attentiveness to the words. I conducted the first and second readings in place of my early morning *Lectio* practice, in the same physical space, and with the same attitude of reverence and coming to something of God, as a 'godly' activity. I approached the texts, therefore, in expectation of discerning some revelation, not by any means from all parts of all texts, but certainly with the attitude that the texts were capable of revelation. However, it is here, after the first two stages of *lectio* and *meditatio*, that my own personal contemplative practice and my academic contemplative practice parted company as I took the women's words into the next 'stages' of *Lectio*: *oratio* and *contemplatio*.

2.9.1   *Theoretical Considerations*

I want now to explore in more depth the issue of whether these women's stories constitute suitable texts for *Lectio*, and also to note the influence of the texts over me—in effect, the continuing power of the women in this process. For Casey, matter suitable for *Lectio* must be such that "it can sustain in us a sense of reverence and submission."[114] In practising *Lectio* with the texts, and in sitting and resting with the words, sentences, and passages that had caught my attention,[115] I was both actively choosing to do this and following Casey's injunction that in *Lectio*, we "safely suspend our critical faculties and freely lay bare our soul to be moved."[116]

---

112   Casey, *Sacred Reading*, 39.
113   Slee, "Feminist Qualitative Research," 20–21; quotation from 20.
114   Casey, *Sacred Reading*, 103.
115   Casey, *Sacred Reading*, 13.
116   Casey, *Sacred Reading*, 130.

Yet it is the voices of the sisters who now speak, and what catches my attention is the stories of their own search for God; they are expert guides in this process. I am indeed submitting myself to be changed; to be "formed and transformed" in this "paschal process"[117] through the confusion of the "not-knowing" inherent in the research process: the transformation to which both qualitative research and practice-engaged theology speak.[118]

Nonetheless, we need to examine the suitability of the texts as source material for *Lectio*. Casey acknowledges that monastic tradition does not limit *Lectio* to Scripture and includes Patristic texts, but the practice has traditionally been limited to works which "express the perennial faith of the Church and not the transient opinions of an individual."[119] Given my inclination to engage with the twelve transcripts through *Lectio*, to what extent, then, could they be considered to be suitable material? Appraising the full extent to which the transcripts would meet this criterion of expressing the "the perennial faith of the Church" is beyond the scope of this book. However, the women religious participating in this study live an ecclesial vocation, vowed to the conversion of hearts and minds to Christ, and represent the kind of "experienced guide" Casey states may lead us to God through *Lectio*.[120] Furthermore, as vowed religious, they are part of the community of interpretation that addresses itself to the question of what is genuinely 'perennial' through ongoing processes of communal discernment.

One factor which may prevent these experienced female guides being regarded as 'suitable' material is that they are mostly excluded from the canon of Scripture and Patristics drawn upon by Catholics in daily prayer and worship. Lectionary readings rarely feature female figures from the Bible,[121] despite the encouragement by the Synod on the Word (2008)[122] to include more writing by and about women, and similarly, the Divine Office,[123] and congregation-specific versions of the Office used by women's monastic communities. Traditionally, as we have seen, these were the sources for *Lectio Divina*,

---

117 Slee, "Feminist Qualitative Research," 24.
118 Terry A. Veling, "Listening to 'The Voices of the Pages' and 'Combining the Letters': Spiritual Practices of Reading and Writing," *Religious Education* 102, no. 2 (2007): 209, accessed January 27, 2017, https://www.academia.edu/227483/Spiritual_Practices_of_Reading_and_Writing?auto=download.
119 Casey, *Sacred Reading*, 103.
120 Casey, *Sacred Reading*, 15.
121 Christine Schenk, "It's Not All about Eve: Women in the Lectionary," in *Catholic Women Speak: Bringing Our Gifts to the Table*, ed. Catholic Women Speak Network (Mahwah, NJ: Paulist Press, 2015), 168.
122 Synod on the Word of God in the Life and Mission of the Church, October 2008.
123 The Liturgy of the Hours according to the Roman Rite is used by Catholics and religious communities to recite or chant liturgy throughout the day.

practised daily by nuns, monks, and other religious throughout the centuries. In recommending reading suitable for *Lectio*, the 'resources' pages of the Order of St. Benedict[124] until recently contained only four female names among a list of nearly forty, and Casey, in his own list of 'recommended reading,' includes only three women. In the later part of the twentieth century, communities of women religious increasingly used writings by women drawn from beyond the official Lectionary or Divine Office books as material for their daily *Lectio* practice. The sisters of one monastic community in the UK have been using their own translation of the Rule of Benedict, written in inclusive language, for at least twenty years, and now increasingly draw on sources as wide-ranging as the writings of their own 'mothers,' such as St. Gertrude of Helfta, and those of Claudine Moine, a seventeenth-century French seamstress.[125] Taking some of these decisions into their own hands at least allows them access to these women's stories, opening up a new canon of 'suitable material.'

Veling claims that a text "of any compelling stature" might be suitable for use with *Lectio*,[126] and, as noted, I did indeed find their texts compelling. Tracy's exploration of the 'religious classic' presents it as text which "both demands constant interpretation and bears a certain kind of timelessness," and which has a "claim to attention on the grounds that an event of understanding proper to finite human beings has here found expression" living as a classic only "if it finds readers willing to be provoked by its claim to attention."[127] This explanation points also to a fundamental exercise in making meaning, which is a task in which the women in this study are engaged. I do not claim that the texts of these women constitute religious or spiritual classics particularly, perhaps, in terms of timelessness, but to a large extent I have experienced and treated them as such. There are parallels in terms of their claim to my attention, to meaning-making, and to provoking and challenging my own understanding of God. Tracy goes on to say, "If the text is a genuinely classic one, my present horizon of understanding should always be provoked, challenged, transformed. ... We are compelled to believe ... 'that something else might be the case.'"[128]

In experiencing both listening and reading in this way, I want to acknowledge that I am also adopting a theological epistemology, meaning that I also understand my research practice as one of discernment, first in relation to what I hear the women say about their lives and their own exclusive search

---

124 http://osb.org/lectio/.
125 Private correspondence with the Abbess of the Cistercian community at Whitland, August 2017.
126 Veling, "Spiritual Practices," 213.
127 David Tracy, *The Analogical Imagination: Christian Theology and the Culture of Pluralism* (New York: Crossroad, 1981), 102.
128 Tracy, *Analogical Imagination*, 102.

for God, and then in listening both for, and to, the voice of God. This is what Cameron and Duce call "creating a conversation in your mind between the data and the Christian tradition," so that I see research itself as a theological task and ask myself whether how I write up my research will "reveal the mark of the Christian tradition on me as a researcher and on my research context,"[129] and, therefore, be truthful to my own stance. "The mystery of Christ is to be found in the *humanum*, within the complex of human experience and history," wrote McDade,[130] reflecting what Sweeney calls "theology's post-conciliar anthropological turn,"[131] and, therefore, I would concur with Sweeney that it is necessary for practice-engaged theology in particular to draw on methods and perspectives of the social sciences. In this study, I have drawn heavily on social science research tools, but to rely solely on these, and not take a theological stance to this work, would neither be truthful to my own stance, nor to what I perceive and hear from these women's lives, in a process and in lives which I understand to be Spirit-filled and driven.

Slee holds that within a feminist qualitative research process, several things are taking place: we are being shaped as "women of faith"; the process itself then "challenges us to dig deep within our own spiritual resources," and it "teaches us how to discern the sacred" in others' lives, as well as our own.[132] I would suggest that through my engagement I am challenged to "dig deep" into my own spiritual resources in discerning both a sense of vocation as a researcher, and a sense of the presence of God through my work, as I work. It is in this context that Slee sees the potential of research to be transformational for the researcher.

Adding two further elements strengthens this point. Veling's texts of "compelling stature" must offer what Ricoeur calls "a proposed world which I could inhabit,"[133] in this case, texts which offer more than simply a description of the women's ministerial lives. They bring us to the 'shared horizon' Ricoeur holds to be necessary for a hermeneutical interpretation to take place, whereby we seek to listen and understand but not explain.[134] In this context, the transcripts

---

129 Cameron and Duce, *Researching Practice in Ministry and Mission*, 106.
130 John McDade, "Catholic Theology in the Post-Conciliar Period," in *Modern Catholicism: Vatican II and After*, ed. Adrian Hastings (London: SPCK, 1991), 424, cited in James Sweeney, "Catholic Theology and Practice Today," in *Keeping Faith in Practice: Aspects of Catholic Pastoral Theology*, ed. James Sweeney, Gemma Simmonds, and David Lonsdale (London: SCM Press, 2010), 17.
131 Sweeney, "Catholic Theology and Practice Today," 18.
132 Slee, "Feminist Qualitative Research," 15–16.
133 Ricoeur, *Hermeneutics and the Human Sciences*, cited in Veling, "Spiritual Practices," 213.
134 Veling, "Spiritual Practices," 213.

as texts lead our gaze towards a way of being that speaks of, and points to, God which is sacramental in making real that which it signifies.

2.10 The Third Component of the Method: Thematic Analysis

Following the thorough process of engagement with the texts through both the VCRM and *Lectio*, I drew on a third element. I again adopted a different mode of working and moved into a more systematic approach to data analysis. Consequently, I employed a method of qualitative data analysis, or more specifically thematic content analysis, as set out by Braun and Clarke. The familiarity with the data gained to date provided "the bedrock for the rest of the analysis."[135] I had first begun to work with the data thematically before I adopted the VCRM, but to an extent, the two were intertwined, and the process iterative.

I read through the data and identified descriptors or codes. Sometimes these codes arose from the data itself and even comprised the actual words of a participant, known as inductive or in vivo codes.[136] Other codes were more deductive in nature, or a priori,[137] and were more theoretically informed. As a new code emerged, I noted it, wrote a short memo explaining or defining the code[138] and logged it. These initial-level codes are called sub-themes by Braun and Clarke.[139] Identifying distinct themes in qualitative analysis is often difficult due to overlap, and consequently some codes were included in or generated multiple themes.

Returning to the reports generated through use of the VCRM, particularly the report which now incorporated the first and second readings, I combed them to cross-check emerging sub-themes. I also then coded the third and fourth readings for relationship and context, following the same process until I reached saturation point.[140]

---

[135] Braun and Clarke, "Using Thematic Analysis in Psychology," 94.
[136] Gery W. Ryan and H. Russell Bernard, "Techniques to Identify Themes," *Field Methods* 15, no. 1 (2003): 89, accessed December 13, 2015, http://www.analytictech.com/mb870/Readings/ryan-bernard_techniques_to_identify_themes_in.htm.
[137] Graham R. Gibbs and Celia Taylor, "How and What to Code," *Online QDA Web Site*, February 19, 2010, accessed June 15, 2015, onlineqda.hud.ac.uk/Intro_QDA/how_what_to_code.php.
[138] Bazeley, *Qualitative Data Analysis*, 131.
[139] Braun and Clarke, "Using Thematic Analysis in Psychology," 88.
[140] Mauthner and Doucet, "Reflections on a Voice-centred Relational Method," 134; and Matthew B. Miles and A. Michael Huberman, *Qualitative Data Analysis: An Expanded*

I then began to search for larger level themes in order to re-focus "the analysis at the broader level of themes."[141] I combined sub-themes to form overarching themes, and I began to play around to see if the largest sub-themes acted as "gathering themes" or "candidate themes."[142] I had ten of these candidate themes initially and gradually refined this down to four. I then returned to them to decide on their relevance and usefulness.[143] I felt it important to reflect on and interrogate examples of inconsistencies, negative instances, contradictions to the dominant themes, and narratives emerging.[144] These included the sisters who found the experience of teaching very positive and apostolic in nature, and also those who did not appreciate the understanding of 'presence.' The deductive nature of VCRM also helped reflect a wider range of issues which emerged, both expected and unexpected.

2.11 Conclusion

My first consideration in designing a method of data collection and analysis for this study was to identify methods which would provide a structured framework and rigour for the analysis. I understood that those drawn from the social sciences, namely the VCRM and thematic content analysis and coding, would perform this function. However, as the women's voices opened up to me, I realized the limit of these tools. I wanted to reflect the depth and the holiness of the encounters at the heart of this study, and was aware of a desire to reflect and express the theological nature of the process. In adding a third element, by incorporating my practice of *Lectio Divina* into the data analysis, and the analysis into my practice of *Lectio Divina*, I have sought to make this stage of the study "theological all the way through."[145] The combining of these three elements provided a method which reflected my experience of the process to date, and confirmed my growing understanding of the godly nature of my research practice.

      Sourcebook, 2nd ed. (Thousand Oaks, CA: Sage, 1994), cited in Bazeley, *Qualitative Data Analysis*, 152.
141 Braun and Clarke, "Using Thematic Analysis in Psychology," 89.
142 Braun and Clarke, "Using Thematic Analysis in Psychology," 91.
143 Braun and Clarke, "Using Thematic Analysis in Psychology," 91.
144 Clive Seale, "Coding and Analysing Data," in *Researching Society and Culture*, 2nd ed., ed. Clive Seale (London: Sage, 2004), 313; and Corinne Squire, "From Experience-centred to Socio-culturally Oriented Approaches to Narrative," in Andrews et al., *Doing Narrative Research*, 57.
145 Cameron et al., *Talking about God in Practice*, 51.

CHAPTER 3

Framing the Apostolic Becoming

3.1 Introduction

One thing that emerged very strongly for me from listening to the sisters' interviews was the sense that I was listening to what I came to recognize as conversion narratives, after "a journey of continual conversion, of exclusive dedication to the love of God" (*vc*, §109).[1] In these stories, I heard two particular threads, both focussing on the sisters' experience of and response to the word 'apostolic.' The first is that of the initial call and the motivations for entering religious life, reinterpreted by them at this later stage in their lives. The second thread charts how the nature of this call and response has changed and deepened throughout their lives. Within this, I noted how the sisters' understanding of an apostolic vocation shifted from one which had earlier been associated with apostolic or charitable works and purpose to one rooted in an experience of self which becomes through helping others become. Perhaps all of this is represented in the sisters' struggles with the term 'apostolic' as they search for language to name this way of life in terms of who they are becoming.

3.2 Making Meaning of Vocation

3.2.1 *The Call Narratives*

By exploring the sisters' call narratives, I hope to illustrate what the 'apostolic impulse' meant to sisters at an earlier stage in their lives. Unsurprisingly, all of the sisters told some form of story of their initial vocation. These cover a period between when this awareness of call was first acknowledged and/or articulated up until their entering their congregation.

The stories of conversion rose up out of the interview texts to confront my assumptions about the sisters' vocations as a place at which they have arrived. The narratives that emerged showed that vocation or call is not a once-in-a-lifetime event or static phenomena. It is a lifelong lived response, experienced and developed on a daily basis, which unfolds before us as we live

---

1 Pope John Paul II, *Post-synodal Apostolic Exhortation: "Vita Consecrata,"* March 25, 1996, accessed November 23, 2015, http://w2.vatican.va/content/john-paul-ii/en/apost_exhortations/documents/hf_jp-ii_exh_25031996_vita-consecrata.html.

it. "I hear my vocation in the harmony between the path that is before me and the mystery that is me."[2] In this, Hahnenberg distinguishes the Protestant theology of vocation as a call to a place from which we respond, from a Catholic theological understanding "as the place to which God calls."[3] It is a call to movement, journeying, and conversion. This struck me powerfully from the sisters' interviews; their experience of call is one of ongoing daily conversion which will continue till the very end of their lives, and this shaped my awareness of, and openness to, their narratives.

3.2.2 Context

As this study considers the lives of a particular generation of religious women and is, therefore, historicized, the context cannot be ignored. Each individual sisters' call was influenced by their own situation and background; but before exploring each sister's call in more depth, I will attempt to locate the narratives in their varied contexts. However, as this is not a historical work, a detailed consideration of the historical context in which the sisters' vocations arose and developed is beyond its scope.[4]

It can be difficult to disentangle cause and effect when exploring motivation to enter religious life, particularly when sisters are looking back fifty years or so and reinterpreting that call. Nonetheless, I have identified two clear motivations in the choice of congregation which can both be situated in the wider socio-cultural context of the period, the Church, and women's religious life: the desire to be a missionary, and family influence.

Of the twelve sisters, five were born and grew up in Ireland, and either entered there or came to England to enter.[5] The other seven were born and grew up in England and Scotland. They all entered religious life between 1945 and 1964, over a period of twenty years following the Second World War. Seven of the sisters were between the ages of sixteen and twenty when they entered,

---

2 Edward P. Hahnenberg, *Awakening Vocation: A Theology of Christian Call* (Collegeville, MN: Liturgical Press, 2010), 156.
3 Hahnenberg, *Awakening Vocation*, 46–47.
4 For a detailed exploration of the context in Ireland in which five of the sisters entered, see Yvonne McKenna, "Forgotten Migrants: Irish Women Religious in England, 1930s–1960s," *International Journal of Population Geography* 9, no. 4 (2003): 295–308, and "Entering Religious Life, Claiming Subjectivity: Irish Nuns, 1930s–1960s," *Women's History Review* 15, no. 2 (2006): 189–211, accessed August 30, 2016, https://www.tandfonline.com/doi/abs/10.1080/09612020500529598. For the English context over that period, see Susan O'Brien, "Religious Life for Women," in *From without the Flamian Gate: 150 years of Roman Catholicism in England and Wales, 1850–2000*, ed. V. Alan McClelland and Michael Hodgetts (London: DLT, 1999), chap. 5.
5 A phenomenon extensively researched by McKenna in "Forgotten Migrants."

and the remaining five between the ages of twenty-three and twenty-seven. Out of the twelve sisters, eleven were themselves educated by sisters at either primary or secondary level, or both. All but one completed a minimum of secondary education, with several completing higher education in the form of either a university degree (three sisters) or specialist teacher training (two sisters). The extent to which they were educated by religious, and the fact that they were able to "look around," often in local congregations, is itself evidence of the widespread presence and numbers of religious in Ireland and England over this time period.[6]

In all these countries, the Catholic Church was a considerable physical presence in the lives of these women. This was particularly the case in Ireland,[7] where there would often have been several convents in each small town, with the Presentation sisters and the Sisters of Mercy being the most widespread,[8] running the majority of convent schools for girls. Sr. Kathleen, for example, mentions there being several convents near her home. The Catholic Church would have been part of the very air that the young women breathed, brought up in Catholic households in Catholic communities, and educated in Catholic schools. This was certainly a "religious atmosphere."[9]

Catholicism was not identified with state or national identity in England and Wales in the way it was in Ireland by the early twentieth century.[10] However, due partly to the Catholic Emancipation Act of 1829 and the restoration of the Catholic hierarchy in England, Catholicism had become physically very present in England and Scotland by the early to mid-twentieth century. Churches and convents were an increasingly visible and numerous element of the geography of small towns. Religious life in England certainly, and in Scotland, was consolidating its presence and expanding its activities. Like the Church, it was

---

6   Barbara Walsh, *Roman Catholic Nuns in England and Wales, 1800–1937: A Social History* (Dublin: Irish Academic Press, 2002), chap. 1.
7   McKenna, "Forgotten Migrants," 299.
8   Mary Malone, *Women and Christianity*: Vol. 3, *From the Reformation to the 21st Century* (Dublin: Columba Press, 2003), 221.
9   McKenna, "Forgotten Migrants," 229.
10 For more on this, see McKenna, "Forgotten Migrants"; Tom Inglis, *Moral Monopoly: The Rise and Fall of the Catholic Church in Modern Ireland* (Dublin: University College Dublin Press, 1998); and James S. Donnelly Jr., "The Peak of Marianism in Ireland, 1930–60," in *Piety and Power in Ireland, 1760–1960: Essays in Honour of Emmet Larkin*, ed. Stewart J. Brown and David W. Miller (Notre Dame, IN: University of Notre Dame Press, 2000), 252–83.

growing in confidence,[11] as if it had always been there, and would always be there, having what O'Brien calls a "rock-like immobility."[12]

The women in this study were part of the "steady and sizeable flow of well-catechised Catholic young women into novitiates,"[13] as the numbers entering in the UK peaked around the middle of the twentieth century.[14] In Ireland, the period of the 1930s to the 1960s forms part of "the peak period of vocations for the religious life amongst women," and vocations reached their actual peak in 1967, with more than nineteen thousand women religious in Ireland by that time.[15]

3.2.3 *The Lure of the Missions*

A strong motivating factor for at least half of the sisters in this study was the desire to go on the missions.[16] As part of that expansion of the late nineteenth and early twentieth century, women's religious orders moved into what were then seen as 'mission lands.'[17] Having established educational and other institutions in countries beyond Europe, sisters frequently returned to their native countries (in this case, the UK and Ireland) to recruit young women to join the order and serve these institutions. Raftery has documented a well-established and structured pattern of such recruitment in Ireland, certainly up until the First World War and after, as experienced by several of the sisters in this study.[18] Sr. Maeve had already decided against entering with the sisters who had educated her, but said of them:

---

11   Susan O'Brien, *Leaving God for God: The Daughters of Charity of St. Vincent de Paul in Britain, 1847–2017* (London: DLT, 2017), 17.
12   O'Brien, "Religious Life for Women," 15.
13   O'Brien, "Religious Life for Women," 17.
14   Carmen M. Mangion, "The 'Mixed Life': Balancing the Active with the Contemplative," in *Gender, Catholicism and Spirituality: Women and the Roman Catholic Church in Britain and Europe, 1200–1900*, ed. Carmen M. Mangion and Laurence Lux-Sterritt (Basingstoke: Palgrave Macmillan, 2010), 165–79.
15   McKenna, "Forgotten Migrants," 296.
16   Tony Flannery, *The Death of Religious Life?* (Dublin: Columba Press, 1997), 13; McKenna, "Entering Religious Life," 196–98.
17   O'Brien, "Religious Life For Women," 122–27; and Deirdre Raftery, "Teaching Sisters and Transnational Networks: Recruitment and Education Expansion in the Long Nineteenth Century," *History of Education* 44, no. 6 (2015): 717–28, accessed August 7, 2017, https://www.researchgate.net/publication/283116476_Teaching_Sisters_and_transnational_networks_recruitment_and_education_expansion_in_the_long_nineteenth_century.
18   Raftery, "Teaching Sisters and Transnational Networks."

They would be the ones who introduced us to the nuns coming round in Ireland looking for vocations. They would always welcome them and bring them into the classroom.

Three out of the five Irish sisters spoke of this call to be a missionary, but it did not only apply to those growing up in Ireland. The influence of encyclicals and appeals by Popes Benedict XV and Pius XI may likely have played a part in encouraging this movement among sisters.[19] It was at this time that Sr. Pamela's congregation opened their first mission in Africa. McKenna explores the appeal of 'the missions' among the women she interviewed, noting both the romance of saving heathens and teaching young children, and the appeal of the foreign and exotic, which she ascribes to a sense of adventure.[20] Flannery writes of "the image of the 'Black Babies'" prevalent in the Ireland of this time,[21] and Sr. Martina recalls being influenced by this missionary fervour:

I was hoping to go on the missions ... because we used to call them the 'Black Babies,' and it was always in the book about the girls going on the missions, and that was really what attracted me to them.

And Sr. Kathleen, who also grew up in Ireland:

The house was coming down with missionary magazines. You'd need to be in Ireland when we were growing up. We sold missionary magazines; we raised money for the missions; it was constantly before us, and I had visions of myself going out to the lepers like Damian [laughter] or something like that. That was the draw. Not to a life of prayer—that never entered my head. It was to do missionary work, you know ... helping these people.

In fact, only one of these sisters was to have her desire fulfilled: Sr. Kathleen spent over forty years living overseas before eventually returning to the UK. Sr. Martina entered a congregation believing she would go on the missions but was never offered the opportunity. She felt this as a source of great regret and talked about it repeatedly during her interview:

---

19 O'Brien, "Religious Life For Women," 126; and O'Brien, *Leaving God for God*, chap. 9.
20 McKenna, "Entering Religious Life," 196–98.
21 Flannery, *Death of Religious Life?*, 11.

It was like we were taken in the wrong, but there was nothing we could do unless we wanted to leave. ... I know the two of us said it doesn't matter; we made our vows to God, so what does it matter? We are here for God, so, there was no more about it and that was it. We didn't go on the missions.

3.2.4 *Family Influence*

A second factor which influenced the women's decision not only to enter religious life but their choice of congregation was the attitude of their families. Half of the sisters described this choice being influenced by their families. For at least two sisters, this family influence both shaped and thwarted the (then) young girl's desire to go on the missions in particular. Sr. Beatrice, from the north of England, experienced a very strong sense of call to a missionary order: an attraction which seems to be both to the exoticism of a particular order, and to the missions itself:

> I was always attracted to missionary work. The White Sisters—they had a gorgeous white habit. Myself and my sister went to what they used to call gospel evenings. ... They were marvellous nuns, and they came from all over the globe ... and I was extremely attracted to their way of life, and I thought, "Oh, I'd love to go out to Africa."

However, her mother intervened and put a stop to this particular dream:

> Three of those nuns came to see my mother. ... She said to me, "Oh, you can't go with those," she said, "they can't speak English." And she said, "No," so that gave me a lot of problems. ... And I went to a priest, and I said, "I want to become a White Sister; I want to go out to Africa and nurse," you know, like Fr. Damian with the lepers. And he said, "Well, if I were you, I'd listen to your mother." They were words I did not want to hear, let me tell you.

Her mother did not stop her entering altogether, but family did impact significantly on her choice of order:

> My mother had two cousins with the order I'm in now. One of them came to see me and I talked to her. My mother would have been quite pleased, she said if I'd entered with them. ... They understood the kind of person I was; they were Irish. And so I read the life of our founder, and I was

quite attracted to her, and I thought, "Isn't she a wonderful woman? Isn't she brave?"

Other writers have also found that the Church was such a dominant influence on the lives of Catholics, both in Ireland and in the UK, that families often had several members already priests and religious.[22] Sr. Kathleen was influenced by having family members who were missionaries overseas, but also who were in the congregation she eventually went on to join, with an uncle on the missions, one aunt in Ireland, one in North America, three in England, and her father's cousin in Argentina.

3.2.5   A Call to an Occupation?

All the sisters in the study offered more than one reason for entering religious life. Among these varied and multi-layered motivations, can any evidence be found of an early acknowledgment/understanding of and attraction to an 'apostolic impulse,' or is there more evidence of an attraction to a particular profession such as teaching or nursing?

McKenna describes Ireland in the period from the 1930s to the 1960s as a place where the belief that a woman's place was in the home, with children, was protected by state legislation.[23] She notes that opportunities for professional training for women were limited, but that religious life itself was regarded as a profession.[24] In Britain, in contrast, this was already changing. In 1950s Britain, the gendered stereotypes of husband as breadwinner and wife as full-time housewife continued to dominate but were increasingly found in tension with other societal changes. Since the 1944 Education Act, educational opportunities for girls and women had opened up, and Britain was experiencing full employment in the period following the Second World War.[25] The first women's colleges in Oxford University had been established in the late nineteenth century,[26] but university education for women became widespread only after the First World War, although it remained limited for many years,[27] often by class.[28] This new development, though, is reflected in the levels of

---

22   O'Brien, "Religious Life for Women," 18; McKenna, "Entering Religious Life", 203; and Raftery, "Teaching Sisters and Transnational Networks," 722.
23   McKenna, "Entering Religious Life," 192.
24   McKenna, "Entering Religious Life," 198.
25   Stephanie Spencer, *Gender, Work and Education in Britain in the 1950s* (Basingstoke: Palgrave Macmillan, 2005), 1.
26   http://www.ox.ac.uk/about/oxford-people/women-at-oxford.
27   O'Brien, *Leaving God for God*, 296.
28   Spencer, *Gender, Work and Education*, chap. 1.

educational attainment some of the sisters had reached before entering the fields of nursing, teaching, or office work, the largest fields of employment for women in the early 1950s.[29] It is likely, therefore, that all could have trained for and entered into a profession, but that on marriage, they would probably have given up work and become a dependent wife and mother. However, this also was changing, as by the 1960s, many married women and mothers began to return to part-time work.[30]

In the narratives, some sisters express an interest in a particular occupation, most notably nursing and teaching. Four sisters wanted to nurse but were told when they entered that the congregation was not in need of nurses. Others, as seen above, expressed a clear longing for the missions, and also possibly nursing. However, it was difficult to separate out the extent to which women were attracted to a congregation because of a specific apostolate from a more general impulse to serve and the desire for God. Two of the sisters spoke of having a 'dual call': for Sr. Martina, it was "I wanted God, and I wanted to go to the missions." Sr. Dorothy, echoing the fascination with the divine referred to in *Vita Consecrata* (§§17–19), the call was to teach and to be closer to God:

> It's a teaching congregation; that's what they do, and I'd be getting to know more about God and having a spiritual life; both those things attracted me … wanting to teach, and the wanting to know more about the transcendent, or the spiritual life.

It is difficult to establish a relationship between a sister's attraction to a particular congregation and her attraction or not to the congregation's corporate apostolate of education. It might be easy to ask why enter a teaching order if you did not want to teach. Three of the sisters were already trained to teach, or already teaching; they were clear they wanted to continue in that field, and this was part of the appeal of the order they joined.

Several other sisters, such as Sr. Collette, said they had no real thoughts of a profession before entering, either being open to whatever would be needed, or experiencing a strong call to join a particular stable community, where they would likely teach, even if this was not what they felt drawn to.

---

29 Serena Todd and Hilary Young, "Baby-boomers to 'Beanstalkers': Making the Modern Teenager in Post-war Britain," *Cultural and Social History* 9, no. 3 (2012): 451–67.

30 Alva Myrdal and Viola Klein, *Women's Two Roles: Home and Work* (London: Routledge, 1956), cited in Spencer, *Gender, Work and Education*, 12; and Todd and Young, "Baby-boomers to 'Beanstalkers,'" 458.

Reasons for attraction to a particular congregation were similarly varied. Sr. Kathleen's choice was influenced by family and her desire to get away, out of Ireland, to somewhere she was not known. For the majority, the attraction to a particular congregation was experienced in very human terms: Srs. Maeve, Pamela, and Bernadette described the sisters they met from their congregation as being fun and human. Other congregations were variously described as being open or broad-minded (Srs. Dorothy and Clare), considerate of their families (Srs. Collette and Maeve), and encouraging them to develop as individuals, with little pressure towards uniformity. Others said that they just felt at home (Sr. Dorothy); for others there was a sense of familiarity and even security during a difficult period in their life (Sr. Susan).

Most of the sisters had not been attracted to monastic or contemplative life: seven sisters said definitely not, giving reasons such as fearing being confined to one place and one way of life, or even that the only monastery they entered smelt too stuffy (Sr. Jayne). Two had considered it and rejected it, but there was still some lingering sense of something lost, or an unfulfilled desire. Sr. Collette said that she had always wanted both: the prayer and the activity. Two of the sisters entered a stable community anyway, and Sr. Anne describes this attraction:

> The attraction to religious life was the personal relationship with our Lord Jesus Christ, which was very personal, and my sense of call was that it was there to which I was being called and which is where I would find Him ... that's where I was being invited to live it out.

3.2.6 A Call to Serve? An Apostolic Impulse?

The majority of sisters spoke of a desire to serve others and to do something useful with their lives. Sr. Bernadette experienced a call to attend to the needs of others and was attracted to the sisters' strong sense of social justice.

> Although the [congregation] nuns' charism is teaching, and I was coming out to be a teacher, I did not see myself being one just like that, because my father was one who always was in the Catholic men's society and studied a lot on the social encyclicals, etc. And so we had been brought up, all of us, to look at social problems and to think about how you could alleviate things like that.

For Sr. Clare:

> Well, I didn't want to teach. I didn't want to be in a classroom. I didn't mind what I did, as long as it contributed to the overall aims of [the

congregation]. ... It was a call to give up the life I was leading and to do something purposeful. ... Well, to have some—some goal, something to aim at.

Sr. Jayne explained:

> When I was about fourteen or fifteen, I had decided I wanted to do something useful with my life. My eldest sister was definitely going to train as a doctor ... but I would like to be a nurse.

Several of the sisters understood their call in terms of service, and the issue this highlights in relation to language is discussed at the end of this chapter. In later chapters, I will also consider some of the consequences of the attraction to 'service' and 'usefulness' later in the sisters' lives.

3.2.7 *A Call to God*

No matter what other motives were apparent, the desire to know or to develop a closer relationship with God, identified also by Schneiders and Wittberg,[31] emerged from the sisters' interviews. The primary call here was to give their lives to God: to give themselves back to God in return for what they had received. Thus, the narrative of self-gift begins early on in their lives, and in their conversion stories. Sr. Anne again:

> For me it was the relationship with Christ. ... And that was personal. ... And I suppose it's one's understanding of God's relationship with us and what God wants for all of us which is for me the apostolic bit.

Sr. Jayne:

> But somehow in the meantime I thought, no. I had this idea of really doing something for God, because I had quite a close relationship with God at that time. ... God, Jesus—meant a lot to me. ... I had this feeling that I wanted to give myself and do something for the God who'd given me so much. Yes, I think those words—what return can I make to the Lord for all he has given to me?

---

31   Sandra Schneiders, *Selling All: Commitment, Consecrated Celibacy, and Community in Catholic Religious Life* (Mahwah, NJ: Paulist Press, 2001), chap. 1; and Patricia Wittberg, *From Piety to Professionalism and Back* (Oxford: Lexington, 2006), chap. 2.

When I asked Sr. Jayne to what extent she was aware of a call to a specifically 'apostolic' congregation, she responded:

> I definitely thought of any religious as giving their life to God. It's appreciation for all he has given to me and what can I do in return. Well, he can use me. ... I didn't think of becoming a religious as really teaching people about Jesus, although I had ambitions as a child to go out to Africa as a missionary—that was a vague thing, but it was more that I was there, that I was giving what I had—my life, my time, and he could use it in any way, and if I was useful, fair enough.

Sr. Susan describes the unfolding of her own call:

> I think it was probably familiarity. I think that there are a lot of hidden motivations. I was twenty-three ... and I could probably tell you *now* what my hidden motivation was, but I didn't recognize it as such when I joined the community. I think I used language like "I think it was God's will" and "I heard God speaking to me"—just traditional language. I wouldn't describe it in those terms now because I think probably one of the big motivations was that we'd had a family break-up and an insecure childhood, and therefore to join the community which had given me a sense of belonging and continuity and security was a good place to come back to.

Both Sr. Jayne and Sr. Clare state clearly that they now understand or reinterpret their motives for entering quite differently. Schneiders similarly found that "most sisters would now repudiate those original motivations,"[32] as we have come to recognize vocation to be a living, developing phenomenon. However, the point is that the place or the life itself provided the sister with the starting place and the anchor from which to venture out and explore this vocation.

3.3 Narratives of a Changed Understanding

The second of the two narrative perspectives I identified is the story of how the sisters' understanding of the word and concept of 'apostolic' changed and developed through their lives, illustrating how the sisters arrived at the understanding they have of their vocation in later life.

---

32   Schneiders, *Selling All*, 13.

In understanding a narrative as a story "that gives shape, significance and intentionality to experience," I identified that ten of the twelve sisters present a clear thread or "a patterned whole" of how their response to their "call" to live an active life has changed.[33] The narratives are set against the backdrop of the post-conciliar period in religious life, lived out and responding both to the Church in their country of residence, and to the changes taking place within their own congregations. It is hard to attribute the changed understanding of 'apostolic' to a specific event, but many sisters mentioned particular experiences which took on significance, as something which triggered a shift in their understanding of their vocation. Srs. Anne, Martina, Pamela, and Susan said that a key event was going on sabbatical, and as part of that, on a long retreat (usually the Ignatian Thirty Days Retreat). However, the shift in understanding took place over a longer period of time, and took the form of a recognition of a growing or changing awareness within themselves, often set within a process of active discernment: listening to what God wanted of them.

3.3.1 *From Corporate Apostolates to Individualized Ministries*

The sisters in this study lived through a period when, from the 1960s onwards, "the very meaning of religious life was reinterpreted."[34] The changes which took place particularly in the twenty years following the Second Vatican Council affected every aspect of their lives as religious sisters,[35] particularly their occupations, as they made the shift from congregational apostolates to individualized ministries. For ten of the twelve sisters in this study, teaching or education was their main occupation up until formal retirement. Seven of them either taught in their congregations' own schools, or (as with Sr. Kathleen) teaching together with her own sisters in a diocesan-owned school in a mission setting. These are among the last generation of sisters in this country to have this experience of congregational apostolates. Sr. Collette, for example, was the last sister in her Province to teach in school.

For most of the sisters, this move from 'apostolates' to ministries was linked to, and part of, the change taking place within their congregation or community. As I noted in chapter 1, the post-conciliar period was, for many congregations, a time when they responded not only to the call to *aggiornamento*,

---

[33] Nicola Slee, *Women's Faith Development: Patterns and Processes* (Guildford: Ashgate, 2004), 67.

[34] Anne O'Brien, "Catholic Nuns in Transnational Mission, 1528–2015," *Journal of Global History* 11 (2016): 402, https://doi:10.1017/S1740022816000206.

[35] For in-depth explorations of the changes, see James Sweeney, "Religious Life after Vatican II," in *Catholics in England, 1950–2000: Historical and Sociological Perspectives*, ed. Michael P. Hornsby-Smith (London: Cassell, 1999), chap. 14.

but also to that of *ressourcement* urged on by *Perfectae Caritatis* (1965).[36] This decree, issued by the Second Vatican Council, called for the recognition of the congregation's founding spirit and aims: "Let their founders' spirit and special aims they set before them as well as their sound traditions—all of which make up the patrimony of each institute—be faithfully held in honor" (PC, §2b). This was in contrast to the norms of the earlier *Conditae a Christo* (1900), which sought to impose some common and standardized forms of life upon the congregations.[37]

The initial response did not immediately transform these congregations into the ministerial religious life of which Schneiders writes,[38] but it did lead to an ongoing series of reviews of their apostolates, as sisters sought to explore and put into practice what their founding charism had to offer to the contemporary world.[39] Over the period from the late 1960s up until the current time, change for these congregations has, rather ironically, become a constant. O'Brien notes at least three significant reviews and renewals of ministry undertaken by the British Province of the Daughters of Charity between 1971 and 2009.[40] In this study, two sisters talked specifically about their congregation carrying out a review or 'audit' of ministries which led to the first of what would have been several changes in ministry for sisters. As Sr. Bernadette explained:

> We did a ministry evaluation back in 1981, and what we did was to get every sister to look at their ministry in the light of Justice and Peace ... and were they actually serving the poor, and then a couple of sisters came out of their ministry—one or two went to teach in areas that they knew were poor—and others changed direction and went into social work.

---

36 Pope Paul VI, *Decree on the Adaptation and Renewal of Religious Life: "Perfectae Caritatis,"* October 28, 1965, accessed April 15, 2012, http://www.vatican.va/archive/hist_councils/ii_vatican_council/documents/vat-ii_decree_19651028_perfectae-caritatis_en.html.

37 D. I. Lanslots, *Handbook of Canon Law for Congregations of Women under Simple Vows* (New York: Fr. Pustet, 1922).

38 Sandra Schneiders, *Finding the Treasure: Locating Catholic Religious Life in a New Ecclesial and Cultural Context* (Mahwah, NJ: Paulist Press, 2000); and Schneiders, "Discerning Ministerial Religious Life Today," *National Catholic Reporter*, September 11, 2009, accessed November 9, 2012, https://www.ncronline.org/news/discerning-ministerial-religious-life-today.

39 See Diarmuid O'Murchu, *Religious Life: A Prophetic Vision* (Notre Dame, IN: Ave Maria Press, 1991); Flannery, *Death of Religious Life?*; O'Brien, "Religious Life for Women"; Schneiders, *Finding The Treasure*; Schneiders, *Selling All*; Wittberg, *From Piety to Professionalism and Back*; and Carmen M. Mangion, "The Nuns' True Story," *The Tablet*, February 7, 2015, 8–9.

40 O'Brien, *Leaving God for God*, 280–81.

The shift out of institutional apostolates in schools, hospitals, and orphanages to more individualized ministries was driven both by demographic changes (fewer, elder sisters) and the embracing of renewal.[41] Schneiders sees the desire for congregations to "jettison baggage" as the main motive for divesting themselves of large institutions.[42] Srs. Bernadette, Collette, Dorothy, and Beatrice were happy in teaching, but even so, for them and for other sisters, coming out of the school environment was liberating. These sisters either asked for, or responded eagerly to, an invitation to explore and follow their own interests and talents outside of the school environment. For Sr. Bernadette, coming out of school meant the opportunity to work with women in interfaith engagement; for Sr. Maeve, to work in catechesis with adults; and for Sr. Beatrice, to run a retreat centre.

3.3.2 The Rise of the Justice and Peace Paradigm

We see from Sr. Bernadette's words above that concern for social justice was also a motivation that drew congregations away from the maintenance of institutions. The period of change and exploration in the post-conciliar period coincided with what Van Heijst has termed the rise of the justice paradigm, as the concept of 'charity' came to be seen as old-fashioned and paternalistic. Van Heijst writes that "from the 1960s onwards, a new slogan claimed 'no charity but social rights.'"[43] This growing interest in social rights and justice was fostered by a changing environment within the Church internationally, and the publication of *Justice in the World* (1971) by the World Synod of Catholic Bishops, a document which embraced elements of liberation theology. This gave the sisters' movement further impetus, and Flannery notes the rise of a similar justice-focussed movement in Ireland.[44]

An emerging preference to attend to social justice or justice and peace-related issues which moves to the forefront of sisters' lives as a result of their lived experience is a significant element in the narratives of four of the sisters. Sr. Susan is one of several who describe how they began to feel the 'itch' of concern for social justice, and experienced this as a tension with teaching in a private school.

---

41 O'Brien, "Religious Life for Women," 131–32; and Wittberg, *From Piety to Professionalism and Back*, introduction, chaps. 1–2.
42 Schneiders, *Selling All*, 271.
43 Annelise Van Heijst, *Models of Charitable Care: Catholic Nuns and Children in their Care in Amsterdam, 1852–2002* (Boston, MA: Brill Academic, 2008), 356–57.
44 Flannery, *Death of Religious Life?*, 36.

> Well, one of the things that happened early on, during my teaching, I had become very convinced about the whole thing about justice and peace, and in those days [the 1970s] it was considered a bit fringy and freaky ... you know, how things come about gradually ..., but in the days we are talking about, I was straining at the leash.

She continues with her story by recalling that the unease continued through 1976 and 1977, when she took a sabbatical, out of school, and out of the community; but when she returned, she continued to experience the tension between her growing interest in justice and peace, and staying on in school. She named her efforts to live with this sense of contradiction—"squaring the circle"—and it continued for some years until an opportunity to move presented itself.

3.3.3   *The Missionary Context*

For Srs. Kathleen and Pamela, the two sisters in the study who served for many years as missionaries overseas, this new awareness of a justice and peace perspective arose in that missionary context, and mirrored their own personal response to the poverty and injustice they saw around them in their "reading or scrutinising the signs of the times," as encouraged by *Gaudium et Spes* (1965, §4).[45] Sr. Pamela also experienced a sense of contradiction between being in a school for children of wealthy parents and her awareness of a call to respond to needs she saw in the community, and "to begin to address needs that no one else was meeting and their congregations had not yet corporately addressed."[46]

> I said to myself after ten years, "What am I doing here? Whether I'm here or not, these children are going to get an education because their parents have money. Their parents are moving in high society, and there's so much poverty, so *why* am I here?" So, I thought the only other thing I can do here now is—I need to make them aware that the [Country x] they know is not the only [Country x], and they need to be doing something for the people less fortunate than them—the disadvantaged—to awaken their social conscious. So that's what I started to try and do.

---

45   Pope Paul VI, *Pastoral Constitution on the Church in the Modern World: "Gaudium et Spes,"* December 7, 1965, https://www.vatican.va/archive/hist_councils/ii_vatican_council/documents/vat-ii_const_19651207_gaudium-et-spes_en.html.
46   Schneiders, *Selling All*, 236.

This impulse felt by Sr. Pamela led her, in the mid-1980s, to ask to be transferred into a school in one of the local slum communities, where she became involved with a movement of priests and religious who were prepared to put their lives on the line to fight for justice. This was a profoundly transformative experience for her, and one which ultimately took her back into education, but to work from a very different perspective of 'conscientization' and education for justice.

Sr. Kathleen taught in a country badly affected by the AIDS epidemic in the 1980s, and her growing awareness of the need to respond was nested within the experience of the sisters who were on mission with her.

> Then, we had the AIDS epidemic which hit [Country Y] very, very badly, and it was a time when all the congregations were looking for new ways of being, and this really challenged us. People were just dying of AIDS; it was just beginning to get very bad.

Similarly, Sr. Pamela, when asked what prompted her to think differently about her apostolic work, responded simply: "What I saw all around me." Her gradual awakening to the poverty and injustice around her was further nurtured by the Latin American Bishops Conference embracing the home-grown liberation theology movement, with the expressed preferential option for the poor welcomed through statements issued by two episcopal conferences held at Medellín, Colombia, in 1968, and Puebla, Mexico, in 1979.

> We worked a lot with those documents—Puebla and Medellín; those documents were very powerful, and we used those in church and in school.

Sr. Kathleen and Sr. Pamela's experiences of awakening to the poverty and injustice around them, and the needs of the most marginalized, affected both of them deeply, shaping the remainder of their lives and their understanding of what it means to be an apostolic religious.

3.3.4 *Back to the United Kingdom*

The majority of the sisters in this study, however, spent their lives in the UK and Ireland, and although this setting may seem to lack the stark contrast between poverty and wealth found in developing countries, and the apparently clearer moral choices faced in such situations, the sisters nonetheless often found themselves part of dramatic shifts and movements. The impulse towards social justice-oriented ministry is equally evident in these shifts, as seen in the experiences of two UK-based sisters in two different congregations. Both congregations underwent significant upheaval between the 1970s and 2005, when private schools and institutions were handed over to lay control as the congregations re-focussed their mission on work with the poor and marginalized.

Sr. Anne describes the impetus for the profound change process which took place in her own community:

> We had been involved in education, but since we didn't have people who came to join us, we didn't have the personnel to go on running a large independent school, which is why we decided to hand it over to lay governors, so it did mean that we had to find our way into a way of being that was not associated with a particular apostolate, if you like to call it in the old-fashioned sense.

She goes on to say that the community experienced

> The call to be apostolic in a different way. ... We were already beginning to get the idea of having smaller groups in areas which we identified as areas of deprivation, so it was a big shift from running our own private school into situations of deprivation which required that we use not necessarily specifically the skills and experience we'd gained in the school, but skills and experience which could be adapted to the needs of the surrounding areas.

Sr. Anne found teaching children very challenging, and she was delighted to have the opportunity to be involved in a new congregational ministry: opening a centre for spiritual retreats and education in 1993. Both her and the community's lives changed radically over a period of ten years and, as a result, led to a very significant change in their self-understanding.

> One of the things that we have rediscovered is the true character of what it means to be a [sister of x], which is to be among the people, to be people of prayer, and to have this community life and be there at the service of the people among whom we live. So, there's definitely been a shift in how we understand ourselves.

Sr. Beatrice taught until the statutory retirement age. She describes the movement through several stages of development of 'apostolic' religious life in her congregation, from a semi-monastic institutional life to external apostolates, to how she now lives, in her late eighties, in a small 'inserted' community on a housing estate:

> The way we used to be as apostolic religious, we were monastic religious, and our doing was inside, and not so much as an evangelization or a thrust towards people, but a thrust towards first of all cleaning our houses and making it beautiful, praying, and sharing among ourselves—very good, all good things, but that was in the beginning many, many years ago.
>
> Today I live in this small house—well, we call it small—it is four bedrooms, and most of our families think it is quite big. We are in this house ... in a housing estate very close to our neighbours. ... This is a completely new experience for us, and I would say in our congregation we are an ageing congregation—this side of the Atlantic anyway. This is the future: the thing is smaller houses close to our neighbours, close to people we serve, and also people we are just friendly with, and that is a tremendous apostolate.

3.4 Naming Their Way of Life

The preceding section has presented some of the events, change processes, and movements shaping the sisters' lives and bringing them to a new, deeper awareness of what it means to be apostolic. It has also highlighted two important elements of this awareness: the growing inclination to pay attention to issues of social justice, and the importance of relationships with people whom they encounter as their lives have become more 'ordinary.'

In the introduction to this chapter, I highlighted a third phenomenon which emerged from the data, which is that many of the sisters seemed to have difficulty in naming the way of life they have chosen, and who it is that they are called to be, particularly at this later stage in their lives. I want now to specifically link some of the change in the sisters' lives shown above, both with how their understanding of apostolic changed, and how they struggle to name what they do and how or who they are. I argue that the changes in way of life experienced by the sisters are reflected in how they respond to the word 'apostolic' and search for other ways of describing the reality of their call and response.

When asked what they understand by the word 'apostolic,' five of the sisters immediately explained it as a way of life rooted in the lives of the apostles: Sr. Anne, for example:

> I understand 'apostolic' to encompass a way of living which is rooted in the models that are given to us in the letters of Paul particularly, [and] in the teachings of the gospel and in the Acts of the Apostles specifically.

Although this was a relatively common response, many sisters were either negative in their response to the word or were reluctant to use it. Sr. Clare, when asked, simply said, "I have no idea … I don't know what it means"; and Sr. Kathleen said, "Even now the word 'apostolic,' I never think of it; it never crosses my mind." Sr. Beatrice felt it was "narrowly religious" but happily used the term "apostolic thrust," a term somewhat akin to Sweeney's discussion of the fundamental impulse of the apostolic religious life.[47]

Several sisters noted that it just feels plain old-fashioned, reflecting the journey they themselves have undertaken to individualized ministries—for example, Sr. Dorothy:

> We use the word 'ministry'; we say 'ministry.' [CS: *Do you ever use the word 'apostolates'?*] No, not now. It just seems a bit of an old-fashioned word … a bit dated.

Sr. Beatrice similarly:

> 'Apostolate' is a nice word because it is like the apostles. I rather quite like it, but it has gone very old-fashioned now, but we talk mainly about ministering because that is much more like a servant.

However, reflecting on the journeys they have experienced, several sisters demonstrated a deeply changed understanding of the 'apostolic' call and looked back on the former (or still prevalent) understanding as being too narrow. In the early 1990s, Sr. Susan obtained permission to take a sabbatical from teaching to go and experience a new ministry.

> By the time I came back [in the mid-1990s], the community was being facilitated through our exploration of what we were doing about this change in the community, and it became an experimental house. But before that, I think perhaps I'd understood what 'apostolic' is in a too-channelled way, like teaching, nursing, that sort of way.

---

47   James Sweeney, "Religious Life Looks to the Future," in *A Future Full of Hope?*, ed. Gemma Simmonds (Dublin: Columba Press, 2012), 139.

Many sisters rejected the association between 'ministry' and 'doing,' usually in the sense of helping others 'out there.' Sr. Kathleen said she used to understand it as "going out" and "helping these people," and now she laughs at the language she used because 'apostolic' for her now means something less 'done to' people and more 'being with.'

Sisters refer to how their earlier religious lives were habitually dominated by a 'work ethic,' often firmly planted during their novitiate. Sr. Beatrice describes how they used to be driven and defined by this 'work ethic':

> We always got the impression that you had to be 100% into the work ethic. I always felt that this was wrong because I felt that, if you were a sister ... I could do that anywhere, but, within the work that you're given to do—like, I was a teacher, there are an awful lot of possibilities for actual apostolic thrust in your work. ... That work ethic always remained with me. If I wasn't there doing my job, I wasn't a proper nun. It sowed the seed of it, because it seemed to me that they put that at the top of their priorities.

Sr. Kathleen agreed but used even stronger words:

> We felt that if you weren't working all the time—and by working, I mean physically working, or out in a school or something—if you weren't occupying every moment of every day, then you were a failure.

When I mentioned the term 'apostolic impulse' to Sr. Susan in her first interview, she responded positively to my use of the word 'impulse' as a way of shifting the emphasis away from task.

> The first thing that came to my mind was a charge of energy ... which is I suppose an activation of the gift that one has, that I've received, but also knowing that that can go to and link with the other person—an interconnectedness ... yes, make a connection with—relate—make a relationship with.

She continued:

> The word 'impulse' actually helps enormously because it takes away the sense of work, in the sense of a defined work, so that's why this is really helpful, because the apostolic impulse of our charism is to take out the

good news that Jesus lives ... and to use the word 'impulse' rather than work, frees me ... enormously.

Most sisters noted that the use of 'ministry' is now more widespread than the language of apostolates, or even of apostolic activity, and were more positive about this, such as Sr. Maeve, and Sr. Beatrice, here:

> I think you can know what ministry is and do it, without using that word, but I can't think of a substitute word. I certainly don't like 'apostolate.' It's lifted from a book, 'apostolate,' isn't it?

Sr. Dorothy revealed mixed feelings:

> I can remember when the word 'ministry' came in and it seemed to me stiff and artificial. I used to think of C of E clergymen having ministry, but it's something that's come into the Catholic Church, isn't it? ... I used not to like the word 'ministry' at all; it was years before I used it. ... But now I'm more comfortable with the word, but for years I didn't like it. ... I thought it was an affective sort of word for years.

However, other sisters have now also become less inclined to use the term 'ministry' to describe work or an occupation. Many have clearly begun to question the appropriateness of the word, and to explore how to talk about their 'ministry' and their 'active' vocation, as they have had to give up 'active' ministry themselves, as seen in Sr. Jayne's response and the questioning of what this means for her future:

> I don't like this word 'ministry,' but to come to be of service to, well—hopefully to God, the Lord ... but that has to come into the very word 'apostle,' this idea of being sent out to carry the message somewhere, and that is where the problem of feeling you have got to have a special job to do, no matter how small or how big, the very idea of being apostolic comes in, so how does it work out with being apostolic to the end?

She continues:

> An awful lot was made of it in our, may I say, recent years, I am going back twenty years or so, or maybe after the change, what was your ministry, you had to have a definite ministry. ... Why don't I like 'ministry'? Because there was too much emphasis on the doing something, so it has left a

legacy of feeling that unless you have, yes, that connection with people outside your small group that you live in, in community, that unless you are doing something, it is this doing thing that is my objection to the word 'ministry,' because I am linking it all the time with a definite job, and that unless you are doing that, you are no good, you are not being apostolic.

In her struggle to describe what she 'does' now that she is largely housebound, one sister singles out her spiritual accompaniment work from the rest of how she is in community. She uses the term "recognizable ministry" to describe it. This provoked some marked reactions when reflected back to sisters in the second round of interviews. They seemed to associate "recognizable ministry" with apostolates or work, and their discomfort perhaps again suggests that continued use of 'ministry' can be problematic for older sisters who struggle with a loss of a sense of purpose and value to the congregation.

Sr. Beatrice explained her view:

> We came from a situation that we had recognizable ministries, teaching, nursing; as you say, 'walking with people,' giving them, helping them, in those many, different ways. Many religious ... we ... have experienced it when they retire from that, or are no longer able to do it physically because they are not strong enough. They feel of no account and stay living in the past—oh, I used to do all that, it was lovely, and now I don't do anything.

Sr. Dorothy similarly struggles with it, but finds no alternative:

> I don't like the phrase, which comes in a few times—"recognizable ministry." I'm sure some people use it—some people know what it means. I know what it means, but I think it's a very ... cold, stark phrase really. In fact, come to think of it, I'm beginning to not like the word 'ministry' [laughs], but I don't know what I would use in its place.

Another sister felt disinclined to use either 'apostolic' to describe her activity or 'ministry'/'ministerial,' feeling that they both seem "confined" due to the association with work. Overwhelmingly, sisters resisted the association between apostolic activity or ministry and 'doing,' and articulated a concern for a balance between 'being' and 'doing.' Sr. Pamela noted that

> 'Apostolic' has so much more to do with being who you are than anything that you do, and I would feel very much identified with that. Yes, I would.

This seemed to strike a chord with several sisters, but also pointed to some confusion about language and terms used in relation to religious life for women. The sisters seem to welcome the use of 'apostolic' as an adjective describing who/how they are rather than what they do. This relates both to the shift from corporate apostolates to individualized ministries, and the association between apostolic activity/ministry and 'doing.'

Interestingly, some sisters recount how in the years following the Second Vatican Council and the call from *Perfectae Caritatis* to return to their founding charism, they were simply told that the nature and identity of the congregation had changed. Srs. Jayne and Dorothy both relate having a visitor from the congregational leadership "telling" them that they were now returning to their roots as an apostolic or active congregation rather than being what they regarded as contemplative or semi-monastic, and this creating some considerable confusion. This reflects both the ambiguity of these terms and how little differentiation was made between 'contemplative' and 'monastic,' overlooking the understanding that many apostolic/active congregations and religious also regard themselves as being contemplatives, and conversely, that many monastic communities understand their life to have an apostolic dimension.[48] It also reflects how congregations gradually were able to emerge from the uniformity imposed on them by *Conditae a Christo*.[49]

Later in the women's religious lives, the nature of the apostolic life became more fully understood, particularly for those congregations who were 'contemplatives in action' by virtue of their often newly rediscovered apostolic or specifically Ignatian-related charism and spirituality.[50] Thus, Sr. Kathleen recounts:

> That was a period of criticism that we went through—that that's all you're interested in; that's what we were always hearing; it's not a matter of just doing; it's a matter of being as well, and we were always told that we were contemplative religious as well as active, but they never explained what that was.

Some sisters reacted badly to hearing that they were now suddenly both contemplative as well as active, fearing that they didn't personally have a

---

48   For more on this, see George A. Aschenbrenner, "Active and Monastic: Two Apostolic Lifestyles," *Review for Religious* 45, no. 5 (1986): 653–68, accessed September 19, 2015, http://cdm.slu.edu/cdm/singleitem/collection/rfr/id/298/rec/11.
49   The Apostolic Constitution *Conditae a Christo* of 1900 and its *Normae* of 1901 were both incorporated in the new Code of Canon Law of 1917.
50   See Aschenbrenner, "Active and Monastic," 664–65.

'contemplative' vocation. In a related point, several sisters described how the emphasis formerly placed on work and 'helping' in the earlier stages of their religious life had then shifted to 'being,' and it may be that this partly reflects the changing demographics of membership. Sr. Beatrice also spoke about 'guidance' from her community on the nature of their life:

> Now that's what we talked about, and the emphasis always used to be on doing. Now it's much more on being.

However, as the congregations have worked to uncover their original nature and identity as intended by their foundress, returning *ad fontes*, the nature of their lives has become clearer. These words from Sr. Dorothy capture the sense of balance between 'doing' and 'being' very well:

> "Our [congregation]'s primary mission is to live the incarnation by being God's merciful love in the world. This takes priority over any specific work," and I think that sums up very well the charism and what we are about, so the apostolic work—"live the incarnation by being *God's merciful love.*"[51]

I would like to end this section with the voice of Sr. Anne. The excerpt is lengthy, but what she says seems to capture the dilemma the women face in naming.

> I know that the sort of traditional way of talking about apostolic ministry is rather narrowed down to people being actively outside; I would like an idea of apostolic ministry to embrace some of the more interior ways of being with people, so quite a lot of my time is taken up with individuals who come for spiritual direction, and that's very private, but I still see it as apostolic ministry. ... If we narrow down apostolic ministry to a rather formalized concept, we would miss perhaps 90% of what apostolic ministry can be.
>
> I think, therefore, that my role is somehow to become, as a member of this community, a person who is a channel of the love of God. Richard Rohr has this wonderful image of the water wheel, and I think that if the millpond is the damming up of God's love, it then turns the water

---

51 The quotation is taken from a document circulated in the Society of the Holy Child Jesus on the occasion of Cornelia Connelly being declared Venerable in 1992. The author is thought to be Radegunde Flaxman SHCJ.

wheel, and that's me, and that then turns the mechanism which grinds the wheat, but the water flows on, and it can feed another water wheel as well, so it's much more this, being a channel of the love and the grace of God.

She goes on to ask a very pertinent question:

> I just wonder whether we have to find a completely new set of vocabulary, because if we use the words that have been applied to religious life in the past, they're freighted with quite a big weight—understanding—which has been transferred perhaps unknowingly to people in the twenty-first century.

3.4.1 Name and Identity

It appears from the range of comments above that the sisters are uncertain what to call their form of life. It may be that this struggle to name and describe is gendered. Srs. Beatrice and Dorothy explain ministry as 'service,' but they do not use the word '*diakonia*'—a contentious term in itself in the Catholic Church in relation to women's ministry.[52] Sandra Schneiders has done more than almost anyone to reframe and rename apostolic religious life for women, including claiming the use of the term 'ministry' and renaming apostolic religious life as 'ministerial.' O'Brien suggests that the naming of this form of life for women has long been problematic. She attributes this partly to the Church's reluctance to recognize this form of religious service by women in the world, a struggle which is acknowledged and well documented by a number of writers.[53]

Sr. Dorothy's association of the word 'ministry' with male clergy (particularly in the Church of England) may illustrate this issue. Similarly, Sr. Jayne admitting that she did not have enough confidence in herself "to think that I could be an apostle" may be because of the historical association of this role with men. We do not know. This study lacks sufficient data to do anything

---

52 For further discussion of this issue, see Susan O'Brien, "'Yes, But What Do You Do?' What is Distinctive about the Exercise of Ministry by Religious?," paper presented at the Compass Catholic Vocations Projects study day, St. Mary's Church, Moorfields, London, June 6, 2015.

53 O'Brien, "'Yes, But What Do You Do?'"; Diarmuid O'Murchu, *The Seed Must Die* (Dublin: Veritas, 1980); Mary Wright, *Mary Ward's Institute: The Struggle for Identity*, Sydney: Crossing Press, 1997); Jo Ann Kay McNamara, *Sisters in Arms: Catholic Nuns through Two Millennia* (Cambridge, MA: Harvard University Press, 1996); Mary Malone, *Women and Christianity*: Vol. 3, *From the Reformation to the 21st Century* (Dublin: Columba Press, 2003); O'Brien, *Leaving God for God*; and Clarence Gallagher, "The Church and Institutes of Consecrated Life," *The Way Supplement* 50 (1984): 3–15.

other than ask whether this points to a specific experience of women religious rather than also of male religious.

It may also be that the difficulty in naming relates to the uncertainty of identity noted in the introductory chapter to this study. Work has always been central to the identity of apostolic women religious, and as women's apostolic congregations have emerged from their semi-monastic existence, the nature and role of work has changed as sisters have moved into individualized ministries. Wittberg argues that the move out of institutions with which congregations were often identified has caused the loss of clarity of identity.[54]

Schneiders, on the other hand, believes that this has strengthened the women's identity. In post-institutional religious life, she sees work as no longer "a secondary end, but absolutely central to their vocation and identity."[55] For her, the concept and experience of ministry has become central to the self-understanding of women in 'ministerial' religious life; it was "not something they did to express who they were but was intrinsic to who they were."[56]

The sisters' hesitancy to embrace either of the terms 'apostolic' or 'ministry' in relation to activity and charitable works may indicate that they are still caught between the two worlds of post-institutional or ministerial religious life, particularly as they move into a stage of their life when their ministerial lives are not so obviously identifiable. They also question the long-held associations between work and identity, between doing and individual worth. Their responses seem to point to their seeking a way beyond the 'being and doing' dichotomy discussed earlier. This may be a consequence of the changes being forced upon the women through physical and social diminishment, and through the declining membership of their congregations in the UK and Ireland, challenging long-held certainties. They highlight the question whether religious life for women in this time and context is less about the binaries of being/doing or apostolic/contemplative, and even diminishment/vitality, and indeed less about "recognizable ministry" and more about ways of being such as channels, signs, eschatology, and most importantly, witnessing as themselves.

3.5 Conclusion

Given the divided opinions and ambivalence I heard from the sisters about the term 'apostolic,' readers may well ask why I have continued to use this word so

---

54   Wittberg, *From Piety to Professionalism and Back*, 59.
55   Sandra Schneiders, *Buying the Field: Religious Life in the New Millennium* (Mahwah, NJ: Paulist Press, 2013), 271–72.
56   Schneiders, *Buying the Field*, 271–72.

prominently and consistently throughout this book. I offer several points by way of explanation.

First, Sweeney, writing of the need "to explore the fundamental impulse of the apostolic religious life" more fully in order to understand the recent and future development of apostolic religious life, particularly in its embracing of 'the ordinary,' caught my imagination.[57] This exhortation made sense to me, and like Sr. Susan, I found the use of the word 'impulse' quite helpful. It prompted me to wonder what exactly was the impulse that had driven these sisters into religious life, and what had kept them there.

Second, and as an extension of the first point, what else to call the sisters' vocation but an impulse to the apostolic, literally to be apostles and followers of Christ? I am not convinced personally that, for this group of sisters, their call was ever to the 'ministerial' as Sandra Schneiders proposes and uses this term, nor, indeed, has it come to be so.

Third, the language used to describe the sisters' charitable works or service is also contested. In certain parts of the world, particularly the United States, Europe, and the Global North, the language of 'apostolates' is, by and large, no longer used. The actual history of moving away from the use of 'apostolates' to 'ministries,' and the varieties of usage in different parts of the world, is interesting in and of itself, but beyond the remit of this book. Nonetheless, I have found among this group of sisters that much of the hesitancy associated with use of either 'apostolate' or 'ministry' seems to be based on the discomfort with the association of both words with specific tasks and activities. As the sisters age, none of 'apostolic work,' 'apostolates,' or 'ministry'/'ministries' quite fits. Either these terms are experienced as being too old-fashioned or too 'corporate,' or they over-emphasize 'doing.' I believe that the word 'apostolic' as an adjective for the sisters themselves offers us a way beyond both. It also offers a way beyond the dichotomy, identified in chapter 1, between being/doing and apostolic or contemplative forms of religious life.

Giving high prominence to 'activity' in the definition of this form of religious life[58] seems unhelpful for the group of women with whom I have worked, nor perhaps suitable for many future forms of religious life. Sr. Anne identified the need for a "completely new set of vocabulary." She may be right, but it cannot be identified by those who are living a form of religious life which finds

---

57 Sweeney, "Religious Life Looks to the Future," 139.
58 *Ecclesiae Sanctae* refers to the "apostolic activity of members of Institutes of perfection who lead a life which is not totally contemplative"; again, the emphasis is on activity. See Pope Paul VI, *Apostolic Letter: "Ecclesiae Sanctae,"* August 6, 1966, §36.1, https://www.vatican.va/content/paul-vi/en/motu_proprio/documents/hf_p-vi_motu-proprio_19660806_ecclesiae-sanctae.html.

itself in the midst of so much change; it must surely come from the renewal, when and if it comes. Any contention from me that 'apostolic' could be resurrected has been challenged by hearing the need for "crafting anew."[59] There is no going back, only forward; the question is to what.

This discussion about language has begun to uncover a central point about the sisters' identity, which is that they reject being defined by what they have done, or what they do, or even by what they are. Thus, the naming of the way of life reflects issues of identity and self. What has begun to emerge is the role of the self and a desire to assert an identity in spite of what and how others might name you. For now, and for my use, 'apostolic' as a descriptor for these women, who they are, and how they live their vocation, serves very well, and it is to a deepening exploration of this that I now turn.

---

59   Martin Poulsom, "Sustaining Presence: Religious Life in the Midst of Creation," in Simmonds, *A Future Full of Hope?*, 56.

CHAPTER 4

Becoming Apostolic as Themselves

4.1 Introduction

In the book to date, I have established that the sisters' own understanding of the meaning of 'apostolic' in relation to religious life changed during the course of their lives. Within this, I have found that sisters experience 'becoming' apostolic as themselves, and therefore the concept of 'becoming' is a particularly helpful lens through which to illustrate the development of their responses to the word and concept of 'apostolic.' These responses have often changed in line with them accepting opportunities to draw on, realize, and develop their own gifts and interests. This chapter will explore this 'becoming' through two related themes. The first is that of the sisters establishing their identity, which I argue they do in relation to others' attempts to define them as Catholic sisters. The second tells the story of the degree to which the sisters were fulfilled or, conversely, what I have called 'thwarted' in their ministerial lives.

I found the sisters demonstrated a clear concern with identity and self and argue that this can be attributed to, and is reflective of, the changing context in which they lived, particularly when viewed through Taylor's work on the development of the modern identity.[1] Their concern can also be interpreted in the light of two further factors. The first is that their reading of, and responses to, the signs of the times is constitutive of their growing prophetic witness. The second is this growing focus on the self as a response to their own earlier experiences of religious life, and of the theology of self-denial as a means to achieving perfection, a dominant theological paradigm in the earlier years of their time in religious life. The sisters did not necessarily embrace self-denial but understood it as vital for their growth towards God. However, their increasing concern for their selves has actually been fundamental to their understanding and practice of being apostolic as an exercise of self and presence as they have aged.

---

[1] Charles Taylor, *Sources of the Self: The Making of the Modern Identity* (Cambridge: Cambridge University Press, 1989); and Taylor, *A Secular Age* (Cambridge, MA: Belknap Press of Harvard University Press, 2007).

4.2 The Context

The sisters' concern with the self is shaped by the changes that have taken place in wider society (western Europe and North America) in the second half of the twentieth century, and which eventually influenced the Catholic Church and the religious congregations themselves. For our purposes, the most significant perspective through which to consider the sisters' growing awareness of themselves and their needs is through Taylor's exploration of the modern identity, as he traces and builds on the turn to the self as it affected society and latterly, the Church and religious life.

Taylor locates the beginning of the development of the modern identity in the demise of the "enchanted world."[2] He claims that up to the Reformation, all aspects of life were viewed through a sense of the transcendent. The loss of this framework as part of the gradual shift to a 'disenchanted' or secular world drove and shaped the need to make sense of and fulfil ourselves. Along with this, Taylor identifies the affirmation of ordinary life or the turn to the ordinary.[3] He locates this in Luther's realignment of what constituted a good Christian life away from 'higher' callings in the Church and towards one centred on work and family, whereby production and reproduction take on a new value. Ordinary life is affirmed with the development of the idea that our destiny is simply to engage fully with what lies in front of us, and live in the world well. This idea has taken hold in Western society since then so that the sisters' own desire to be 'ordinary' can be understood in terms of this societal shift.

Alongside the disenchantment of society and the affirmation of the ordinary, Taylor plots the rise of the inward turn, from Augustine onwards, towards an increasing emphasis on the self.[4] He builds on modernity's 'turn to the subject' and Descartes' siting of the self within and calls it the 'turn to the self,' thus bringing us to the modern concept of selfhood as one which values freedom, authenticity, and individuality.[5] This concern with self is further nuanced by Taylor's identification of the "age of authenticity," characterized by our embracing and displaying an ethic of authenticity which places great value on our being our 'real' selves and always acting out of our 'real' selves.[6] The sisters' 'becoming' takes place in the light of this turn, both in society, and as recognized and responded to by institutions and the Church.

---

2 Taylor, *A Secular Age*, 25–27, 268–69.
3 Taylor, *Sources of the Self*, 211–34; and Taylor, *A Secular Age*, 79–81, 144.
4 Taylor, *Sources of the Self*, 127–42.
5 See also James Sweeney, "Religious Life Looks to the Future," in *A Future Full of Hope?*, ed. Gemma Simmonds (Dublin: Columba Press, 2012), 132–33.
6 Taylor, *A Secular Age*, 475–83.

The extent to which religious life itself would be impacted by these societal changes became evident during the Second Vatican Council. It could be argued that the main documents of the Council which influenced the lives of sisters can be seen as part of the shift towards the ordinary, as religious life lost its special status, with its apparently superior way of life, and was re-classified as within the lay state. At the same time, the role of the laity and the ministry of the laity were given new prominence. Furthermore, the shift to world-engagement and the sisters' eventual emergence from the 'total institution' meant that they came more into contact with 'ordinary' life. They came to see themselves as part of, rather than set apart from, ordinary life, and to accept that as a good thing. The period following the Second Vatican Council saw the emergence of the individual sister with her personality, experience, talents, interests, and an interior life; and furthermore, there were signs that this development was increasingly accepted and valued in congregations. As Sr. Collette explains:

> It's so different from the past when decisions were made by our superiors and people that were in charge of us, but the Holy Spirit is working in individuals, and we need to listen to and be open to and respond to whatever is coming from them.

4.3 Free to Become Oneself

Schneiders, in a discussion of vocation, posits that religious life is not a profession or an organization, but a "state of life": "Religious Life is not really something one 'enters' or 'joins' so much as a life one lives. One *becomes* a Religious. Being a Religious is not primarily something one does but something one is."[7] She emphasizes the being over the doing, reflecting the shift she saw both happening and needing to happen in apostolic religious life. However, from my experience of engagement with the sisters' narratives in this study, I would take that one step further and suggest that being a religious is some*one* rather than some*thing* one becomes, or even in the present continuous, is becoming.

Hahnenberg's work refocussing Catholic theology of vocation on the notion of call towards a place offers further insights into the sisters' stories of becoming in response to their call. He charts the development of vocation theology from the Protestant Barth towards the Catholic Rahner, identifying

---

7 Sandra Schneiders, *Selling All: Commitment, Consecrated Celibacy, and Community in Catholic Religious Life* (Mahwah, NJ: Paulist Press, 2001), 9.

a trajectory towards a link between "who I am and the God who calls."[8] He understands vocation as "forward movement—the 'whither' of vocation" which resonates with the dynamic generativity of the concept of becoming.[9] Hahnenberg grounds this observation in the recent reception of Karl Rahner's theology of grace, and particularly in the possibility of an immediate experience of God being available to each of us. Hahnenberg styles this, after Rahner, "*Selbstmitteilung Gottes*," or that God self communicates to each of us on a very personal, individual level. "God gives God's very self to us,"[10] dwelling within us, and this has influenced the development of an understanding of both grace and vocation or 'call' as inductive, rather than something visited upon us externally.

It is the very personal, individual nature of this experience and call which is of relevance to us here: that God speaks "through *me*—through the dynamism of my own personality and inner life," calling each of us as we are, rather than as someone we ought to or could be.[11] We only have the freedom to make choices, as ourselves, if we are deeply rooted in a self-awareness which is in turn rooted in God's indwelling. Hahnenberg interprets this as there being a place of freedom, out of which we make our own choices, located in between our creaturehood, and our acting out of the power of grace. This is how we arrive at and live out our individual personality and self: "so, by freedom we become unique."[12] There is a paradox in following the gospel, the word of God, and in being open to being conformed to God's loving purposes: "There is a freedom in this limitation, the freedom to be me, marked as I am by all the particularities of the existence granted to me by God."[13]

In the narratives which follow, the sisters strive to establish their own identity, wanting to make choices for themselves. In doing so, they are seeking to be both religious and apostolic as themselves: the person God has called them to be. Hahnenberg's points help to interpret the meaning in the sisters' stories: the sense of forward movement; the desire to become as oneself; the realization that this has to be inductive as they look within and their becoming some*one*, and not some*thing*.

---

8 Edward P. Hahnenberg, *Awakening Vocation: A Theology of Christian Call* (Collegeville, MN: Liturgical Press, 2010), 123.
9 Hahnenberg, *Awakening Vocation*, 231.
10 Hahnenberg, *Awakening Vocation*, 132, likely relying on Karl Rahner, *Foundations of Christian Faith: An Introduction to the Idea of Christianity*, trans. William V. Dych (New York: Crossroad, 1978).
11 Hahnenberg, *Awakening Vocation*, 143.
12 Hahnenberg, *Awakening Vocation*, 150.
13 Hahnenberg, *Awakening Vocation*, 120.

4.4   First Set of Narratives: Claiming and Asserting Identity

These narratives demonstrate a strong thread of constructing and conveying a sense of identity. This is unsurprising, as this weaving of patterns of experience to project or claim identity is a fundamental function of narrative. The self is constructed in its locating of itself in relation to and its telling of itself to others.[14] It is through talking to me, and how I reinterpret their story, that the sisters construct their identity, and in this sense, are continuing to 'become.'

While this book does not seek to provide an exhaustive exploration and analysis of the projected or claimed identity of each of the participants, some consideration of this issue is relevant. Taylor provides a helpful definition of identity.

> To know who I am is a species of knowing where I stand. My identity is defined by the commitments and identifications which provide the frame of horizon within which I can try to determine from case to case what is good, or valuable, or what ought to be done, or what I endorse or oppose. In other words, it is the horizon within which I am capable of taking a stand.[15]

In other words, identity helps supply us with a framework or ethic in which we can be, to which we can respond. The first reason why identity is relevant here is that the sisters also use this opportunity to expand upon their frame of horizon, or where they stand. They are at pains to point out that they are very much connected to others, but some do this in relation to who others say they should be. Taylor goes on to qualify the definition above by adding that we can only be a 'self' in response to some defining community or framework:

> We cannot but orient ourselves to the good, and thus determine our place relative to it and hence determine the direction of our lives; we must inescapably understand our lives in narrative form, as a "quest."[16]

He then continues with an alternative:

---

14   Taylor, *Sources of the Self*, 25–52; and David Pellauer, *Ricoeur: A Guide For the Perplexed* (London: Continuum, 2007), 84.
15   Taylor, *Sources of the Self*, 27.
16   Taylor, *Sources of the Self*, 51–52.

> Because we have to determine our place in relation to the good, therefore we cannot be without an orientation to it, and hence must see our life in story.[17]

This latter point sheds some light on the sisters' understanding of 'apostolic,' which has changed from being an adjective used to describe activity and work, to an adjective used to describe a person, being for and in relation to others. This I reinterpret as becoming apostolic as themselves.

The second reason why identity is relevant here is that I believe the sisters are establishing the importance of being 'free,' or allowed to be themselves. Turning again to Hahnenberg:

> Empowered by grace in the core of our personality, we freely shape our own individuality. What God is calling me toward, what God wants for *me* is to be *myself*.[18]

Hahnenberg's point helps explain why the sisters say that it is important to be apostolic as themselves, and not as someone they are not, as they respond to God's call to be more fully themselves.

4.4.1 *Resisting Externally Ascribed Identities*

The sisters all made use of a variety of devices to build up a picture of who they say they are. These included self-descriptors; examples of how family, friends, and others describe them; anecdotes; experiences; and relationships with others and institutions. Seven of the twelve sisters appear to do this in reference to other voices or forces ascribing identity to them, to 'who others say I should be' as a nun. Sometimes this 'other' is the public in general, or people outside of religious life. Sometimes this 'other' is named. For Srs. Martina, Kathleen, and Jayne, it refers to other sisters in their community or congregation, or the community or congregation itself. For Srs. Bernadette and Maeve, their family is a strong voice in defining and describing them; and for Srs. Bernadette, Clare, and Jayne, the Church is a strong external force, particularly in setting expectations of who and how women religious are expected to be.

Brock states that "notions of what it is to be woman are constructed on multiple sites in the social, political, religious and economic world," and in her work, she explores the extent to which the Catholic Church has created and

---

17 Taylor, *Sources of the Self*, 52.
18 Hahnenberg, *Awakening Vocation*, 151, emphasis original.

regulated the 'norms' of identity for Catholic sisters.[19] However, despite these constructs and norms being set and accepted, women can claim identities for themselves which are not bound by those constructed for them by the Church, their congregations, or more widely. In Taylor's terms, they can choose their own ethic.[20]

One group of sisters claimed their own identities, and their first act of claiming is expressed in terms of 'I'm me: I'm different, but I've always been allowed to be different,' and 'I'm not a conventional nun.' Three sisters in particular described how they broke the mould when younger, being the unconventional sister who, despite wearing a habit and, therefore, conforming externally, taught sport or refereed matches. Sr. Beatrice tells of challenging others' expectations:

> When I appeared in a full habit and things, they said to me, "Oh, your meeting is down the corridor in the library," and I said, "What meeting is that?" "Something to do with books." And I said, "Actually, I've come for the sports meeting"—to do with netball, it was, and they said—absolute total silence.

Later on, she describes being invited for an interview on a sports programme on local radio:

> They said, "No nun has ever been on [this programme] before," and I said, "Oh, I'd like to be the first." ... He wanted me because it would have been a big coup for him, to have got a nun coming on doing this. Lots of people would have laughed, but there would have been an interest. ... And then he put on the most popular ones for the new year, and mine was the top of the list—not because of me, but because I was a nun [laughter]. They didn't expect a nun to be like that.

Sr. Pamela similarly challenged convention and appeared energized by having done so.

> [I was asked] so would I teach football, so I taught football ... my photo was in the [national newspaper]—we've had the singing nun and something else nun, and now we had the soccer nun. So that went viral; it went all over the papers and ... the photograph that they took at the primary

---

19 Megan P. Brock, "Resisting the Catholic Church's Notion of the Nun as Self-sacrificing Woman," *Feminism and Psychology* 20, no. 4 (2010): 486.
20 Taylor, *Sources of the Self*, 27.

school, at a football match, ended up in one of these books "when I were a lad"—about the north of England, well I'm in one of those; they called me Sr. [x] and said I could swear like a trooper.

Sr. Bernadette was also keen to demonstrate that she is "not the usual type of nun," contrasting herself with another nun in her family whom she describes as pious, but also showing an awareness and rejection of prevailing stereotypes regulated by the Church.

> I'm interested in football. ... I have a very good sense of humour, and it kind of shows in all sorts of ways. I will dress up at the drop of a hat. I'm no introvert, and a lot of nuns are introverts.

She used comments by her family, with them joking that the congregation would never be able to cope with her, in order to reinforce what an unlikely nun she makes. She recounts that unlike others, her family never put her on a pedestal:

> There was no artificial adulation in any way, so I think that was why I didn't have to act out in any way or look like I was walking on wheels.

In doing so, Sr. Bernadette acknowledges the kinds of expectations those outside of religious life might have of sisters, and to which other sisters were subjected:

> It can be a bit daunting to live up to that [expectation] all the time, when you'd really just want interaction. But it's the way people were brought up in the fifties and early sixties, to respect the religious and the priest and all the rest of it.

The sisters above almost delight in 'being themselves' in a way that challenges prevalent stereotypes. Srs. Kathleen and Jayne, on the other hand, show how the expectation or actual experience of negative responses can restrict their identity or curtail behaviour, particularly when it comes to revealing that they are in fact sisters. None of the sisters interviewed now wears a habit, although most wear some external sign such as a ring or cross, or can be identified in other ways, as Sr. Kathleen explains:

> I don't feel the need to tell other people that I'm a nun. ... I would never hide it, and in Church circles I would always say, and to parish people, because I've no trouble explaining it ... maybe Irish people my own age ...

often when I'm chatting to people on the buses—the gossip that goes on there, on the bus, and I say I was in Africa for so many years, and they say now how was that—they ask what kind of person would go and live that long in Africa and then come back here, and I would then say, "Well, I'm a nun"—you know, for Irish people, that's no problem, but for other people it only deepens the problem!

Sr. Jayne gives several examples of feeling challenged by others' responses to her being a Catholic sister:

On the whole, I would rather be just myself, an ordinary person, rather than being a member of an institution, especially as we got rather a bad press recently, child abuse and the rest of it. It's either the abuse or the sentimental good little sister who's a bit naive. So I have been much happier since I took off my veil and wimple or whatever you call it.

I'm talking to somebody I've never met before and I'll say well, you know I'm an RC sister—I'm a nun. Oh, you're wearing trousers—that sort of thing comes out. Okay—but they don't mind—well, some of them do; some of them will say, "Oh, I was taught by nuns and oh, I didn't like them."

These excerpts articulate not only a concern about how others might react, but also an expression of a desire to be perceived and accepted as ordinary women, a point I will return to later in this chapter.

4.4.2   *Resisting Internally Ascribed Identities*

In contrast to the group in the previous section, a smaller number of sisters showed some resistance to identities being ascribed to, or imposed on, them by their own congregations. Initially, I treated these sisters' experiences as outliers or exceptions, as they seemed to be in a minority. However, on encountering Brock's work, I realized that these sisters, although few in number, had a real significance. Brock identified independent living as one of the main markers by which sisters in her study demonstrated personal agency. Two of the sisters in this book live singly, and Brock's work offers a framework for viewing these sisters' experiences.

Sr. Kathleen lived in small mission-based communities in Africa for many years, the informality of which contrasts with the institutional community life she encountered on returning to the UK just five years previously. She elected to live alone, but close to her community. However, her lifestyle and decisions to continue to work and move around independently, attracted what Brock terms "the disapproving disciplinary gaze" of her own sisters.[21]

> And the older sister, who's a very well-educated, experienced, with-it person, she said something when I came in: "Oh, so you've been out, and you never told us where you were going," and that sums up an attitude that—our dear sister has been out, and she hasn't told us where she's gone. I thought my answer was a bit sharp, but I think it was the right one. I just said, "Your dear sister is back now." I wasn't getting drawn into it, but that lack of freedom—that's going on all the time for years and years, and you internalize the criticism that's going to come to you. And then you behave accordingly so they don't ever have to say to you, "You're stepping over the line." This is the idea of community, and if you're not conforming ... those hidden things, little things—that would be what I found hard—I anticipated what they [her community] were going to say to me.

This expectation of conforming to norms of behaviour she did not herself espouse was a leading factor in Sr. Kathleen's decision to live alone, and she says of that move: "the happiest day of my life; the freedom of leaving that situation." Problems she had experienced earlier in her religious life still dogged the way the community saw her: "Still, it was on my CV, if you like; it was there, and it's there today even still." Her independent lifestyle, refusal to conform, and the way the community viewed her, point to her being judged not a 'proper nun,' and she is paying the price for her separation and perhaps alienation from her community.

> You know the thing that 'nuns don't behave like that'—that sentence was thrown at us so much when we were young and then—talk about your mother's voice talking to you!—the voices of our Superiors go on speaking to us in our old age.

It is clear that in these cases, the sisters' own congregations had absorbed the Church's regulating of the women's identities and establishing what constitutes a 'proper nun.' This was made explicit in myriad ways, such as judging other members of the community for not conforming, and an implicit expectation that sisters ask, if not permission, then seeking some kind of informal consent.

---

21 Brock, "The Nun as Self-sacrificing Woman," 484.

These cultural norms and restrictions which were "petty and out of date … [and] ritualism for its own sake" governed every aspect of the sisters' lives.[22]

Sr. Clare lives singly and also seemed something of an anomaly among a group of sisters who appear by and large content to be living in physical community with their sisters. She was the only sister in the cohort who was a member of a teaching order who had never taught but forged a path of ministry in a new field.[23] Although she did not experience disapproval or judgement from her congregation, she does speak of not feeling understood. She is also very outspoken about the way the Catholic Church both views and treats women generally, and women religious in particular. She is critical of her own congregation, and women religious more broadly, for having been very passive in their acceptance of this. Viewed alongside these other factors, her choice to live alone, not teach, and live a different form of religious life, could well be seen as a form of resistance.

Sr. Jayne, on the other hand, lives with her community but talks of feeling out of step with them on several important issues. She confesses to being slightly envious of the sisters in her congregation who live singly, but who come together regularly for prayer and a meal. "In their acts of resistance, [they] create new discursive truths and material practices about what community is and how it best functions for them."[24] Sr. Jayne feels that it is now too late for her to be part of creating "new discursive truths" herself, and indeed for her congregation to do so, but nonetheless sees hope for new forms of religious life in the future, where this may be encouraged.

4.5   Second Set of Narratives: Fulfilment and Frustration

The extent to which sisters appear to find fulfilment or not in their apostolates and ministries emerged as a significant second narrative running through the majority of their interviews. Certainly up until the late 1970s, congregations were under a lot of pressure to staff their own institutions. They came to regard, perhaps unintentionally, their sisters as a work force; they had "instrumental goals."[25] This instrumentalization of the sisters served not only congregational

---

22   Suzanne Campbell-Jones, *In Habit: An Anthropological Study of Working Nuns* (London: Faber and Faber, 1979), 121.
23   With the exception of Sr. Martina, who was a lay sister and never expected to teach.
24   Brock, "The Nun as Self-sacrificing Woman," 485.
25   Campbell-Jones, *In Habit*, 128.

needs, but also the 'works' of the Church at parish and diocesan levels.[26] This was a practice that tainted the true nature of apostolic religious life up until the Second Vatican Council, by carrying out what Schneiders terms "external 'apostolates' such as administering and staffing Catholic institutions … exercised exclusively within the context of the institutional Church to support, sustain, and implement the ministerial projects of the hierarchy."[27] Elsewhere, she contrasts "the hierarchy's understanding of Religious as a dedicated 'work force' within Catholic institutions" with the emerging self-understanding of religious as they moved closer towards claiming their "fully apostolic character."[28] So, both individual and collective identity are being reshaped. However, in the early lives of the sisters in this study, their congregations were still caught up in this dynamic, which often obscured the congregation's true nature and founding charism. Sr. Susan was a member of a community that continued to live a mixed life, or hybrid form of religious life, until the 1980s, and explains how her Superior justified the need for her to teach:

> [She] told me, "We are a contemplative order that teaches." Now that's not exactly true; in a sense, there you can hear the lack of clarity that I spoke about, and it's almost a contradiction anyway.

What follows below are narratives of 'thwarted desires' or loss, and satisfaction, where individual sisters are caught up in this dynamic. I take the example of teaching as the means of exploring fulfilment and frustration in their ministerial lives, as so many of the sisters taught. However, through the stages of thwarted desire and acceptance, all come to a point of growing agency.

Ten of the sisters taught, and nine of them spent the majority of their 'professional' lives (that is, until retirement age) in school. Of the other two, one was a lay sister and domestic worker, and one chose not to teach and worked in the probation service. Five sisters enjoyed teaching and seem to have felt fulfilled in this apostolate, loving both the contact with children and teaching their subjects. They appreciated the opportunity to influence the lives of young people and build a wide range of relationships. They understood this as a real opportunity for apostolic work. This experience needs to be acknowledged,

---

26   Catherine Sexton and Gemma Simmonds, *Religious Life Vitality Project: Key Findings*, report for the Conrad N. Hilton Foundation (London: Heythrop College, 2015), 4, 5, 11.
27   Sandra Schneiders, *Buying the Field: Religious Life in the New Millennium* (Mahwah, NJ: Paulist Press, 2013), 356.
28   Sandra Schneiders, "The Radical Nature and Significance of Consecrated Life," UISG Bulletin 146 (2011): 23, http://www.uisg.org/public/Attachments/doc_semteol_schneiders_2011_en.pdf.

and the analysis presented here is not intended to undermine that in any way. However, alongside the positive experiences of teaching, there are some striking alternative stories which are less commonly heard, indicating that there were many sisters unhappy in school-level education. Mostly these sisters taught out of obedience, even when either they did not feel a particular call to teach or felt they particularly excelled at it. Sr. Anne was not attracted to teaching, and yet felt a strong call to a particular stable community which ran a school. For her, agreeing to teach, even though it was not her personal choice, was just what you did at the time.

> It would be pretty much automatic that you would go into the school to teach ... it was just one of those things. When I joined the community, I accepted what was asked of me, so I suppose if I had been asked to go off and train to be a nurse, I would have said mm, yes, okay. It was a very different mentality we had.

Sr. Anne narrates and locates her own shift to self as having begun from a very different focus on seeking perfection through obedience and participating in the congregation's apostolate.

> I would never have chosen to be a teacher but I was asked to be a teacher, so in obedience [laughs] I did it. I can't say that I didn't enjoy some aspects of it, but I didn't really on the whole enjoy it that much.

Sr. Susan described herself as not a "theoretical educationalist" but found the relationships fulfilling.

> Perhaps it's better to say that teaching never attracted me as such, when it came about that I taught, it was the engagement with the children and colleagues ... the human bits rather than the notion that attracted me.

Other sisters either taught happily, or did not teach, but were clearly aware of the level of dissatisfaction among others who had to teach. In the second round of interviews, I fed back to sisters what I had heard of this unhappiness, and it prompted many comments. Sr. Bernadette taught until formal retirement age and loved it. Nevertheless, she talked about sisters who were told to go into ministries which were not "always what they had thought for themselves," or who were not properly trained for jobs, or moved from one community to another: "Like a square peg in a round hole, it would be so debilitating. I think it does resonate with some of the things that we've all met in religious life."

Sr. Martina noted

> how many nuns had to teach when there was nothing in them for teaching; it was the last thing they thought of—to teach.

Sr. Dorothy had also loved teaching but nonetheless noted the unhappiness of others from her experience of being a head teacher.

> Some of ours were [unhappy], and it was quite obvious, if one was put on your staff, that she should never be here. There were quite a few who were not suited, and they've blossomed since they were able to find another outlet. ... I think you either loved teaching or you didn't, and if you were not at ease with it, it must have been agony, really, to be in the classroom. I've had some of them on my staff.

For many sisters, this being assigned to a profession you were not suited to must have meant many long, unhappy, and unfulfilled years. Others undoubtedly left as a result of the "talent-stripping" which Campbell-Jones observed among congregations she studied,[29] when sisters were sent to do work which made no use of their talents, and where they had no other outlet for personal interests and gifts. The sisters, by and large, did what they were told and what the congregation needed. As Sr. Martina says, "That's how I understood obedience—in the old days, the obedience was 'do it.'" However, this gradually began to change from the late 1960s onwards, as congregations revisited their founding charism, rewrote their constitutions, and in the 1970s, began to widen the sphere of their apostolates in response to both interest and need.[30] As part of the gradual breaking open of the 'total institution,' many sisters became aware of new possibilities: the possibility of taking the dust sheets off their 'selves,' or even of beginning to discover what that 'self' was for the first time. This was a clear point in the move from an ethic and theology of self-denial to self-discovery and self-development.

4.5.1 *Examples of Thwarted Desire*

The stories of several sisters, particularly Srs. Jayne, Maeve, and Martina, illustrate the development from total, unquestioning obedience to expressions of desire. Sr. Jayne had originally wanted to go into nursing, but when she entered

---

[29] Campbell-Jones, *In Habit*, 82.
[30] Teresa White, *A Vista of Years: History of the Society of the Sisters Faithful Companions of Jesus 1820–1993* (n.p.: Society of the Sisters Faithful Companions of Jesus, 2013).

in the 1940s, she was assured that the congregation had no need of nurses, already encouraging her to suppress her 'desire' in support of its own needs. She told her Superior that she was "scared stiff of teaching" and thought she could only cope with the youngest children. She was pleasantly surprised, therefore, to be sent on a three-year course to train to teach young children.

However, there then followed in her narrative a series of at least six of what I term 'institutional buts' or obstacles. Each time she was either told where she was to be sent next, or each time she began to articulate a desire for herself, this was met by a 'but' from the institution, such as:

> But the Provincial at the time had other plans for me, really without much, without any discussion. ... I was a bit dropped on because it came in a typed letter that said I was going; so anyway, I went.

This expression in her narrative of a desire, then blocked by a 'but' indicating an institutional need, manifested itself throughout her interview as a series of waves met by a hard, straight line, so that I waited for the next 'but' to arrive. On each of these six occasions in her ministerial life, her plan came into conflict with an institutional need so that her own desires were thwarted. Sr. Jayne never actually said no to any of the requests or directives which came from her Superior. Indeed, the degree to which it was possible to say no would have varied between congregations. Sr. Pamela, for example, says that she could have said no to a mission posting because it was overseas, whereas Sr. Maeve felt unable to say no to being sent to the United States.

Sr. Jayne relates that on occasion she tried to say no, but in obedience she accepted each 'missioning.' There is, however, some irony to the final 'but.' In accepting the challenge of a difficult prison ministry, at quite a late stage in her working life, she then found herself engaged in what turned out to be "the best bit of apostolic work I ever went into."

The interviews offered at least two other narratives of thwarted desires or loss, from Sr. Martina and Sr. Maeve, and they share some similarities. They were either given no training at all for work they were then sent to do, or they were trained for something in particular and then sent to do something else, or repeatedly sent to play roles they were either unsuited to, or were unhappy doing. There is a sense of the "talent-stripping" referred to earlier. In both cases, they showed their unhappiness. On being pulled out of teacher training midway through her course, Sr. Maeve said:

> I was in [teacher training] college and I was very happy there. At the end of the year, I was sent for—the God of surprises—I was out on teaching

practice, and when I came home, Mother [name A] was looking for me. She wanted to speak to me, and it was to say that I wouldn't be going back because they needed me—I would be going to [place name] because they were opening a house in [place], and there were two sisters ready to go, and I was qualified to go also, as a third. I mean, it wasn't asked in those days; she just told Mother [name B] that I wouldn't be going back.

When asked how she felt about this, she responded:

> I was heartbroken; I cried for a whole week. I loved [college name] ... but that was the way it was.

A further common point across the narratives is the sisters' use of language, particularly passive forms, and their use of 'they.' Sometimes this is in reference to a faceless, anonymous Superior, and sometimes in reference to the congregation itself: "and I stayed on in London for another year, and then they changed me"; "they took me out of it"; "they sent me" and "they asked me to"; and "they were still deciding. And then I was told by—before officially I was told—that I was destined to go to [x]."

These all suggest a clear experience of lack of agency earlier in their lives: of being 'done to' in order to support an institutional need. As they got older and more confident, and in concert with the changes taking place around them, the sisters' being 'done to' was gradually transformed into expressions of agency and collaborative responsibility. This also took place in the context of the *aggiornamento* within congregations whereby they turned their attentions to the needs of the wider world, and the collective locus and ethic for the sisters' identity was formed within that larger story.

4.6 Using Voice to Exercise Personal Agency: from Obedience to Discernment

The journey through obedience to discernment emerged as a narrative interwoven with the two earlier narratives of claiming an identity and fulfilment in apostolates. The sisters in this study have lived through very radical changes in the understanding of the vow and the nature of obedience. This issue has been extensively documented elsewhere.[31] In its earlier form, obedience was

---

31 Campbell-Jones, *In Habit*; Barbara Fiand, *Living the Vision: Religious Vows in an Age of Change* (New York: Crossroad, 1991); Judith Merkle, *A Different Touch: A Study of*

largely understood as 'keeping the rule' and as absolute and unquestioning obedience to a Superior who represented the figure of Christ in the community or congregation, whose will governed almost every aspect of a sister's life. The shift in understanding of obedience in religious life was again rooted in societal changes, particularly those relating to the socio-cultural understanding of, and increasing mistrust of, authority and obedience. This was coupled with an embracing of psychology which taught that human development continues throughout life.[32] A third contextual factor was the unfreezing of the 'total institution' of the post-conciliar period. As a result of these changes, obedience is now interpreted as listening to and for what God wants for sisters as individuals, and being open to hearing the Spirit from and through a variety of sources.

Conversely, while the traditional idea of absolute obedience to a Superior was being questioned, Schneiders relocates authority from Church hierarchy to within the congregation itself, but to be expressed and explored communally through discernment processes.[33] Discernment has become the 'how' of obedience, so that often decisions are taken after a long period of careful prayer and reflection together.

Sr. Collette explained:

> The understanding of [obedience] has changed, but in a deep-down way. You are more involved in the decisions, and you take the responsibility on yourself as it is collaborative—it's kind of together we make the decisions now—it's not the leaders ... whereas in the past, the Spirit said you go to such and such a place, and in obedience to that, you went.

Apostolic women religious have struggled both to reshape internal understandings of obedience, and with how authority is exercised within the Church, especially in relation to their own lives. These struggles have played a crucial role in enabling congregations to reclaim their fully apostolic nature. Schneiders has argued that a new understanding of religious life as a prophetic calling, wherein obedience is exercised in response to an identified ministerial

---

Vows in Religious Life (Collegeville, MN: Liturgical Press, 1998); Sandra Schneiders, "Discerning Ministerial Religious Life Today," *National Catholic Reporter*, September 11, 2009, accessed November 9, 2012, https://www.ncronline.org/news/discerning-minister ial-religious-life-today; and Schneiders, *Buying the Field*, chap. 10.

32   Vivienne Keely, "Aspects of Mission in Religious Life Since the Second Vatican Council," in *A Future Built on Faith: Religious Life and the Legacy of Vatican II*, ed. Gemma Simmonds (Dublin: Columba Press, 2014), 81–102.

33   Schneiders, *Buying the Field*, chap. 8.

need, was an important factor in enabling this to take place. A ministerial sister is obedient to her call to bring about the reign of God as an alternative reality in a particular time and in a particular place. Schneiders writes of religious "re-imagining the obedience they profess and live" so that obedience becomes "life-giving for themselves and prophetically effective in Church and world."[34]

Although for Schneiders the primary aim of this response to the word of God is through and for ministry which points to an alternative reality, she also acknowledges that "developing and living their life in and for their own times is in and of itself a form of prophetic witness."[35] Comments in interviews evidence the sisters' changes in attitude and self-understanding, as they begin to ask for things for themselves. I argue that in doing this, they are exercising a form of prophetic witness to the role their constructed self can and will play in their ministry in later life. Sisters move from unquestioning obedience and submission as part of a workforce serving a congregational need to an awareness of need in the community and society around them, an increasing expression of self and desire, but within their community and in response to others. This is coupled with the growing sense of freedom which allows them to identify their own gifts and interests and articulate their desire to follow these.

In contrast to the earlier lack of agency in some of the sisters' stories, there is a growing sense of agency across almost all of the narratives. Sr. Maeve wanted to train to be a nurse, but it took her many years before she felt able to ask. As a lay sister, she was always needed in a school kitchen, or as housekeeper. However, finally, unable to face another intake of children into the school, she asked.

> And I said, "Oh, I can't bear that, because I'd never get out of it." [laughter] … And then I thought, I'll go and ask again if I can go nursing before it's too late. I had my last shot with it. I wouldn't have any more … and so this time I asked them again, and I got permission, but I was just lucky to get in, in Scotland, with [religious congregation], because I was too old for being accepted, but they took me.

She did not ask until she was aged fifty. Although her request was received positively, her age made getting a place difficult, and the only course that would accept her was run by another religious congregation. Furthermore, qualifying in her mid-fifties, she found it hard to find work. She eventually found nursing

---

34   Schneiders, *Buying the Field*, 423.
35   Schneiders, *Buying the Field*, 432.

work for a short time, and says she could have resented what happened, but seems now to have come to a position of acceptance.

This slow acquiring of agency in the sisters' religious lives has not always been a smooth trajectory from total obedience to asking and having their requests granted. There seems to have been a long period of testing this out, and a gradual move towards more joint (Superior and sister) or more communal discernment processes prior to decisions being made, such as when to retire from teaching. It is possible that the stories demonstrate a growth towards genuine obedience to their call to become Christlike, and the witness that this form of obedience can offer. Sisters ask, but generally they are only asking for a new form of ministry, or training to increase their ministerial effectiveness.

The sisters also never spoke of the need for fulfilment directly; rather, it was me who introduced language such as 'satisfaction' in my feedback to sisters on the first round of interviews. For some, this seemed to open up the possibility of discussing fulfilment in ministry and elicited a lot of comments, particularly in relation to the consolation felt on retiring from school and being able to explore a new form of ministry. Sr. Clare relates the sense of relief and release from other sisters:

> Others told me about their experience in later life ... of being released from working nine to five in school and preparing kids for exams, and they found a new life dealing with people, and they did various things in retirement.

Sr. Anne, when asked how the decision was made for her to come out of school, said:

> I think I had become increasingly unhappy, and that people recognized that and offered me ... I was just *so* relieved I was able to get out of the school, and I happily said, "Yes, I'd love to go to the [new centre]."

In her second interview, she expanded on the significance of this for her, and also then for her sisters.

> That was a transition which opened up a whole different way in which I might be more happy and at home with myself, because it was then that I realized that the study of Scripture was something I was being drawn to—that was 1972 to 1974—but I went on teaching in the school for another fifteen years—and by that time we'd opened the centre, and that gave me the opportunity to offer Scripture courses, and from 1989

onwards, that has been my focus, so that gradual transition from school teacher to adult education has ... fulfilled something that I knew instinctively was more in communion really with my inner being. ... So, yes, I suppose, the gradual freedom that was extended to any members of the community to pursue a course which seemed to resonate with their inner being and helped them to develop more.

The language used by Sr. Anne and other sisters emphasizes being drawn and being fulfilled and points to more than simply meeting a hitherto unmet ministerial need; it is rather an expression of a desire to meet a hitherto unmet need within themselves. Viewing this through Schneiders' lens, it could be seen as a form of prophetic obedience in that this is what was needed at that time and in that place. The forms of, and understanding of, apostolic ministry into which the sisters were to move as they aged rely and draw on a strong self-knowledge and awareness, so that one can be fully present to and a resource for others.

Hahnenberg recognizes the importance of opportunities to use God-given talents and interests, saying that "God calls us as we are"[36] and, therefore, does not work against who we are.[37] However, he goes on to say that talents and gifts "are but cues—we should glance at them but should not stare," and that "God can always call us to transcend our context and our personal limitations. The call to faith and obedience cuts across all human spheres. Faith is our first and greatest calling."[38] This desire for a form of self-fulfilment is nonetheless an important and very human element which, if completely disregarded, can cause considerable damage and pain. Like all Christians, the sisters are still on that path in between their call and their response, and their longings are very ordinary.

St. Paul in Eph. 4.22–24 exhorts Christians to

> put away [their] former way of life, [their] old self, corrupted and deluded, and to be renewed in the spirit of [their] minds, and to clothe [them]selves with the new self, created according to the likeness of God in true righteousness and holiness.

This is the call to all Christians, and the sisters, through the profession of public vows, have made an additional, single-minded commitment to this lifelong conversion. One wonders whether thwarted self-actualization or even damage

---

36 Hahnenberg, *Awakening Vocation*, 122.
37 Hahnenberg, *Awakening Vocation*, 134.
38 Hahnenberg, *Awakening Vocation*, 123.

reflects on us as the *imago Dei*, and whether the lifelong process of conversion is able to embrace and convert this disappointment.

The concept central to these words of St. Paul above, that of the old self contrasted with the new self, has been taken up, in line with the 'turn to the self,' and even the 'therapeutic turn' in modern psychology and spirituality, as a true self/false self binary by more popular writers such as Richard Rohr.[39] In contrast, Taylor identifies the strong Augustinian roots of the notion of the human "good" being based on our desire for, and orientation towards, God.[40] For Merton, holiness consists of being able to "offer to God the worship of our imitation."[41] This well-known passage from his *New Seeds of Contemplation* may shed light on what he means by this, and on the process the sisters are embarked on, particularly in expressing the choice they are making:

> For me to be a saint means to be myself. Therefore, the problem of sanctity and salvation is in fact the problem of finding out who I am and of discovering my true self. ... God leaves us free to be whatever we like. We can be ourselves or not, as we please. We are at liberty to be real, or to be unreal. We may be true or false, the choice is ours.[42]

4.7 Encouraged to Be Themselves

In contrast to the two groups of sisters considered so far—one claiming their identity in the face of external stereotypes, and one in response to internal expectations—there was a third group of sisters who claimed an identity in which they are very much 'themselves.' Srs. Bernadette, Clare, Dorothy, and Maeve all emphasized that either their school or congregation placed value on their individuality as a person as opposed to trying to 'mass produce' nuns from a mould. Even before we began recording the interview, Sr. Dorothy wanted to stress that she believes she is the person she is regardless of being a sister, and reiterated this several times during the interview.

> I think I'd be like that as a person—I always enjoyed people, and meeting different people, so I think that's me—not necessarily [the congregation], though it may have been nurtured, fostered, whatever.

---

39 Richard Rohr, *Hope against Darkness: The Transforming Vision of Saint Francis in an Age of Anxiety* (Cincinnati, OH: Franciscan Media, 2001).
40 Taylor, *Sources of the Self*, 127–33.
41 Thomas Merton, *New Seeds of Contemplation* (New York: New Directions, 2007), 32.
42 Merton, *New Seeds*, 32.

She attributed this largely to the fact that from the earliest days of being with them in school, her congregation had always encouraged her to be an individual.

> There was never, either at school or in the initial training, any putting you into a mould. We weren't moulded in any way at all.

Sr. Dorothy felt this was related to her congregation's charism which is rooted in incarnational theology, understanding each human person to be made in God's image. This recognizes that God calls us to be ourselves, but also proposes that the call is to become that self that God wants us to be, recalling Hahnenberg's earlier point that discernment begins with being fully rooted in the awareness of God's presence. The more we come to know God and accept that we are made in God's image, the more 'real' our self is, and the more freedom we have, and thus we come to know our 'true self.'

The sisters appear to hold this as a truth for themselves as they turn inwards to the self, more fully reflecting God's image. Taylor draws our attention to the paradox at the heart of this search: it is "where I strive to make myself more fully present to myself, to realize to the full the potential which resides in the fact that knower and known are one, that I come most tellingly and convincingly to the awareness that God stands above me."[43] The sisters know and recognize that this inner, God-based freedom is how they can realize their unique God-given self or creaturehood. Furthermore, they seem to have been aware of this since the early stages of their discernment to become a sister. The desire to be accepted for who they were was an important factor for many of the sisters in considering which congregation they joined.

Excerpts from the sisters' interviews have already established their belief that 'apostolic' means so much more than doing. Furthermore, they claim that being apostolic is part of their identity and an expression of their deepest desire, which is to love God. They are keen to establish that they draw on their deepest selves in being apostolic, and that in being apostolic, they are drawing on their deepest or 'true selves.' As evidence of this, Sr. Bernadette told me:

> I exercise ministry just by being the Jolly Green Giant—opening the door, welcoming people, making them a cuppa and showing that I'm happy and just being myself—that's my ministry of presence.

---

43   Taylor, *Sources of the Self*, 135.

Sr. Jayne also explained:

> I think it's over the years that I've come much more to think of being apostolic as being a sort of human, Christian, religious, just person, just me.

Some sisters went slightly further than simply making the connection between being apostolic and being themselves. Both Sr. Martina and Sr. Beatrice seemed to be saying that this apostolic impulse was in some way innate to their being. Sr. Martina explained about being apostolic: "It's part of my nature; it's because it's in me, it's in me by nature." Sr. Beatrice talked about praying for, and doing things for, others and being apostolic, and said, "Without it, I would die"—implying in some way that it is such an integral part of her that she could not live without it, and would certainly not be the person she is without it.

Sr. Brenda was keen to emphasize that nuns are 'real' people:

> Nuns are not people who are not real, who have not had experience, who have not been in love; they are real human beings with human desires.

In this she displays, along with many other sisters, a desire to be seen and accepted not only as themselves, but as 'ordinary.' This is a noticeable theme in the sisters' interviews.[44] In one sense, the Second Vatican Council's removal of the superior status and holiness of religious, and their reclassification as lay, set the scene for this change. It may also be a response to a form of class system among religious orders, with those owning and running prestigious schools being seen as grand or superior in some way. Another factor may be the negativity of Western attitudes towards the Church and religious in the context of numerous sexual abuse scandals, and sisters' fear of a response rooted in these negative experiences, as expressed by Sr. Jayne and Sr. Beatrice.

However, it must be seen most clearly in relation to Taylor's affirmation of the ordinary life where the 'ordinary' has taken on a moral relevance as we judge both ourselves and others by how 'ordinary' we are.[45] This affirmation of the ordinary has given us an ethical direction. In spite of our celebrity culture, the 'ordinary' is good, and Catholic sisters are not immune to this. They are keen to portray themselves as ordinary Christians, with the same call, and making the same journey in response, and several of them really wrestle with any notion that they or their life is in any way chosen or 'special.' This is of relevance, as the desire to self-describe as 'ordinary' is so evident in the sisters' own

---

44   See Sexton and Simmonds, *Religious Life Vitality Project*, 7.
45   Taylor, *Sources of the Self*, chap. 13.

words. Sr. Beatrice, for example, celebrates her new 'ordinary' life in a small community on a housing estate: "You are just part of what everyone else is doing. I find that very freeing." This is an expression of release, of relief, and of the freedom of just being able to live as and be received as oneself, narrated and located in the ordinary.

4.7.1 A Concern with Freedom

The theology articulated in teaching documents on religious life such as *Vita Consecrata* (1996)[46] and *Starting Afresh from Christ* (2002)[47] is based on a belief that the call from God and the 'special consecration' which distinguishes vowed religious are sufficient rewards in and of themselves. The religious does not therefore need to look for affirmation from other people.

> Consecrated life does not need praise and human appreciation; it is repaid by the joy of continuing to work untiringly for the kingdom of God, to be a seed of life which grows in secret, without expecting any reward other than that which the Lord will give in the end. It finds its identity in the call of the Lord, in following him, in unconditional love and service, which are capable of filling a life to the brim and giving it fullness of meaning.[48]

This claim contrasts with the sisters in this study who speak, in very human terms, of unfulfilled desires and a sense of not being appreciated for who they were, nor what they had to offer. Sr. Collette presents her perspective on this:

> I don't know, maybe before this I just focussed on my work as a teacher and how I could do that to the best of my ability. I put so much into that, whereas I felt maybe my own self was left out of it, I know I was always thinking of others.

At the beginning of this chapter, I noted the post-conciliar turn in religious life away from external compliance, authority, and structure towards 'the subjective' and an acceptance of the importance of the individual call, personal discernment, and relationship. This acceptance has enabled the transition

---

46 Pope John Paul II, *Post-synodal Apostolic Exhortation: "Vita Consecrata,"* March 25, 1996, accessed November 23, 2015, http://w2.vatican.va/content/john-paul-ii/en/apost_exhor tations/documents/hf_jp-ii_exh_25031996_vita-consecrata.html.
47 Congregation for Institutes of Consecrated Life and Societies of Apostolic Life (CICLSAL), *Starting Afresh from Christ: A Renewed Commitment to Consecrated Life in the Third Millennium* (London: St. Pauls, 2002).
48 CICLSAL, *Starting Afresh from Christ*, §13.

to individualized and diversified ministries. The sisters I encountered were taught not to consider their own needs, interests, or self-fulfilment, but that varying degrees and forms of self-sacrifice would contribute to the sanctification of their own souls, and those of others. This would have been inculcated from early on within their novitiates, as illustrated by Mangion: "The abnegation of self and the taming of one's self-will demonstrated their dedication to religious life."[49]

This explains the level of concern with freedom, primarily, or superficially at least, in terms of being *free from* past strictures, rules, and regulations, and being *free to* be apostolic religious as themselves. The stories of frustration and loss demonstrate why sisters show interest in choice and freedom, and why use of these words in their stories is surprisingly common. They also express a longing for, and appreciation of, the 'freedom' they were given to explore and respond with their own gifts and talents, and a sense of loss or grief for what they were not able to do.

The sisters use the language of freedom in several ways. First, the recent-found freedom to explore interests in a new and individual ministry making use of their gifts is evident in the excerpts presented above, and even among the sisters who loved teaching. Sr. Beatrice, at the age of eighty, is finally free to make choices for herself.

> She [the Provincial Superior] said I could go where I like—imagine that! ... She said, "I want you to use your gifts," and I said, "Oh, thanks very much." And she said, "You have a gift for writing," which I knew I did have, and she said, "I want you to spread the Word through your writing."

Sr. Bernadette and Sr. Collette both speak extensively about the importance of being free to be oneself, and to live one's own life, and Srs. Collette, Maeve, and Kathleen all contrast this with their previous lack of 'freedom.' Sr. Collette, for example, comments on being *free from*, in terms of contrasting the present situation of religious life with that of the past, and locates this 'freedom' in the experience and context of her own congregation.

> Whereas you know in the past we'd have had a day of recollection once a month, but now I'm free to choose whatever, and I find that's a strength for me as well, to be able to choose.

---

49   Carmen M. Mangion, "Laying 'Good Strong Foundations': The Power of the Symbolic in the Formation of a Religious Sister," *Women's History Review* 16, no. 3 (2007): 412.

In her second interview, two years on from the original interview, she talks about freedom in a different way again, showing a concern to pay attention to her own needs in a more intentional way. She understands that freedom is a prerequisite of responsibility and choice: "Yes, only in freedom can a person assume responsibility for her life." The theology operant in her speech emphasizes being free to witness as herself.

> It's not somebody else's life I am trying to live, it's just to live my own as best as I possibly can.

A religious is a witness by virtue of who she is, through herself. In response to my asking if it is important to witness as a religious, she replies:

> I'm not sure its witness as a religious, but as a human being; you're a developed human being … you're not just a religious, but a spiritual, religious person, and you're recognized for that, that you're a whole human being; I think that's the witness in society today, that you can enjoy, that you can socialize and develop all parts of you yourself and then go out and help to develop, help others. I think that speaks more to people—that we are human beings, and not people up in the clouds and can't relate to them. That's the witness I feel called to give now; I don't want to pretend I am somebody else. … I want to be true to my own commitment.

In the second round of interviews, Sr. Kathleen reacted quite strongly to my 'finding' that being or becoming free to choose appeared to be important to the sisters. She judged this subjectivity as overly individualistic, seeing it as a negative development among religious:

> The people who made this … it's all of us, but I was just kind of shocked at how individualistic we have become. Like … all mission, ministry, whatever we call it, apostolate, it has become very, my pain, my being true to myself, what I have to offer individually.

She acknowledged, however, that she recognized herself in this:

> They see their strength is in their own being free, finding themselves, and I am one of the people who contributed to that, and when I saw it coming back in such an abundance I was thinking, my God, is that where we are now?

In response to Sr. Collette's (among others) delight in being free to choose how she prays, she noted:

> Even in the way we pray there is an awful lot that suits me individually, like in older times listening to readings, say, from the Old Testament, Jeremiah, Isaac—it challenged us; but now we choose the prayer we want to say, that suits me for the day, there is a lot of that having a nice setting ... and finding nice words maybe in a song or poem or something that looks, I don't know what, but it's more, I am not allowing myself to be challenged from the outside.

4.7.2 *From Self-Denial to Self-Gift*

The extent to which religious life has been affected by the individualism which is now such a feature of the culture of western Europe and North America has been noted and explored elsewhere.[50] However, I do not interpret the desires for choice, freedom, and to be themselves expressed by the sisters in this way, nor indeed as Sr. Kathleen has done. Rather they seem to form part of their response to their own past and the experience of a form of self-abnegation. Schneiders suggests that religious, in moving away from the pre-conciliar ideal of "self-denial," had to then move through a period of self-realization or self-fulfilment, when many believed they had succumbed to the temptations of individualism.[51] She argues that, to the contrary, they have emerged through this dark night into a place of "legitimate and life-giving personal development which is the *sine qua non* of a mature capacity for self-donation."[52]

In the second round of interviews, I asked sisters what they thought of Schneiders' proposal. Of the ten sisters who responded, two said quite firmly that they did not recognize the experience of self-denial or self-abnegation. Sr. Dorothy laughed heartily, and Sr. Jayne said:

> Well, I am not sure that I ever did have that experience of religious life—self-abnegation or self-denial—that to me is not a very good starting point. Maybe I did start from that, but I didn't think of it that way,

---

[50] See David J. Nygren and Miriam D. Ukeritis, "The Religious Life Futures Project: Executive Summary," *Review for Religious* 52, no. 1 (1993): 6–55; Patricia Wittberg, *The Rise and Fall of Catholic Religious Orders: A Social Movement Perspective* (Albany, NY: SUNY Press, 1994); Tony Flannery, *The Death of Religious Life?* (Dublin: Columba Press, 1997); James Sweeney, "Prophets and Parables: A Future for Religious Orders," *Informationes Theologiae Europae: Internationales ökumenisches Jahrbuch für Theologie* 4 (2001): 273–92; and Sweeney, "Religious Life Looks to the Future."
[51] Schneiders, "Radical Nature and Significance of Consecrated Life," 25–26.
[52] Schneiders, "Radical Nature and Significance of Consecrated Life," 26.

it was more … if you are in love with somebody, you don't immediately think of denying something that you would like … and that is where to me religious life starts.

Five sisters, however, agreed with Schneiders' depiction quite strongly; they recognized this as a path they had travelled themselves. From the perspective of an outsider, it appears to map onto the sisters' 'thwarted' narratives quite strongly. Even those sisters who felt they had been encouraged to be themselves identified aspects of self-denial or self-abnegation in the shape of all the petty and pointless regulations of their earlier lives. Many sisters in this study, however, noted that although their novitiate was hard, they did not take it too seriously, as they had their eye on the greater prize. They understood that in some way this path would lead to growth (at least for many who stayed), and for the sisters in this book, it could be argued that it did. Their desire for some form of self-fulfilment is a sign of a healthy, mature self-awareness. It is also a response to the signs of the times, and of prophetic obedience, both operating out of, and embracing, free will as self-determination. I argue that this has been fundamental to their understanding and practice of the forms of ministry of later life, which I will come to explore in the following chapters, and whereby they give of themselves so freely and knowingly.

4.8 Conclusion

The pre-conciliar theology of religious life considered self as something to be denied. The material I gathered from my interviews with sisters presented in this chapter has shown some of the impact of this theology on their lives and, furthermore, how the sisters have resisted the Church's and their communities' efforts to shape their identities. Through this process, they have become apostolic as themselves.

The great French ethicist Paul Ricoeur would recognize in this process the three elements of the self's own desires, and the self being shaped with, and for, others, and in concert with a just institution, as "the ethical constitution of the person."[53] The reality of living for others through relationship that has been implicit in this chapter will be made explicit in the next chapter, as I consider the sisters' understanding of 'apostolic' as being with and for others, expressed through the gift of themselves. These elements point to the heart of the apostolic vocation and how it can be lived in later life.

---

53 Paul Ricoeur, *Oneself as Another*, trans. Kathleen Blamey (Chicago, IL: University of Chicago Press, 1992), 45.

CHAPTER 5

Being With and Being For

5.1 Introduction

In our exploration of the sisters' journey of conversion, the time has now come to consider their current context. This does not mean looking at a point of arrival, as the theology at the heart of this study indicates that the sisters are still and always becoming. However, their current context has a direct bearing on the ways in which they understand themselves to be apostolic at this stage in life. In this chapter, I will begin to explore the sisters' context of being largely housebound or in a care community and engaged in no or only limited external activity and how this shapes their attitude to living out their vocation in later life. Taking a group of sisters who are for the most part no longer in active, recognizable, or external ministry allows us to focus on who they are, as they find themselves being apostolic largely in and through relationship with others outside of the framework of formal employment. It highlights an orientation of being with and being for, interpreted with the help of the concepts of self-gift and availability.

Schneiders refers to the 'new normal' of religious life which is being shaped by a demographic shift in western European and North American society with the growth of an ageing population.[1] Over the course of the lives of the sisters featured in this study, the demographic profile in these parts of the world has changed from those over sixty-five being a minority to them rapidly forming a very significant sector of society.

Schneiders claims that this new normal of longevity means the human lifespan can no longer be viewed in terms of a childhood and an adulthood followed by an old age characterized by inactivity. Rather there will be a second adulthood, which she terms "Adulthood II," which may last from the mid-fifties into the late seventies or early eighties, and that sisters in their second adulthood will continue in active ministry probably throughout that stage.[2] Schneiders says it is, therefore, inappropriate for sisters in their seventies to be considered in retirement. Today, sisters in this age bracket and over

---

[1] Sandra Schneiders, "Religious Life Evolving Faithful and Free," paper presented to the Conference of Religious of Ireland, Dublin, April 25, 2014.
[2] Sandra Schneiders, *Buying the Field: Religious Life in the New Millennium* (Mahwah, NJ: Paulist Press, 2013), 21.

are often "not retirees psychologically, socially or ministerially, even if they might be such in terms of society's employment structure."[3] The sisters in this study would concur, as several state that religious do not retire, and they do not see themselves as retired from ministry. If we accept Schneiders' claim that religious life is not an organization but a state of life,[4] then the sisters clearly cannot retire from being religious. As Sr. Maeve says:

> I am maybe retired, but what am I retired from? I haven't retired from being a sister and our way of life and the values that have been passed on and have been imbibed by me over the years.

The question, then, for consideration in this and the following chapter is this: If the sisters' state of physical health and stage of life mean that they are no longer able to be involved in formal, paid, or external ministries, what is the ministry they are involved in, and what does ministry at this stage of life look like?

5.2 Context

The factors that have led to a changed demographic profile and reduced visibility and, therefore, social influence of religious in the UK and beyond have been discussed at various points in this book. However, two factors have a particular bearing on how sisters continue to be apostolic, and on their understanding of ministry at this stage in their lives. The first is the extent to which they continue to be involved in ministry outside of their own community. At the time of the first interviews, four of the sisters were still involved in some form of voluntary ministry outside of their community. The remainder are now no longer involved in external ministries, although three are still involved in prayer and retreat work and spiritual direction, or working with their congregation's Associates, which is done from within their own community and so can be regarded as home-based.

A second factor is the extent to which a sister is being cared for. By the time of the second round of interviews, five of the sisters were largely housebound due to a change in their health, and two were resident in their congregation's care community. Both these factors appear to influence how the sisters talk

---

3 Schneiders, *Buying the Field*, 572.
4 Sandra Schneiders, *Finding the Treasure: Locating Catholic Religious Life in a New Ecclesial and Cultural Context* (Mahwah, NJ: Paulist Press, 2000), 54.

about their current understanding and experience of being apostolic. Their activities are now largely home-based, domestic, focussed on other members of their community or carers, or taking place entirely through relationship-based ministries.

My analysis of the interview texts shows two findings. First, it shows that the sisters understand their being apostolic in terms of both breadth and particularity of relationships. This is unsurprising, because being in relationship does not depend on physical mobility, although it may depend on having good speech, hearing, and other faculties. The second finding is that the sisters see their ministry, and perhaps their lives, now in terms of self-gift. These findings are not unexpected, as both enable sisters to make meaning of an active vocation within the physical limitations of their lives. Even if a sister can no longer leave her own community, she can understand what she does and who she is in these terms, and continue to find her life meaningful.

The extent to which the sisters are realistic about their physical limitations and abilities is perhaps an indicator of their being obedient to their changing context. It was my impression that none of the sisters in the study is unrealistic about her capabilities, nor do they speak of a reluctance to let go of things they can no longer do. They appear to embrace relinquishment, an intentional letting go and emptying, rather than see themselves as being defined solely by diminishment.[5]

5.3 Ways of Being Apostolic

5.3.1 *Evangelizing*

Within these ever-reducing spheres of activity, mobility, and social influence, sisters speak about being apostolic in a number of ways: apostolic as relationship, and as being with and being for, and articulating these as both self-gift and reciprocity. It can be difficult to separate these concepts out from each other because they are so closely intertwined, both in the sisters' words and in reality, but overall they reflect their self-understanding in terms of intersubjectivity. Sr. Bernadette's explanation of 'apostolic' is typical in its setting out a self-understanding as apostolic which encompasses all of these concepts.

> Bringing Christ to others … following in the footsteps of the apostles in that you try to preach, or rather to live the word of God, in a world that isn't always open to it, so you have to become all things to all people, to

---

[5] For more on the distinction between relinquishment and diminishment, see Schneiders, *Buying the Field*, chaps. 10, 6.

try to get the message across that what you are saying and what you are living has relevance, and has an ultimate purpose and goal, the kingdom of God, and that you really believe that is where your ultimate destiny will be. You've got to do your best to express that in terms of your living, your being, so it's just more outward looking.

Sr. Bernadette here describes her understanding of 'apostolic' in more traditional terms such as through following in the footsteps of the apostles and preaching, but integrates these into the way she lives her life and who she is, and all the while looking outwards to others.

Seven of the sisters used the more traditional language of 'evangelization' to explore the meaning of 'apostolic,' although none used this word to describe what they believe themselves to be engaged in, with Sr. Jayne and Sr. Beatrice (see below) noting how much they disliked the term. The sisters used a group of frequently recurring words used to denote their apostolic activity: bringing Christ to others; bringing God to people; preaching; taking out or spreading the good news or the gospel; drawing people to a life of prayer; and bringing others with you, showing them the kingdom, and spreading God's love. Sr. Anne sees spreading the good news as an essential part of her mission.

> "Go, tell the brothers where I am, what you have seen, what you have heard," and that model of the women at the tomb being told to go—that's a missioning—go and spread the good news, and when Jesus appears to the disciples in the upper room in John's Gospel—"as the Father sent me, I have sent you."

Sr. Susan links 'taking out the good news' very clearly to the apostolic impulse towards others and to her congregation's charism.

> The apostolic impulse of our charism is to take out the good news that Jesus lives—he lived the human life that we live; he died a real death, and he lives in the new way that we are all being invited to enter into.

Although the language used by sisters, such as spreading, bringing, and taking out, speaks of a one-way action, a central element of the sisters' view of this 'activity' is that it involves sharing the good news with others, through a clear outward orientation, towards and with others, as articulated by Sr. Beatrice:

> To be apostolic is to be an evangelist, I think. I hate the word 'evangelist,' because it has other connotations that I don't like, but if you're talking about an apostolate, you can't keep it to yourself; you've got to share it

with others. And it's just as our lady carried Jesus wherever she went—she carried him before he was born. We *must* do that. To be apostolic is to be a prayerful person, and second, it's to share that prayer and the joy of the gospel with others, in whatever way we can do, we are allowed to do, or we are called to do.

This suggests the sisters can 'be' through doing—for example, through spreading the gospel and sharing the good news. There are, however, other ways in which they do this which are less explicitly missional.

5.3.2   *Availability in the Everyday*
Although sisters describe specific activities as expressions of being apostolic, these all form part of the gift of their time. In turn, they are also all aspects of self-gift through availability and give expression to the sisters' self-understanding as focussed on gift of self. The sisters' greater availability at this stage in their life reflects not only the changes in attitude which have taken place in religious life, but also that they have more time to give to others now they are no longer in full-time ministry. Sr. Collette explains:

> It's feeling not quite guilty, but should I be doing something else because of my ministry? Now I feel that whenever I meet people, I can have time to share—to smile, and to say good morning. I often meet people around here now, taking their dogs for a walk and things like that, and I feel that that's part of my ministry now, and I'm not saying, "Oh, it's a waste of time or whatever," whereas before I'd have thought, "Oh, I should be doing something else, I should be doing something for preparation for school for tomorrow," or something like that, but I don't feel a bit guilty now.

Sr. Kathleen also appreciates the benefits of no longer being in full-time ministry: "it's not like when we had piles of exercise books to correct or running around here and there." Sr. Pamela recalls how in earlier religious life, simply sitting and listening to someone would have been viewed as "a waste of time." Sr. Dorothy notes that with old age, time has come as a gift to her:

> At least I have time on my side; I can give them time. I can't go running around the country now, but I can give them time.

In this time that they give, the sisters listen actively to others, and they also share their own stories, in what is often described in terms of deep conversation and mutual exchange. Furthermore, they say they are consciously trying not to judge, but to welcome and accept others for who they are. Sr. Collette explains this below:

> The more I hear peoples' stories, the more I think, "Oh my gosh, who am I to judge in any way their life and how good it is or how bad it is?"—so I tend not to do that, but just accept them as they are and see if I could in any way help their situation by sharing.

This reflection from Sr. Collette explores not only being welcoming and accepting what the person offers, but gives us an insight into the sisters' belief that they in turn have something to offer, in an exchange of experience and perhaps vulnerability.

In a demonstration of the complexity of the concept of 'being,' much of the sisters' understanding of being apostolic is described or explored in terms of specific activities which have come to express being apostolic at this stage in their lives. These fall largely into the following categories: helping others become; hospitality and welcoming; and listening, which is sometimes exercised through the particular ministry of spiritual accompaniment. These are all activities which can be undertaken within their own community, and with those who come in to see them. As Sr. Jayne says of being apostolic: "You don't have to have a job to do it, do you?"

The common thread through these activities is being in relationship with others. I have referred to this as both being with and being for, and this now forms part of their own self-understanding. Consequently, I suggest that this turning towards others be recognized as an attitude or orientation rather than a series of acts or practices, something Marcel describes as *disponibilité* or availability, which he explores in the first volume of his two-part work, *The Mystery of Being*.[6] A relevant feature of Marcel's philosophy here is his central concern with the individual human person and the importance of her experience as a starting place for philosophical enquiry,[7] along with his examination of individual identity in relationship with others.[8] According to Blundell, Marcel works out of this "primacy of concrete existence of the embodied person,"[9] not so much as a rejection of abstraction per se, but more from a

---

6 Gabriel Marcel, *The Mystery of Being*: Vol. 1, *Reflections on Mystery* (London: Holden, 1950).
7 Boyd Blundell, *Paul Ricoeur Between Theology and Philosophy* (Bloomington, IN: University of Indiana Press, 2010), 58–60; and Helen Tattam, "Atheism, Religion, and Philosophical 'Availability' in Gabriel Marcel," *International Journal of the Philosophy of Religion* 79, no. 1 (2016): 19–30, https://doi.org/10.1007/s11153-015-9547-9.
8 Gabriel Marcel, *The Mystery of Being*: Vol. 2, *Faith and Reality* (London: Harvill Press, 1951).
9 Blundell, *Paul Ricoeur*, 58.

belief that the abstract and the conceptual need to be considered in concert with the concrete experience. Rather like the concern among practice-engaged theologians that theological theory begin with and be rooted in everyday lives, Marcel worked out of a dialectic between the concrete and the abstract, lest the reality and dignity of the individual be overlooked in the face of abstractions such as political systems.

Marcel's philosophical concept of availability to and for others arises as he explores how to determine identity. His concern is "highlighting the intersubjective community in which man [sic] is situated and exploring how existential 'availability' can be promoted between the self and others."[10] Thus, for Marcel, questions of human identity can only be resolved through relationship with others and the ability to respond to the "calls made upon [him] by life" or by others.[11] He sees it as essential for humans to be oriented towards life's call as it is lived in relation to, and in communion with, others.[12] One reason why this 'availability' is so important to Marcel is because "rendering the self open and available to the otherness of others"[13] involves risk, and relies on an act of faith on the part of the individual as she makes herself open to an encounter with the unknown. For Marcel, life only has meaning when lived in intersubjectivity: through being 'with' others, we find communion.[14] This echoes the call in *Vita Consecrata* whereby "consecrated persons are asked to be true experts of communion and to practise the spirituality of communion as 'witnesses and architects of the plan for unity which is the crowning point of human history in God's design'" (VC, §46).[15] Sr. Pamela commented:

> It's just accepting that we are all one family, and by that I include the earth and the planet and the cosmos; we're all part of the same kin-dom, without the 'g.'

Another form by which sisters express being apostolic and self-gift is through helping. Sr. Pamela explained her understanding of the apostolic call of all women religious in this way:

---

10 Tattam, "Atheism, Religion, and Philosophical 'Availability,'" 23.
11 Marcel, *Mystery of Being* 1: 163.
12 Marcel, *Mystery of Being* 1: 163–64.
13 Tattam, "Atheism, Religion, and Philosophical 'Availability,'" 24.
14 Marcel, *Mystery of Being* 1: 172–77.
15 Pope John Paul II, *Post-synodal Apostolic Exhortation: "Vita Consecrata,"* March 25, 1996, accessed November 23, 2015, http://w2.vatican.va/content/john-paul-ii/en/apost_exhortations/documents/hf_jp-ii_exh_25031996_vita-consecrata.html.

We're all in the process of being the people that God would want us to be, and helping other people to be the people that he wants them to be.

This is echoed by Sr. Jayne:

It's really the idea that we are to show to other people that God is *in* people—in humanity; he is here amongst us, living, and living through us.

Thus, they claim that this process of becoming their true selves involves not only their own becoming, but helping others on that journey of becoming. Sr. Bernadette's words demonstrate this:

I wouldn't put the emphasis on saving my own soul but on trying to help others on their journey to God, and finding God in their lives, and anything I could do to help.

Over half the sisters are now primarily home- and community-based, and unsurprisingly, welcoming and hospitality play a substantial role in the meaning they make of their apostolic call. Sr. Bernadette has a formal 'welcoming' role with guests in her community, and she explained:

Being here in the house and welcoming guests—hospitality is a ministry, and people can come at any time and need to be welcomed, given a cup of tea, chatted to, or listened to.

When I asked her about the older sisters in her community, she said, "Some are ambulant, but can't do much … but a ninety-year-old can still be there to welcome people"; and in her second interview, she affirmed my recognition of welcoming as a ministry.

I thought that was good—thank God somebody was on the ball for that one. … That's exactly how, in many ways, you saw yourself; you had to give your time, your gifts, and the listening, helping, welcoming, hospitality—I would certainly see that as very important in religious life.

Sr. Maeve is in her late eighties and housebound since a recent fall, but sees much of her everyday activity in terms of ministry.

The time was when we were outside, caring for others, and now a number of us are in, but it is amazing what we can do … the Associates, the prayer groups, we are all involved in some of that, working with the poor at the door, making sandwiches, giving them tea.

Listening plays an important role in sisters' ministry and can be engaged in anywhere or at any time. Many of the sisters see the act of listening as very much needed in today's world and, therefore, a relevant part of being apostolic. Sr. Bernadette expresses it in these terms: "The listening ear is the important part—where in today's world so few listen." Sr. Clare concurs: "there's a great need for people to be listened to"—a need also endorsed by Sr. Susan. Several sisters, including Sr. Collette, Sr. Clare, and Sr. Beatrice, identified this as a role religious can helpfully fulfil at this point, both in society and in the history of religious life. Sr. Jayne spoke of the role of listening in a former ministry of hers in prison chaplaincy, in a situation where often she had little else to offer:

> I wasn't talking about God to them—maybe with the prisoners occasionally in some very vague way, he would come up, but on the whole, it was what that man said to me; it was listening to them; trying to be understanding; seeing the good in them, as well as the fact that they'd murdered somebody, or supporting them. To me, that is what Jesus really wants from people: it's being with people; it's listening to them … that is being apostolic.

5.4 Facing towards Others

In this orientation towards others and self-understanding as being in relationship with and available to others, the sisters see themselves as ordinary practising Christians, as they reminded me repeatedly during interviews. They follow the commandments of loving God and loving their neighbour and anchor their sharing with, and doing things for, others in their relationship with God, seeing it as a fruit of that relationship.

However, the sisters are also vowed religious and have embraced a form of life which places seeking God through the following of Christ at its heart, with all the turning towards the Other and others that this entails. Apostolic works in the form of service to, for, and with others have long been part of the identity of the apostolic or active religious. Furthermore, the vows publicly professed by active religious include that of chastity, or celibacy, which is understood by contemporary writers on religious life as a vow of availability for and to others, and increasingly as a vow of or for right relationship with others, which includes intimacy, but also healthy self-development through relationship.[16]

Hahnenberg holds that God's call is always mediated through others so that the sisters hear their call shaped or determined by and through the needs of others.[17] He also contends that our contemporary, postmodern world, which is almost defined by diversity, demands "a particular kind of conversion … namely, the conversion that comes through openness to 'the other.'"[18] The 'other' in this sense extends beyond the familiar, pointing to those who are different, and therefore challenges us to step beyond the comfort of ministering to those who are like us. The sisters' conversion depends on others for both its progression and realization. "We grow in this openness to God who is *the* Other precisely by growing in openness to others."[19]

Volf also recognizes a contemporary need to be open to the other. He calls for an openness, as God is open to the other, drawing on the imagery of the open arms of the cross as a metaphor for God's openness, and an invitation to, and embrace of, the enemy.[20] Thus, the call here is to be inspired by divine openness. Writing in the years following the conflict in the Balkans in the late twentieth century, Volf was concerned with reconciliation but draws heavily on the recent revival of Trinitarian theology. He makes particular use of Moltmann's work highlighting the character of self-donation inherent in the Trinity, and in Christological self-donation, and draws on this for his model of how we might make space in ourselves for, and to relate to, the other.

> At the centre of the New Testament lies the narrative of the death and resurrection of Jesus Christ understood as an act of obedience toward God and an expression of self-giving love for his followers as well as the model for the followers to imitate.[21]

---

16   For more on the contemporary treatment of the vows taken by apostolic religious, see Barbara Fiand, *Living the Vision: Religious Vows in an Age of Change* (New York: Crossroad, 1991); Diarmuid O'Murchu, *Religious Life: A Prophetic Vision* (Notre Dame, IN: Ave Maria Press, 1991); Judith Merkle, *A Different Touch: A Study of Vows in Religious Life* (Collegeville, MN: Liturgical Press, 1998); and Schneiders, *Buying the Field*.
17   Edward P. Hahnenberg, *Awakening Vocation: A Theology of Christian Call* (Collegeville, MN: Liturgical Press, 2010), 159.
18   Hahnenberg, *Awakening Vocation*, 160.
19   Hahnenberg, *Awakening Vocation*, 173.
20   Miroslav Volf, *Exclusion and Embrace: A Theological Exploration of Identity, Otherness and Reconciliation* (Nashville, TN: Abingdon Press, 1996), 126.
21   Volf, *Exclusion and Embrace*, 30.

In Volf's and Hahnenberg's theology, both influenced by liberation theology, there is an element which could be described as activist. For Volf, the call is to work actively for reconciliation in the face of conflict; Hahnenberg seeks to call his readers away from the comfort of ministering to the familiar in order to engage with the other who is different and discomforting. Several of the sisters, notably Sr. Bernadette and Sr. Collette, have been able to respond to the call to open themselves to the other through involvement with multi-faith women's groups, particularly in urban contexts where the neighbour is increasingly of different ethnicity and faith. However, the sisters in this study are now largely limited to encountering those who are able to come to them, and often these are the known and the familiar. Furthermore, not all sisters are activists in this sense, and even those who are, and continue to be so well into their later years, come to a stage where this is no longer practical for them. I would contend that for sisters at this stage in their lives, and for those who are perhaps less activist in nature, a theology of service to others based on activism does not serve them or their congregations well in terms of providing a framework to give meaning to those years when they are beyond activism and activity. As Sr. Dorothy says, "I can't get out as much now and go out and do things for people, but there are other ways people can come to me."

There is a third model for this orientation to others. Moltmann's model of 'open friendship' calls on Christians to be in communion with all others.[22] Moltmann draws our attention to what he sees as a central tenet of Christianity, that is, to be open to the other, the one who is different, and offer friendship. Friendship should not be limited to those who are like us, but we should strive for "acceptance of others in their difference, for it is this experience of our neighbours, and only this, which is in line with the Christian experience of God,"[23] as modelled by Christ in the New Testament. Moltmann claims that "the difference is experienced in the practical encounter which mutually reveals what we are and what the other is,"[24] and points to a mutual recognition of each other, rather than loss of identity in the face of others. In contrast to the forms of engagement with others being offered by Volf and Hahnenberg, there is no activism inherent in open friendship. In fact, Moltmann is explicit about the fact that open friendship is simply about welcoming all.

---

22 Jürgen Moltmann, *The Spirit of Life: A Universal Affirmation*, trans. Margaret Kohl (London: SCM Press, 1992), 255–59.
23 Moltmann, *The Spirit of Life*, 258.
24 Moltmann, *The Spirit of Life*, 258.

> The motive for this is not the moral purpose of changing the world. It is a festal joy over the kingdom of God which … has thrown itself wide open for "the others."[25]

I will return to Moltmann in my later exploration of reciprocity, but for now, I want to note that while I have argued that being with and for is fundamental to the sisters' self-understanding, a theology with activism at its heart may not be the model which best represents their form of self-gift. However, what Hahnenberg, Volf, and Moltmann have in common is a call to openness to those with whom we share elements of life, and those who are unfamiliar. I have noted that as sisters are increasingly housebound, the range of 'difference' with which they can engage becomes reduced. However, at the same time, their choice of whom to engage with is reduced, and so perhaps the task of availability and openness to the other becomes in some ways more difficult and demands an ever-greater commitment to self-gift. In light of this, I want to turn to Sandra Schneiders' work on ministry as gift to consider whether this gives a theological expression to the sisters' lived experience.

5.5   Ministry as Gift: Fit for Purpose?

Engaging with the main features of Schneiders' theology of ministry as gift will help us to reflect a little more deeply on the nature of sisters' ministry at this stage in their lives. The first feature of this theology relevant here is Schneiders' interpretation of the three vows of poverty, obedience, and chastity as a combined articulation and expression of self-gift, modelled on Christ's self-giving, and with the aim of being "in union with Jesus in his total self-gift to God in the Spirit for the salvation of the world."[26] Second, she locates her theology of ministry as gift specifically within the vow of poverty. She understands religious to be both living in, and pointing to, an alternate world which is the kingdom of God. Their life within that world operates within an economy of gift,[27] as opposed to an economy based on commodity and profit. Ministry for Schneiders is understood not as something a religious undertakes in order to earn payment either for herself or her congregation, but rather as prophetic action to bring about the kingdom.

---

25   Moltmann, *The Spirit of Life*, 259.
26   Schneiders, *Buying the Field*, 291.
27   Schneiders, *Buying the Field*, chap. 5.

In a further feature of Schneiders' model of ministry, she reads Arendt's understanding of action, in her distinctions between labour, work, and action, as "transformation of persons and society through structural change,"[28] and sees this as the basis of ministerial activity for the contemporary world. While there is great coherence in Schneiders' theology of ministry, it also forms part of her aim to show the emergence of a new form of ministerial religious life, and mark the break with the past form of apostolic life. Schneiders here puts 'action' at the centre of her theology of this form of life, centred not on charity and alleviation of the effects of poverty and injustice, nor on listening and being with an individual person's pain, but on tackling the fundamental causes. In this, she is setting out a clear demarcation in the evolution of apostolate into ministry. There is also a slightly didactic element here as she appears keen to encourage religious to move on from seeing ministry primarily as work to support themselves and an institution, and view it instead as service and gift.[29]

In her consideration of ministry, Schneiders' emphasis is not, however, entirely focussed on 'action.' In the final part of her trilogy on religious life, she makes it clear that ministry is now intrinsic to the very identity of ministerial religious, and notes furthermore the primacy of being: "What Religious are ... is at least as important as what they do."[30] Again, I would challenge her to say that the focus should be *who* religious are, rather than *what*, and one wonders whether the emphasis on action to tackle structural causes of poverty is a theology that easily maps onto the reality of the women in this study. Although one or two of the participants continue to look outwards and engage in actions such as online petitions or lobbying Parliament, the majority were facing increasing physical limitations and health needs that may limit their capacity for 'action.' They may no longer be able to lobby Parliament and yet still live meaningful lives filled with expressions of concern for others. Is Schneiders' theology of ministry, therefore, sufficiently extensive to offer meaning to a sister with an apostolic calling in her later years?

5.5.1   *Ministry as Gift*

Despite the physical limitations they now face, the sisters in my study understand their ongoing ministry in terms of both gift and reciprocity. In discussing how they are apostolic with others, they use the language of giving and receiving. A question to ask at this stage is this: What is it about their motivation and their relationships that enables both them and the reader to identify

---

28   Schneiders, *Buying the Field*, 271.
29   Schneiders, *Buying the Field*, 274.
30   Schneiders, *Buying the Field*, 248.

their ministry as gift? I will turn to Marcel, Ricoeur, and Milbank to explore this question. All of these writers support Schneiders' own differentiation between gift and income generation. Both Marcel and Ricoeur identify and discuss the distinction between gift-giving and commercial exchange.[31] For Marcel, gift is more than simply transactional, as it has to be unconditional in nature in order to be gift. Although the sisters do speak of what they receive in return for their giving, they do not appear to be seeking a return, nor do they know what the return might be; it is unconditional. Milbank similarly sees the purpose of gift to establish exchange and relationship in some way because "though there is equivalent return, the same thing does not come back. Something passes never to return at all."[32] Gift is both, therefore, one-way and reciprocal, as although it elicits a return, its nature cannot be known. Marcel traces gift back to generosity in the soul and claims that generosity itself is not the cause of gift, but makes gift possible. "Generosity ... seems itself to be a gift," that is, a manifestation of grace.[33] Sr. Anne recognizes this in her understanding of being apostolic as "being a channel of the love and the grace of God."

Ricoeur also differentiates between commercial exchange and gift-giving and identifies "a form of recognition that announces itself to be immanent in personal transactions."[34] He interprets Anspach's "transcendent third term" present between the giving and receiving which, "even if nothing other than the relation itself, impos[es] itself as a separate actor entirely."[35] He seeks to identify this 'third element,' which Marcel has interpreted as grace, present in the gap between giving and receiving. Ricoeur names this as a form of mutual recognition between the giver and the recipient, whereby the two parties identify, recognize, and accept each other. Within this, Ricoeur also identifies a paradoxical cycle of expectation built into gift-giving, which sees the recipient experience an obligation to return the gift. In order that mutual recognition itself does not become an obligation, Ricoeur, like Marcel, recognizes the role of generosity, and suggests focussing on the generosity of the giver.[36] "Gratitude lightens the weight of obligation to give in return and reorients this toward a generosity equal to the one that led to the first gift." However, unlike Marcel,

---

31 Marcel, *Mystery of Being* 2: 117–24; and Paul Ricoeur, *The Course of Recognition*, trans. David Pellauer (Cambridge, MA: Harvard University Press, 2005), 225–26.
32 John Milbank, *The Future of Love: Essays in Political Theology* (London: SCM Press, 2009), 257.
33 Marcel, *Mystery of Being* 2: 120, 151.
34 Ricoeur, *Course of Recognition*, 227.
35 Mark Rogin Anspach, *À charge de revanche: Figures élémentaires de la réciprocité* (Paris: Seuil, 2002), 5, cited in Ricoeur, *Course of Recognition*, 227.
36 Ricoeur, *Course of Recognition*, 243.

who identifies this as grace, Ricoeur claims that what makes this ultimately possible is the "giving without return" of *agape*, love which does not demand any return, and which ultimately has a role in establishing a state of peace.

Ricoeur sees the presence of *agape* in mutual recognition as the factor that helps turn a potentially vicious cycle of giving and obligation to return into a virtuous cycle. Milbank also does not see gift as a one-way action or movement, nor even as a complete circle; "rather it is a spiral or strange loop ... there is no first free gift, because to give to another one must have received at least her presence."[37] The sisters' understanding of gift is rooted in what they themselves have received from God: the first gift. Their sense of gratitude for this moves them, as posited by Ricoeur, to respond not reciprocally, but with another first gift. Sr. Collette speaks of having received the "gift of faith" and feels called to share this and her God-given gifts with others. Sr. Maeve also links giving and receiving.

> I feel it's only right and proper that I should [give]; we've been given so much. When I look at the situations outside, and the boat people and all, you just feel such sorrow for them, and I think that is important, to be involved, in so far as we can.

Sr. Susan talks of the apostolic impulse as "the activation of the gift I have received," and Sr. Jayne explains her initial motivation to enter religious life in terms of giving her life to God:

> It's that phrase—what return can I make to the Lord for all he has given to me? It's an appreciation for all he has given to me and what can I do in return—well, he can use me.

So, sisters give not in return for a gift in a transactional sense, but as another first gift. Sr. Susan, in her second interview, explained this:

> The good news of Jesus Christ is that he came with a message of what God wants for all of us and the grace of God is given to us through Jesus Christ, to receive what God actually wants for us, does that make sense? ... Because we don't have anything that is ours to give, we witness for God. ... We need to follow what he is actually gifting us, because we are not going to get there on our own or by our own good ideas.

---

37   Milbank, *Future of Love*, 257.

In reference to Milbank, none of the sisters explicitly recognize the first gift from God in terms of their presence, but they do acknowledge that they are nothing in and of themselves: they accept their dependence on God, in an attitude of poverty of spirit, as Metz terms it.[38] Sr. Beatrice expresses this utter reliance on the gifts of the Spirit several times:

> I have never ever had anyone who didn't like it in this house; they love it when they see you laugh and smile at them, and they say when you read you become so alive, and I thought, that's the Holy Spirit, it is not me. … I tend to say it because I get scared then, and I say, "Oh, well, that is the Holy Spirit," anyway. I don't want them to think I'm doing it, that I mean this, and it is my gift; it *is* my gift, but it is a gift that God has given me for them, and tomorrow if I had a stroke, I wouldn't have it, would I?

For Schneiders, this ability to accept our utter dependency on God is not just at the heart of, but a prerequisite for, ministry through self-gift: "In experiencing their very being as gift, ministers reach out to foster, promote and enable the very being of those to whom they are sent."[39] She offers a hermeneutic of Jesus' call for us to receive the gift of life and the kingdom of God "as a little child," which invokes and invites "us to embrace our ontological contingency, our very real total dependence on God not only for all that we have, but for all that we are,"[40] which for the sisters means accepting that "they are called and *gifted* to participate in the Reign of God."[41] The emphasis on 'gifted' in this last quote from Schneiders is my own, as it links into the sisters' understanding that they need to draw on their selves in order to minister and serve.

There are, therefore, several identifiable movements within this desire to give. First, sisters acknowledge their first gift from God and also want to give back to God. There is clearly a desire for mutuality within this, but they also recognize that they cannot 'do' things for God or give God anything; they can only do this through first gift to others. Sr. Martina tries to connect her desire to do something for God with her desire to do things for others.

> You were doing it for God, but you were doing it through people—you're not doing it direct—you can do it in several ways, apostolic. … You are giving part of your life … you are doing something for somebody, not

---

38   Johann Baptist Metz, *Poverty of Spirit* (Mahwah, NJ: Paulist Press, 1968).
39   Schneiders, *Buying the Field*, 305.
40   Schneiders, *Buying the Field*, 304–5.
41   Schneiders, *Buying the Field*, 305.

necessarily a job for earning money, or doing anything, [you are] just [going] some way beyond yourself.

Second, the movement apparent here is towards others: doing something for somebody else beyond themselves, without reward or expectation, and thus making themselves available to others. Schneiders sees self-gift as centred in the vows, lived out as a lifelong commitment to availability. Linking this to Marcel's idea of *disponibilité*, or availability, discussed above, shapes this as a fundamental, almost existential, orientation on the sisters' part.

In an analysis which complements Schneiders' own understanding of economy of gift, Milbank also understands giving as both a sign or feature of, and pointing to, the alternate world and thus imbues it with a sacramental quality. Christianity has, by virtue of the incarnation, made all things sacred: "everything is a sign of God and His love," and "in Christ this is shown again."[42] This provides the continuing means by which all can be sanctified, emphasizing the sacred nature of the relationship established, as givers and receivers are one in Christ. Milbank identifies gift-exchange as one of the constitutive features of St. Paul's vision of *ecclesia*: "a kind of universal tribalism of gift-exchange over-against both local polis and universal empire," between those who are no longer strangers, but sisters and brothers in Christ.[43]

5.5.2   *Reciprocity*

The recognition, noted above, that reciprocity or mutuality is at the heart of the nature of gift, is deeply embedded in the sisters' apparent orientation towards others. Sr. Anne described it thus:

> My concept of apostolic ministry would be something which encloses, gathers together more than doing the soup run and going out; it's a little bit like the disciples and Mary going back to Jerusalem to await the coming of the Holy Spirit; it's something which is all part of one movement.

Sr. Anne's words bring to mind the concept of *perichoresis* drawn from Orthodox or Eastern theological traditions, which recognizes the divine interpenetration of and, therefore, reciprocal relationship between the three persons of the Trinity. This has formed part of the rediscovery of Trinitarian theology

---

42   Milbank, *Future of Love*, 257.
43   Milbank, *Future of Love*, 256.

in recent years within Western theology.[44] This theology informs the sisters' recognition of their dependence on God and on others, and that in giving they receive, as sisters say below. Their seeking out of the other reflects their awareness that in doing so, they become more closely united to God, and part of establishing Milbank's *ecclesia* and Schneiders' kingdom, as explained by Sr. Anne:

> What I've learned through my own experience is that you can only give what you have received, and if the most important thing is that I become a channel of the Holy Spirit and God's love for other people, then I have to have a certain space in which I do open myself and allow myself to be invaded by the Spirit so that my response to people, individuals, or to any ministry that I've undertaken is based on that inner relationship. ... I think this is the establishing of the "God space": I don't like the word 'kingdom' because I think it's got too many attachments to it, but the whole question of the kingdom of God—[British New Testament scholar] Tom Wright actually has got a very nice phrase—he said to think of it as the God space—are you helping to create the God space—in collaboration with God?

Returning to Moltmann, the theme of self-gift or self-donation in his work is inspired by a recognition that the self-giving love of Christ is rooted in the self-giving love of the Triune God,[45] which in turn inspires Moltmann's concept of "open friendship."[46]

> The reciprocal self-surrender to one another within the Trinity is manifested in Christ's self-surrender in a world which is in contradiction to God; and this self-giving draws all those who believe in him into the eternal life of the divine love.[47]

At times, sisters speak of this reciprocity and mutuality as if they are being completed or made whole by the intersubjective nature of their relationships. They do not give in order to receive, but recognize that they are nonetheless

---

44   For more on this topic, see Catherine Mowry LaCugna, *God for Us: The Trinity and Christian Life* (New York: HarperSanFrancisco, 1991); Moltmann, *Spirit of Life*; Volf, *Exclusion and Embrace*; and Gregory Collins, "Giving Religious Life a Theology Transfusion," in *A Future Full of Hope?*, ed. Gemma Simmonds (Dublin: Columba Press, 2012), 23–37.
45   Volf, *Exclusion and Embrace*, 25.
46   Moltmann, *Spirit of Life*, 255–59.
47   Moltmann, *Spirit of Life*, 137.

enriched by what they receive. In Moltmann's understanding of *koinonia* or fellowship of the Spirit, the Spirit gives itself and enters into fellowship with believers, drawing them into fellowship and thus into community. "Fellowship means opening ourselves for one another ... fellowship lives in reciprocal participation and from mutual recognition."[48] There are two points of note here. First, as with his concept of open friendship, Moltmann believes that fellowship can exist not only between those who are alike, but between those who are truly different, as the Holy Spirit's fellowship is open to all. Second, that fellowship "is never unilaterally determined. It is always reciprocally defined";[49] those in fellowship must share some element in common. Moltmann notes that through the fellowship of the Holy Spirit, God enters into a relationship which is both reciprocal and mutual, thereby allowing those with whom he enters into relationship and influences to influence him (Godself) in return.[50]

LaCugna supports this, saying that it "provides a dynamic model of persons in communion based on mutuality and interdependence," pointing to the dynamic nature of that relationship.[51] If we are made in God's image and likeness and can understand God as "an eternal movement of reciprocal giving and receiving,"[52] then surely, Collins muses, humans are invited "in love to enter its communion."[53]

> God self-reveals as a communion (*koinonia*) of divine persons united in an eternally self-constituting/self-sacrificing web of mutual relations. God is a flowing circle of inter-penetrating, self-giving lovers, whose source is the first person, the Father. The divine life is a communion of giving and receiving ... so absolute that with each one dwelling within the others through *perichoresis* ... there is but one subject, God.[54]

The sisters become more closely formed to the *imago Dei* in their ongoing process of conversion, and the love they show towards others reveals another aspect of the nature of God. Sr. Kathleen's experience of volunteering with asylum-seekers demonstrates this.

48　Moltmann, *Spirit of Life*, 217.
49　Moltmann, *Spirit of Life*, 218.
50　Moltmann, *Spirit of Life*, 218.
51　LaCugna, *God For Us*, 271.
52　LaCugna, *God For Us*, 272.
53　Collins, "Giving Religious Life a Theology Transfusion," 35.
54　Collins, "Giving Religious Life a Theology Transfusion," 34–35.

I'm helping those people, and in return I'm getting a life that I love; a way of life that's giving me so much happiness. ... There's a man in the very beginners' class, and he's a very fast learner. He really needs to go up because he's too fast for us, and I told him one morning, I said, "We've decided that now you're ready for this class." Well, he turned round and he hugged me, and he hugged me and he loved me, you know.

When Sr. Collette was asked by the Superior why she wanted to enter their particular congregation, she responded:

I said to save my soul and that of others—that was the usual answer, but I must have felt that I would be doing both really—how they complement each other.

Even at that point, she had begun to see how the two movements were inextricably linked, and this has continued.

For me to try and help them to live their lives as best they possibly can, and for me to gain from helping them as well; that they help me as well—a two-way thing.

In her second interview, she welcomed my feedback that sisters give and receive in return.

That is true, we give and we receive in life all the time, right now I am receiving, you know, no matter what we are doing, where we are, or who we are sharing with, or what is happening in our lives.

Sr. Bernadette speaks of "giving empowerment we ourselves have received as women religious to other women"—a channelling; but she also notes:

I get a lot more from people—family, friends, casual acquaintances—than I give. I'm a people person, and I like observing people, and I get my energies from interacting with them.

The concept of the ordinary again makes itself known. Sisters want to feel ordinary themselves; it is important to them to be among ordinary people and part of a local community, immersed in a spiral, or virtuous circle, of giving and receiving. Sr. Kathleen derives "a lot of nourishment from listening to people—again, this is where the ordinary people come in." She speaks movingly of the experience, in southern Africa, of visiting ordinary homes and simply sitting with, and being among, people affected by AIDS. Sr. Beatrice understands the presence of her community on an inner-city estate in similar terms.

> People around here, a lot of them, would never have been brought up to know much about God, but they know an awful lot about caring, about being with you when you are in need, and that is something that we have to work out together. I found that very wonderful and they are bringing us with them as well as, it works both ways, doesn't it? We are an apostolic community; we are meant to be part of people all around us, and yet at the same time, we are also meant to be, I was going to say guides, but we are not really, it is a mutuality. It sounds very posh, really, but it is a reaching out and a mutual outreach. ... We will of course be there with you through the whole thing, and there is that freedom to talk about not to be holy, but to say yes, let us see what we can do together in this.

Sweeney sees sisters' embracing the ordinary in this way as an indication that, after the years of turmoil, and wrestling with identity in the post-conciliar period, apostolic religious are turning towards what he terms "the prophetic way."[55]

> Their value is in the fact that the religious "are there," close to ordinary people, inserted in local neighbourhoods. Their credibility lies in the relationships and friendships they strike up; they are seen to value individuals, families and communities who on a routine basis are socially disregarded and used to being discarded. Their mission is to witness to hope in the midst of what seems like hopelessness.[56]

5.6 Self-Gift

The theological concepts of *perichoresis* and *koinonia* or communion, explored above, have already been helpful in understanding the movements involved in sisters' ministry and relationships with others. As a contribution towards

---

[55] James Sweeney, "Prophets and Parables: A Future for Religious Orders," *Informationes Theologiae Europae: Internationales ökumenisches Jahrbuch für Theologie* 4 (2001): 273–92; and Sweeney, "Religious Life Looks to the Future," in Simmonds, *A Future Full of Hope?*, chap. 9.

[56] Sweeney, "Prophets and Parables," 284.

establishing *koinonia* or communion, LaCugna identifies the connection between these concepts.

> "Toward-another" ... God is self-communicating, existing from all eternity in relation to another. The ultimate ground and meaning of being is therefore communion among persons: God is ecstatic, fecund, self-emptying out of love for another, a personal God who comes to self through another.[57]

This is echoed by Collins, for whom some form of *kenosis* on the part of the individual is a necessary component of movement towards communion.[58] Collins' linking of *kenosis* and communion expresses what appears to be at work in the sisters' understanding of their apostolic ministry in terms of both gift and reciprocity. In theological terms, *kenosis* is recognized as an attribute of the divine, as Christ emptied himself to become human, and so cannot, therefore, strictly speaking, be applied to human self-emptying, as the concept and movement are of a different order. Kilby makes the point that *kenosis* is best used only when invoking the originating verse in Phil. 2.6–7 and God's own self-emptying.[59] Schneiders would seem to concur. She uses the term in reference to God's own self-emptying but relates it to her anchoring of ministry in evangelical poverty. The issue to be confronted is the clinging to material possessions as a form of protection against humanity's fragility. She urges religious to adopt "the same existential stance toward our creaturehood" in embracing ontological vulnerability.[60] The response to the self-giving of the incarnation is self-giving in return.

Consequently, it may be more appropriate to use *kenosis* in analogical terms and speak of kenotic-like self-emptying, or giving up, modelled on the Trinitarian self-surrender identified by Moltmann in the previous section. It may even be that Welker's language of "free self-withdrawal" is more helpful in considering the nature of the sisters' self-giving.[61] Welker, as with Moltmann, Volf, and Collins, understands this free self-withdrawal as modelled on the mystery of the self-giving Trinity for the sake of the world. One of the ways in which we see this free self-withdrawal at work among the sisters is in their availability and self-gift, through a form of ministry increasingly termed

---

57 LaCugna, *God For Us*, 14.
58 Collins, "Giving Religious Life a Theology Transfusion," 35–36.
59 Karen Kilby, "The Seductions of Kenosis," in *Suffering and the Christian Life*, ed. Karen Kilby and Rachel Davies (London: T&T Clark, 2020), 166.
60 Schneiders, *Buying the Field*, 311.
61 Michael Welker, *God the Spirit* (Minneapolis, MN: Fortress Press, 1994), 310.

'ministry of presence.' This, and other expressions of self-gift through ministry being practised by sisters in later life, will be explored in the final chapter.

5.7 Conclusion

The sisters' experience of apostolic ministry at this stage of their lives is often situated in a context of reduced social influence and, therefore, limited opportunities for apostolic ministry. However, sisters clearly acknowledge and place reciprocity and mutuality at the heart of their giving of self, both in relationship with God, and to and for others. I suggest that the theology of ministry as gift, and the concepts of Trinitarian *perichoresis* and Christological *kenosis*, offer the beginnings of a theological framework which helps make sense of the nature and form of the sisters' experience of ministry at this stage of their lives. It is clear that there are limitations to the work of Volf, Hahnenberg, and Schneiders as a means of giving voice to the sisters' experience of ministry at this stage of life, but Moltmann's understanding of fellowship, and Marcel's approach to presence and gift, have been helpful, as the sisters' understanding of gift incorporates the concepts of reciprocity and is encompassed by self-gift.

Although we might assume that physical limitations lead to reduced or limited opportunities for apostolic ministry, it is already clear that this is not necessarily the case, and that sisters seek out opportunities to continue to minister. I would like to end here with a quote sent to me by one of the sisters after her first interview, taken from her congregation's constitutions.

> Each succeeding stage of life brings a new invitation to leave all, to follow him and to find the place where He dwells. We take a firmer grasp of the hope His call holds for us.

The final chapter will continue the exploration of that call.

CHAPTER 6

Ministry in Old Age: Apostolic to the Very End

6.1 Introduction

What does ministry mean for these sisters who are now physically infirm in some way and increasingly dependent on others? The range of people with whom they come into contact is decreasing. This may be the stage in later life where Vacek considers the moral priorities to be those of disengagement and completion, and which for Schneiders focusses on relinquishment.[1]

In this chapter, I want, first of all, to consider some of the sisters' attitudes towards older age and being able to do less, and the ambivalence and contradictions heard in connection with this. Then I will reflect on these in relation to the wider social construct of old age, and the context of decline in the membership of religious congregations. In my work with sisters, I have identified three ways in which they continue to be apostolic or in ministry until the end of their lives, and I want to propose that these can be read as sacramental and incarnational. As sisters continue to be oriented towards the needs of others, even in small ways, they continue to be apostolic to the end of their lives through being relational and dialogical in obedience to the context in which they find themselves. Although the sisters experience physical diminishment, they do not experience diminishment in terms of living their apostolic vocation.

6.2 Ministry in Old Age

As I sought to understand how sisters continue to be apostolic when their relationships are largely conducted within a community and with those who visit, I asked each sister whether sisters who are either housebound due to physical infirmity or living in a care community can have a ministry or be apostolic. The majority saw even the oldest or most infirm as continuing to be apostolic in some way. Sr. Jayne, for example, answered:

---

1 Edward Collins Vacek, "Vices and Virtues of Old-age Retirement," *Journal of the Society of Christian Ethics* 30, no. 2 (2010): 161–82; and Sandra Schneiders, *Buying the Field: Religious Life in the New Millennium* (Mahwah, NJ: Paulist Press, 2013).

Yes. I do. Definitely because of your inner being and your acceptance and your friendliness—all inspired by what is deep within you, which is hopefully your knowledge of God.

Despite the clarity about continuing to be apostolic, sisters were less certain what might comprise ministry at this stage of life. Sr. Maeve noted that in her community, which is quite elderly, "there's not one person in this house who hasn't a ministry," including herself. Sr. Pamela articulates the issue at stake:

So in one way, 'apostolic' doesn't necessarily have to be active, does it, or at least I don't think it does, but that is something I have come to, and possibly because of, how I can no longer do actively all the stuff I used to be able to do. So how do I continue to serve?

6.2.1   *Ambivalence towards Old Age and Inactivity*

Despite the overwhelmingly positive responses when asked about being apostolic to the end of their lives, some sisters were conflicted in their attitude to this stage of their life. These sisters appear to struggle to make sense of the experience of ageing and increasing inactivity in at least three ways. First, despite the fact that all say they believe they can be apostolic without a specific role, and that there is no such thing as retiring from being a sister, they have mainly experienced a call to apostolic life which constituted a call to active ministry and to being useful. Sr. Bernadette's words on retirement illustrate this dilemma: "It's a figure of speech. You entered this order to be of service." Sr. Dorothy confirmed this in her comment: "Well, we can't simply sit around all day and fill the dishwasher"; and Sr. Beatrice observed:

Now we're not young any longer … we shouldn't equate retirement with doing nothing, because we don't work then we only say our prayers, and go to bed early and have a nice little life. I think that's the kiss of death to religious life—definitely.

Second, the sisters recognize that purposeful activity in service of others has been the focus of their lives, and to an extent, there continues to be an association between being useful and worth or purpose and meaning in relation to apostolic life, despite *Vita Consecrata*'s affirmation that the "mission continues to be worthwhile and meritorious, even when for reasons of age or infirmity they have had to abandon their specific apostolate. The elderly and the sick have a great deal to give in wisdom and experience … if only the community can remain close to them with concern and an ability to listen" (*VC*, §44).[2] I asked sisters if they were able to say how their congregations viewed older sisters in relation to ministry in old age. Several recognized that this was not always positive. Sr. Bernadette credits this to the association between ministry, purpose, and self-worth.

> I think it will take another period of time to come to the understanding that you ought to be valued till the very end. ... There's a lot of work to be done on that ... because people see themselves as valued for their ministry.

Sr. Collette confirmed this.

> We look at ministry as being out there, whereas we should really see it as here and now. ... This is ministry—what we're doing now. That's my understanding of it, but I don't know that others would view it so positively.

Sr. Bernadette agreed that this association between having a purpose and worth is beginning to change, but that "it's taking a long time to accept." Although this may be true, several sisters observed that this experiencing a lack of purpose can be a cause of suffering for older sisters. Sr. Bernadette, for example, explained:

> There is a great sense of frustration at lessening faculties—and maybe me as well, I can see it—if life gets you down and you can't rise above the petty trials ... not depressed, but disgruntled with yourself that you can't overcome these trials. ... Some older sisters need outside help to deal with their irritability and depression; behind it is a feeling of "I am no use." We need to give them a sense of purpose.

Sr. Jayne also identified the continuing challenge caused by this association.

> The very word 'apostle'—this idea of being sent out to carry the message somewhere, and that is where the problem of feeling you have got to

---

2 Pope John Paul II, *Post-synodal Apostolic Exhortation: "Vita Consecrata,"* March 25, 1996, accessed November 23, 2015, http://w2.vatican.va/content/john-paul-ii/en/apost_exhortations/documents/hf_jp-ii_exh_25031996_vita-consecrata.html.

> have a special job to do, no matter how small or how big, the very idea of being apostolic, comes in, so how does it work out with being apostolic to the end?

She adds that older sisters, particularly those who achieved a lot in their working lives are hit badly in later life as "they see themselves only as *what* they have done and not who they are." The sisters seem to be articulating a disconnect between purpose and meaning, and recognizing that a sense of loss of purpose can lead to a loss of meaning.

Third, sisters acknowledge that they can be apostolic without ministry, but, when pressed, many describe even the most elderly and infirm sisters as having some sort of 'ministry,' as if fearing to accept the idea that without this there may be only the experience of 'undergoing,' as in being 'done to,' and dependency. For most sisters, however, the ministry identified is acknowledged as one of prayer and presence. Sr. Collette described her congregation's elderly as "a powerful praying presence," while Sr. Beatrice said of this, "We felt that that was a good apostolic thrust for old ladies—to pray for the families around us."

While ministry of prayer is valued by, and for, other sisters, it is not necessarily the only one the sisters want or envisage for themselves. They often give an example of the one sister or person they knew who remained active until a very late age who they clearly think exemplifies the ideal of how to age. Sr. Collette remembers:

> There was a sister here once, with me, she lived to be ninety and, my God, she was out doing keep fit and doing this and that. People still talk about her—she was part of the Walking Club.

She gave a further example of her uncle who died at the age of ninety-seven but was still very active and was driving up until two or three years before he died; both are described as "great." Sr. Susan similarly refers to a sister in their community who, in her late eighties, was still actively involved in external ministries, visiting the elderly, volunteering at the hospice, and still driving. The struggle seems to be a very human one: having to accept their own increasing infirmity, diminishment, and approaching death, and yet celebrating those who do not become infirm and remain active.

Sisters are, on the one hand, insistent that one can be apostolic without a ministry, and want to underline the separation between a specific ministry or task and being apostolic. On the other hand, they all refer to the most elderly, even those who are "on a bed of pain" (Sr. Dorothy), as either being apostolic or on mission, as they acknowledge the activity inherent in their undergoing suffering or dependence. Their position seems to be that you can be of value when unable to do anything, yet they seem unwilling not to ascribe activities to even the most infirm. This could point to sisters reading meaning into every life, no matter how actively lived. However, it could also be a further reflection of the difficulties they face in coming to terms with what may lie ahead of them individually, in some form of cognitive dissonance. It may also be another aspect of the question of language and naming encountered earlier,[3] such as whether ministry can only apply to activities and active forms of service, and, therefore, whether the forms of serving in later life can be called ministry. Finally, it may be another example of the difficulties of either not having access to, or claiming a name for, their continuing service.

I note some reluctance among the sisters to describe what older sisters do, or how they live, as ministry, as with Sr. Kathleen saying of the lives of older sisters: "I don't know whether you'd call it ministry." It was the oldest sister in the study, Sr. Martina, herself now living in a care community, who perceived least value in talking about ministry at this stage of her life. Although she described her life in terms of what could be interpreted as activities of service such as prayer and visiting other sisters in her community, spending time with them talking and listening, she did not consider these activities as constituting ministry.

> Who, me? No, not now. ... Well, I don't call that ... kind of I go and visit people. To me, that's just something I enjoy doing. I like sitting down with them, and just to let them talk to me, and see what's happening today and how they are, and it's just something that ... no, it is, it's a ministry but ... it's just for old age.

Vacek argues for the importance of the elderly maintaining contact with others, noting that "people are greatly constituted by their engagement with persons and things."[4] This is likely to be particularly true of sisters who have such an outward orientation and purpose. Vacek also underlines the importance of older people developing a set of purposes for this stage of life so as to avoid unhealthy introspection and even depression. Several sisters suggest that being vowed religious gives an identity and meaning to their later lives that many elderly people lack, so this is a positive belief—"it should really be easier for us" (Sr. Beatrice)—but their struggles are evident. The sisters' ideal is those who have kept going, and they want to be active themselves. Interestingly,

---

3 See chapter 3 of this book.
4 Vacek, "Vices and Virtues," 165.

Vacek notes that many gerontologists view the insistence that the elderly keep active as "anti-ageism."[5]

6.2.1.1 Contextual Influences

There are two key influences shaping how the sisters view independence and dependence. The first of these is the social construct which holds that continuing agency is good, and old age and dependency problematic. Sisters' increased integration into and openness to society since the Second Vatican Council means they are not immune from negative societal attitudes towards the elderly, who are now often regarded in Europe as "a problem," constituting what Marshall calls "the Othered category that is old age."[6]

This may affect the sisters' perception and sense of self-worth, particularly as society often views older women more negatively than older men. This is likely to impact upon their reception of the narrative of diminishment and their self-image as elderly women. Many feminists claim that elderly women are even more likely to be marginalized. Calasanti uses the term "age relations" to describe the systematic inequality which prioritizes the needs of the young over the ageing,[7] and Bennett Moore notes, "Old women are so often treated without respect and indeed may be the last in the queue for material resources too."[8] Arber and Ginn argue that "stereotypes of elderly women are particularly negative and demeaning."[9] Elderly women who are not economically productive, not significant consumers, are past child-bearing age and therefore no longer seen as generative, are not considered relevant in a youth- and body image-obsessed culture. Ageing women are less visible in most areas of society, and their voices seldom heard.[10]

The second of the two contextual factors which may affect how sisters see themselves at this stage of their lives is the discourse about the current state of religious life and individuals within it. In a series of interviews conducted

---

5   Vacek, "Vices and Virtues," 165.
6   Leni Marshall, "Aging: A Feminist Issue," *NWSA Journal* 18, no. 1 (2006): vii.
7   Toni M. Calasanti, "Theorizing Age Relations," in *The Need for Theory: Critical Approaches to Social Gerontology for the 21st Century*, ed. Simon Biggs, Jon Hendricks, and Ariela Lowenstein (Amityville, NY: Baywood, 2003): 199–218.
8   Zoe Bennett Moore, *Introducing Feminist Perspectives on Pastoral Theology* (London: Sheffield Academic Press, 2002), 116.
9   Sara Arber and Jay Ginn, *Gender and Later Life: A Sociological Analysis of Resources and Constraints* (London: Sage, 1991), 1, cited in Laura Hurd Clarke, "'We're not old!' Older Women's Negotiation of Aging and Oldness," *Journal of Aging Studies* 13, no. 4 (1999): 419–40.
10 Fariyal Ross-Sheriff, "Aging and Gender, Feminist Theory and Social Work Practice Concerns," *Affilia: Journal of Women and Social Work* 23, no. 4 (2008): 309–11.

with Provincial Superiors, Sexton found that the sisters rejected the language of diminishment, with one preferring to talk of "there's still life in us yet."[11] Pellegrino spoke to the Leadership Conference of Women Religious (LCWR) of the need to combat a narrative of diminishment which has come to dominate the discourse on religious life within the United States and more broadly. She calls for this narrative to be replaced by a more positive one: "a narrative of deepening communion."[12] The communion she refers to is a global communion, between all religious: those of different nationalities within the US and internationally, and with those who are different in age, culture, and outlook. It is a significant attempt to reframe the discourse.

Schneiders also rejects the use of the language of diminishment in wider theological debates for two reasons.[13] First, she does so because of what she sees as de Chardin's understanding of diminishment as passivity in biological terms, particularly in his 1957 work *Le Milieu Divin*. However, in recognition of the struggle going on within sisters, some in this study acknowledge diminishment, with Sr. Susan as an example.

> I can't get out and about; I'm fairly housebound, but in a way … I suppose it's age, it's all become integrated and merged, and I'm so pleased about what everybody [in her community] is doing at this stage, with the new initiatives and so on, and in a sense now it's hard not to be able to do it, but that's the diminishment of age, which, as the life cycle, is absolutely part of this—Teilhard de Chardin and all that—and it's the fulfilment of the paschal mystery, because it is the moving in the direction of the end of life, and it will come to us all. So, I'm very conscious of that at the moment because of restrictions.

Sr. Dorothy is very matter-of-fact in her acceptance of what she sees as a reality.

> Well, it's a fact, isn't it? We are diminishing in numbers, and people are diminishing in themselves; they are not able to do the things they were

---

11   Catherine Sexton, "Still Life in Us Yet: In Search of a Narrative of Diminishment," paper 2 in partial fulfilment of the Professional Doctorate in Practical Theology (Cambridge Theological Federation and Anglia Ruskin University, 2013).
12   Mary Pellegrino, "The Future Enters Us Long Before It Happens: Opening Space for an Emerging Narrative of Communion," presidential address for the Leadership Conference of Women Religious, Orlando, Florida, August 10, 2017, accessed September 14, 2017, https://lcwr.org/sites/default/files/calendar/attachments/2017_lcwr_presidential_address_-_mary_pellegrino_csj.pdf.
13   Schneiders, *Buying the Field*, 586.

able to do. I still think there's a lot of life amongst the people who are diminishing physically in so many ways.

Schneiders does acknowledge the suffering and loss which may accompany advanced old age and the end of life, but she herself is a member of an apostolic, now ministerial, congregation and presumably wrestling with similar issues.

Her second reason for rejecting the use of diminishment is that she believes that to use the term in this context is to judge according to human criteria, rather than those of God. Those at this stage of life are not diminishing; they are "growing into who they are called to be."[14] This draws our attention to the choice we face in old age: how to engage with and respond to suffering and physical infirmity. In obedience to a physical reality, we can make an active choice about how to engage with physical diminishment, and choose relinquishment, or choose passive diminishment. Schneiders sees this choice sisters must make to offer themselves to God in this way as a following of Christ's cry "Into your hands I commend myself" (Lk. 23.46), the final act of self-gift through obedience: "The obedience of self-surrender takes the form of the final fruit of a life of union with the will of God."[15] There are many merits in these attempts to reframe, but they may also be rooted in a fear of dependency and death.

6.2.2 *In Defence of Dependency and Passivity*

I now want to bring these concerns about diminishment into conversation with Vanstone, who, along with several other theologians, holds that the experience of dependency, vulnerability, and undergoing, rather than 'doing,' is feared in our contemporary world.[16] Swinton argues that society has embraced a form of personhood defined by cognitive attributes and agency, whereby a person's worth is judged according to their capacity for rational and articulated intelligence, economic activity, and independence.[17] Coakley notes "the continuing

---

14   Schneiders, *Buying the Field*, 586.
15   Schneiders, *Buying the Field*, 593.
16   William Hubert Vanstone, *The Stature of Waiting* (London: DLT, 1982); Sarah Coakley, *Powers and Submission: Spirituality, Philosophy and Gender* (Oxford: Blackwell, 2002); John Swinton, "The Body of Christ has Down's Syndrome: Theological Reflections on Vulnerability, Disability, and Graceful Communities," *Journal of Pastoral Theology* 13, no. 2 (2003): 66–78, accessed January 21, 2013, http://www.abdn.ac.uk/cshad/TheBodyofChrist HasDownSyndrome.htm.; Swinton, *Dementia: Living in the Memories of God* (Cambridge: Eerdmans, 2012); and John Cottingham, "The Question of Ageing," *Philosophical Papers* 41, no. 3 (2012): 371–96.
17   Swinton, *Dementia*, 130.

cultural fear of 'heteronomy,' that is of submission, dependency or vulnerability," and interprets this as "not just an intellectual, but also a spiritual, crisis of some magnitude."[18] Vacek sees the desire for and self-definition by autonomy, or the desire to be as independent of others as possible, as one of the factors "which inhibits growth in trust towards others and towards God."[19] Vacek also does not recognize the life of Christ as a model for how to live in old age, presumably because he only sees a life of active ministry. This view sits in stark contrast to that of Vanstone.

Vanstone offers a hermeneutic of the passion narratives in the Gospels where the focus of Jesus's passion is not the physical suffering endured, but the act of handing himself over. Vanstone reads this act as a decision to pass from being an active person who does, to being a passive subject or recipient who undergoes,[20] and therefore as an experience of losing control and making himself vulnerable. He argues that human dignity and worth cannot, therefore, be based solely on the capacity to be an independent, active agent. As we are likely to face dependency at some stage in our lives, Vanstone encourages us to rediscover the innate dignity of undergoing, of being dependent and being vulnerable,[21] rather than associating this with loss of dignity and worth in societal terms.[22]

He singles out the particular vulnerability in being dependent, waiting for others and having to relinquish control of self, noting that "although we acquiesce in practice in our condition of dependence we see no positive worth or value in it; and where it is possible to assert or pretend to independence, we do so."[23] God-in-Christ's embracing vulnerability gives theological significance to the experience of waiting and dependence, claiming that "from a Christian viewpoint [waiting] is never a degraded condition, a condition of diminished human dignity,"[24] but is actually a reflection of the glory of God as "the handing over of Jesus discloses the transcendence of loving over everything else."[25]

This is the place where many apostolic women religious find themselves today—particularly those who were once independent and active—waiting, and increasingly dependent on others. They are ageing, living in a situation of corporate congregational diminishment, decreasing in numbers and influence,

---

18   Coakley, *Powers and Submission*, xiv.
19   Vacek, "Vices and Virtues," 173.
20   Vanstone, *Stature of Waiting*, 16–25.
21   Vanstone, *Stature of Waiting*, 66.
22   Vanstone, *Stature of Waiting*, 54.
23   Vanstone, *Stature of Waiting*, 43–44.
24   Vanstone, *Stature of Waiting*, 109.
25   Vanstone, *Stature of Waiting*, 99.

and cannot know the future of religious life. If religious life is a sign of God's presence and points to it both now and to come, embracing an eschatological attitude of trust and hope in the reality of the resurrection, then God must be present in their situation. If we accept that the experience of diminishment at least relates to the physical aspects of the individuals, and the numerical decline of the congregations, this need not necessarily constitute diminishment in a theological sense. We may be witnessing sisters finding ways of being within a context of diminishment and suffering which would constitute flourishing and being apostolic to the very end of their lives, and this on both an individual and congregational level. The sisters recognize and accept the suffering, but find continuing life within this.

6.3   Forms of Ministry in Later Life

Being apostolic in later life and the use of self therein finds a number of expressions in the narrative texts. When asked whether sisters undertake ministry in later life, the initial and most common response is positive, and the most commonly identified form is the ministry of prayer.[26] However, I also identified three other forms of ministry: ministry of presence, ministering to each other in community, and ministry to their carers. I will now explore each of these and their theological expressions in turn.

6.4   Ministry of Presence

This is both a 'how' and a 'what' in that not only is presence identified as a form of ministry, but it also signifies a way of being and an orientation towards others, and as such permeates and is even constitutive of the other forms identified in this chapter. Sisters use 'present' to describe how they are with individuals, through a ministry of presence. Um writes of the impact religious can have on apostolic ministry simply through their presence: "a contemplative gaze capable of generating communion" by imbuing the situation with an indication of God's presence and love.[27] Listening to how sisters draw on this concept of presence will help demonstrate how it is providing them with

---

26   See also page 138 in this chapter.
27   M. Maximilia Um, "Evangelical Mission," in *The Foundations of Religious Life: Revisiting the Vision*, ed. the Council of Major Superiors of Women Religious (Notre Dame, IN: Ave Maria Press, 2009), 172–73.

a framework through which to make meaning of their apostolic vocation in later life.

If the sisters did not themselves use the word 'presence' in the interviews for this study, I asked for their views on it. Thus, the word was used quite extensively, and most responses were positive. Some sisters, however, understood it in negative terms. Sr. Bernadette thought it indicated passivity; Sr. Kathleen associated it with the work of retreat-giving and spiritual direction and the opposite of activity, and had not thought of herself in those terms. In response to my feedback to sisters in the second round of interviews, several expressed discomfort at describing their ministry as 'presence.' Sr. Maeve, for example, feared that using the word to describe what she or other sisters do would somehow set them apart, as if thinking of themselves as special in some way.

6.4.1 Contexts for Ministry of Presence

Sisters apply the language of 'presence' to at least three contexts. First, and in contrast to Sr. Maeve's fear, they link the term to the ordinary and the experience of being present in and to the local community. Several sisters, including Sr. Beatrice, Sr. Susan, and Sr. Anne, live in communities with an intentional presence on a socially deprived housing estate. Sr. Anne explains the effect she believes this has:

> The ministry of presence is the reality of either an individual or a group of people who live in a particular area, live a particular way of life, and simply the presence of that group can be an almost intangible influence on what goes on around you ... actually being in a place inevitably sends ripples out.

This usage expresses a concern to be both present in and to a local community, and is one which Sweeney regards as being

> coherent with the founding inspiration of many apostolic religious congregations, particularly institutes of women religious and those established in the nineteenth century.[28]

This suggests that this form of intentional presence may well be a reflection of that charismatic impulse and the congregations' own journey *ad fontes*. A number of congregations in Britain during the 1980s and 1990s set up such

---

28   James Sweeney, "Religious Life Looks to the Future," in *A Future Full of Hope?*, ed. Gemma Simmonds (Dublin: Columba Press, 2012), 139.

communities, including the Daughters of Charity, the Infant Jesus sisters, and both female and male Passionists.[29] Experimenting with this form of intentional presence, often in collaboration with other congregations, formed part of an exploration of their commitment to the preferential option for the poor.[30]

A second context where the term 'presence' is applied and practised is in response to a situation encountered which is so difficult that nothing else can be offered. Nouwen used the term to describe his response to situations of abject poverty and injustice in Latin America where he felt that he had nothing to offer except his presence.[31] This understanding of 'presence' recognizes human powerlessness in situations where we have to recognize the limitations of creaturehood. Sr. Kathleen describes being present with those dying of AIDS in southern Africa, and Sr. Jayne, who, in her prison ministry, felt she had nothing to offer the prisoners she encountered other than her listening presence.

Sisters also use the term in a third context, where they feel one needs to be present and listen to people, in a world where, as they perceive it, no one listens any more. Several sisters used it to describe their response to individuals who came to them for support. Sr. Maeve, in her second interview, identified this as a need for our times.

> Compassionate presence ... [is] required because of the violence, et cetera, out in the world, and you have to counteract it by mingling with people, to be that empathetic, compassionate presence.

Marcel's philosophical understanding of 'presence' draws on the concepts of availability (*disponibilité*, as explored in the previous chapter) and communion. Presence, for Marcel, carries a much deeper meaning than simply being physically present, transmitting to, or communicating with, another on an almost transactional basis. Instead, it denotes being fully open, through availability to another, in a way which enriches the presence and fullness of both. This is understood as communion,[32] perhaps as experienced by Sr. Collette.

---

29   Female Passionists belong to the Sisters of the Cross and Passion, and the male Passionists are members of the Congregation of the Passion.

30   For more on this topic, see David McLoughlin and Gemma Simmonds, "Pastoral and Practical Theology in Britain and Ireland: A Catholic Perspective," in *Keeping Faith in Practice: Aspects of Catholic Pastoral Theology*, ed. James Sweeney, Gemma Simmonds, and David Lonsdale (London: SCM Press, 2010), 26–42; and Susan O'Brien, *Leaving God for God: The Daughters of Charity of St. Vincent de Paul in Britain, 1847–2017* (London: DLT, 2017).

31   Henri Nouwen, *Gracias: A Latin American Journal* (New York: HarperCollins, 1987).

32   Gabriel Marcel, *The Mystery of Being*: Vol. 2, *Faith and Reality* (London: Harvill Press, 1951), 201–8.

> To be fully present to the person, and not to think, "I'm meeting this person now, and I'm going to, or he or she is going to, share with me," but to be aware, to look at the person, to respect the person for who he or she is, to bring out what is good in that person as well, bring out something positive, and to explore that and develop that within the person's standpoint.

This form of presence enriches the other in a way that is reciprocal and mutual. Marcel presents a philosophical understanding of communion whereby we participate in each other's experience and being, thus complementing the theological concept of communion identified in the previous chapter. He differentiates between a form of being with another which is simply "a communication without communion," and true presence which "can refresh my inner being; it reveals me to myself; it makes me more fully myself."[33] What makes the difference for Marcel is mystery, which turns the intersubjectivity into something intangible, indefinable: "a something else."[34] Presence expresses Marcel's belief that we can only understand and recognize the self through being with, for, and among others. As Sr. Pamela explains:

> It's a kind of insertion, but it's stronger ... it makes you part of others. ... I'm automatically thinking of a presence which is living, which has an influence, which is not just a stone statue, present.

6.4.2 *Expressions of Presence*

Sisters express several ways by which they are 'present' in this ministry of presence. The first is through attentive listening and being present for and to the other's needs, all of which denote an orientation to the other, and an attitude of availability.[35] Sr. Beatrice described ministry of presence as "being there for them." It points to the role of collaboration and accompaniment which Sweeney claims is now part of the self-understanding of apostolic religious.[36] Sr. Bernadette referred to one of the more active sisters in her congregation's care community who writes letters for sisters no longer able to do this: "To me, that is a ministry of presence because she is making herself available to them."

A second way comprises, for the sisters, an element of drawing very deeply upon oneself, so that the self is a key resource. Sr. Bernadette exercises her

---

33   Marcel, *Mystery of Being* 2: 205, 206.
34   Marcel, *Mystery of Being* 2: 118.
35   As explored in chapter 5 of this volume.
36   James Sweeney, "Prophets and Parables: A Future for Religious Orders," *Informationes Theologiae Europae: Internationales ökumenisches Jahrbuch für Theologie* 4 (2001): 281.

ministry just by being herself. Sisters also describe drawing upon themselves as a sister, as explored in the previous chapter, which indicates a belief that sisters can bring something, perhaps indefinable, to a situation because of who they are. Sr. Susan felt that "we are doing ministry through how we express our being." Sr. Bernadette talked about sisters who go to visit isolated and lonely people in their homes.

> There's that poster on the Underground "Agnes hasn't spoken to anyone for a full week"—this is something religious can do and they have the time—they don't have to come in and clean the carpets and do the physical caring—someone else can do that, but they can come and just be with people and spend time—just by being who they are.

Sr. Jayne, in her second interview, echoes this, indicating a belief that one's self is one's greatest resource, particularly at this later stage in life when a sister may have greater personal resources on which to draw. "It is all part and parcel of you, especially by the time you get to my age, hopefully." She is present to others through who she has come to be at this stage of her life, perhaps ministering out of her true self, and perhaps this 'self' has become more visible to them as they are now without formal employment or work.

A third expression of presence locates it specifically in the experience of old age, recognizing that with age comes physical and social limitations, but that being present to and with is still possible as an expression of being apostolic. This is a form of ministry (if we still want to use that word in this context) that is a practical option for sisters, no matter what their state of physical health, as long as they have good hearing.

The emergence of presence, especially linked to age, as an identifiable form of ministry highlights further tensions. First, presence may have become increasingly popular because this is now the only form of ministry many sisters can offer, and so the sisters may well be making "a virtue out of necessity," something which Vacek notes is often a task of the elderly.[37] Considering the current demographic reality of many women's congregations in the UK, this form of ministry may be something which religious life can specifically offer at this point in its history. Sr. Bernadette contrasts how sisters used to be 'out there' with how they are now called to be present to each other in their care community.

> I think that's what's been given to us now that, in this time of religious life, you know, like when we were in our sixties everything was apostolic,

---

37   Vacek, "Vices and Virtues," 21.

and we were out there and doing things. Now we're ... unable to man the barricades and we're ... having, you know, a more reflective way of living, but it's important for us to realize that that is the way we are.

It may be a question for congregations, and also perhaps for theologians with an interest in this field, whether there is a need to give this stage of life a more structured theological underpinning by which to explore the meaning of an apostolic vocation in later life. This seems to be particularly relevant for sisters who experienced a call to serve others through action and activity, and to do something useful with their lives. Sr. Bernadette suggests above that many older sisters need to be helped to find a purpose. Another perspective is whether or not it is about purpose or about reimagining or redescribing sisters' ways of being as they age. This would mean highlighting the meaning of these forms of ministry in order to help those sisters who need support to understand how they can continue to live their vocation, and what meaning their lives can continue to have.

However, this may also have implications for religious life more widely. As Sr. Bernadette suggested above, 'presence' may have become a form of ministry through which religious sisters, at any time in their lives, have something unique to offer, including the gift of themselves and their time.

6.4.3 *Towards a Sacramental Theology of Presence*

I want to move on now to explore a theological understanding of presence and argue that we can read into the sisters' self-understanding and orientation towards others a theology that is in itself sacramental. If sacraments are "signs of both the Church and Christ, pointing to the action of Christ in the world, and communicating God's grace to that world,"[38] then we can read the sisters' understanding of presence and their form of being apostolic as sacramental.[39]

This claim rests on two points. First, the change in world view articulated in *Gaudium et Spes*[40] led to a recognition that "the locus of revelation is the living experience of humanity."[41] Schillebeeckx's work in 1963 gives us some

---

38 L. Kelly, *Sacraments Revisited: What Do They Mean Today?* (London: DLT, 1998), 22, cited in Susanna Brouard, "Using Theological Action Research to Embed Catholic Social Teaching in a Catholic Development Agency" (PhD diss., Anglia Ruskin University, 2015), 130, accessed November 24, 2016, http://arro.anglia.ac.uk/580464/1/FullThesis%20Susanna%20Brouard.pdf. Accessed November 24, 2016.

39 Brouard, "Using Theological Action Research."

40 Pope Paul VI, *Pastoral Constitution on the Church in the Modern World: "Gaudium et Spes,"* December 7, 1965, https://www.vatican.va/archive/hist_councils/ii_vatican_council/documents/vat-ii_const_19651207_gaudium-et-spes_en.html.

41 Daniel O'Leary, *Begin With the Heart: Recovering a Sacramental Vision* (Dublin: Columba Press, 2008), 59.

conceptual tools to break open and illustrate the shift from traditional sacramental theology to sacramental thinking. Schillebeeckx called for a reconsideration of the "dogma of the perpetuity of the incarnation" so as to understand that although we no longer encounter Christ in his own flesh, his incarnation is made flesh in the world, and "this earthly element replaces for us the invisibility of his bodily life in heaven."[42] He understood the sacraments as "the face of redemption turned visibly towards us, so that in them we are truly able to encounter the living Christ."[43] This was indeed a breakthrough, as Schillebeeckx identifies that previously sacramental theology had understood humans as "passive recipients of sacramental grace which seemed to be 'put into us' automatically."[44] He argues for a sacramentality that sees sacraments as "encounters of men on earth with the glorified man Jesus by way of a visible form, the visible and tangible embodiment of the heavenly saving action of Christ."[45] Therefore, through human encounter, the invisible can be rendered visible.

A second point, which perhaps was enabled by Schillebeeckx's reimagining of the formal sacraments, is that developments in the theology of grace during and since the Second Vatican Council have led to a perspective which views humanity and the created world as having the potential to be imbued with God's grace. This theology, whereby created things and humanity are seen as the locus of revelation, and whereby sacramentality is no longer exclusively located within the seven formal sacraments of the Church, is now widely discussed and recognized. It is essentially what McBrien refers to as "the sacramental principle," wherein "everything is, in principle, capable of embodying and communicating the divine,"[46] and what O'Leary terms "the sacramental imagination," which celebrates Catholicism's capacity to "reconfigure reality by seeing it through an alternative lens, acquiring a new vision of its graced character."[47] If, as Timmerman holds, a symbol or sign (*sacramentum*) "conveys what it contains,"[48] then the sisters, through their approach to presence, are indeed signs in this context. Through their approach to presence, they

---

[42] Edward Schillebeeckx, *Christ the Sacrament of the Encounter with God* (New York: Sheed and Ward, 1963), 43.

[43] Schillebeeckx, *Christ the Sacrament*, 43.

[44] Schillebeeckx, *Christ the Sacrament*, 1.

[45] Schillebeeckx, *Christ the Sacrament*, 44.

[46] Richard P. McBrien, *Catholicism* (Minneapolis, MN: Winston Press, 1980), 731, cited in Susan Ross, *Extravagant Affections: A Feminist Sacramental Theology* (New York: Continuum, 2001), 34.

[47] O'Leary, *Begin With the Heart*, 175.

[48] Joan H. Timmerman, "The Sacramentality of Human Relationships," *The Way Supplement* 94 (1999): 11.

make real that which they convey through a practical process or experience of "knowing relationships as sacramental and oneself as graced by them."[49]

However, while these theologians have done much to develop a broader sacramental theology, none, with the exception of Orobator, pays attention to the exclusion of women from the sacramental life of the Church.[50] Ross argues for a feminist sacramental theology, which views women's lives and experiences as constituting a suitable locus for sacramentality.[51] Although I do not here address Ross' central concern of ensuring that the formal sacraments of the Catholic Church more fully represent the lives and experiences of women, I do share her starting point: "to begin by acknowledging the revelatory character of the world, of human beings, and deliberately to focus on the importance of the experiences of women."[52] My concern is to recognize the "sacramental beyond the liturgical" in the lives of the women in this study.[53] This further builds on the reference to religious as signs in both *Vita Consecrata*, which refers on several occasions (VC, §§20, 25, 27) to consecrated women as signs ("they will become true signs of Christ in the world … a living sign of God" [VC, §25]), and Pope Francis' call to religious to be "a credible sign of the presence of the Spirit who inspires in human hearts a passion for all to be one."[54]

6.4.4 *Presence as Incarnational*

Building on the above, I claim that the sisters' understanding of their presence as embodying Christ can be read as an articulation of an incarnational theology. Earlier, I suggested that Marcel's understanding of presence complements the theological understanding of communion. I have shown how Marcel understands presence as both rooted in the lived experience of the person, in the here and now, and yet also mysterious, as the experience of presence can transcend the physical.[55] The sisters similarly demonstrate an understanding

---

49   Timmerman, "Sacramentality of Human Relationships," 12.
50   Agbonkhianmeghe E. Orobator, "A Global Sign of Outward Grace: The Sacramentality of the World Church in the Era of Globalisation," *Catholic Theological Society of America Proceedings* 67 (2012): 14–22.
51   Ross, *Extravagant Affections*, 10–13.
52   Ross, *Extravagant Affections*, 31.
53   C. Watkins and H. Cameron, "Epiphanic Sacramentality: An Example of Practical Ecclesiology Revisioning Theological Understanding," in *Explorations in Ecclesiology and Ethnography*, ed. C. B. Scharen (Cambridge: Eerdmans, 2012), 89, cited in Brouard, "Using Theological Action Research," 140.
54   Pope Francis, *Apostolic Letter to All Consecrated People*, §1.2, November 21, 2014, accessed January 12, 2015, https://www.vatican.va/content/francesco/en/apost_letters/documents/papa-francesco_lettera-ap_20141121_lettera-consacrati.html.
55   Marcel, *Mystery of Being* 2: 207–18.

of presence which is concrete in its embodied nature, but given meaning by its expression of the presence of God, pointing beyond themselves.

In earlier chapters, I established that with age, the sisters' self-understanding develops beyond one associated with undertaking defined apostolic activities towards being apostolic through an embodied presence of self. As Sr. Pamela said in her second interview:

It's going back to St. Francis of Assisi ... preach the gospel and if necessary, use words. That's what he's supposed to have said. It's about *who you are*.

As seen earlier in chapter 3, Sr. Dorothy referred to "being God's merciful love" as an aspect of her congregation's charism.[56] Sr. Anne, echoing *Vita Consecrata* §72, similarly uses the language of 'being' to communicate a highly developed sense of the embodied presence of God.

> Simply *by being we can be* mission. ... We can be a mission, like, the example we always say, well, you know, I was just having a conversation with the woman in Tesco who does the checkout, or whatever it happens to be.

Although not directed as intentionally at those living religious life, the sisters' words echo and reflect those of Pope Francis in his 2013 apostolic exhortation *Evangelii Gaudium*.

> My mission of being in the heart of the people is not just a part of my life or a badge I can take off; it is not an 'extra' or just another moment in life. Instead, it is something I cannot uproot from my being without destroying my very self. I am a mission on this earth; that is the reason why I am here in this world.[57]

Second, sisters also indicate their understanding of the paradox inherent in their ministry: that in being truly present, in being mission, by virtue of being fully themselves as consecrated women, it is not they who are present, but Christ, as experienced by Sr. Beatrice.

> The presence is the presence of Jesus—that where two or three are, there am I in the midst; that feeling that there is a presence other than who

---

56   The quotation is taken from a document circulated in the Society of the Holy Child Jesus on the occasion of Cornelia Connelly being declared Venerable in 1992. The author is thought to be Radegunde Flaxman SHCJ.

57   Pope Francis, *Evangelii Gaudium* §273, November 24, 2013, https://www.vatican.va/content/francesco/en/apost_exhortations/documents/papa-francesco_esortazione-ap_20131124_evangelii-gaudium.html.

we are ... because you are empowered by the Spirit. Not because you are anything, but because Jesus in you is everything.

The theology articulated in these two aspects is incarnational. The sisters understand their ministry of presence as incarnating or embodying God, being God's presence, being a channel for God's grace, and, for Sr. Beatrice, being nothing but what God has given her. These are all facets of the "embodied Christianity" that O'Leary says characterizes Catholicism.[58] In my feedback to sisters from the first interviews, I reported having heard an understanding of ministry at this age expressed in terms of physical embodiment, and the majority of sisters responded by saying they understood this in explicitly incarnational terms. Sr. Susan explained:

> It's one's understanding of God's relationship with us and what God wants for all of us which is for me the apostolic bit, you know, reaching out to people in Tesco ... it's being counsel ... incarnation—bearing the gifts and the purposes of God for his people.

Sr. Jayne spoke very powerfully of her recent experience of prison ministry as an example of what Welker described as "the public person of God's spirit concretized and realized in this communion."[59]

> I was really the Catholic presence on the staff. Looking back over my life, that is the time that I think I was most apostolic ... does it sound awful to say I was God's presence among these damaged people? That's what I mean by 'being apostolic'—it's being, just bringing God to people, isn't it, not so much in words?

In order to explore this sense of the self as incarnational a little further, and something of the paradox of self-empowerment through self-gift, I want to explore Coakley's understanding of *kenosis*, which, she claims, is compatible with Christian feminist theology, as a means of embracing the paradox of "losing one's life to save it." She refers to a "right" *kenosis* based on Christian contemplation, whereby silent prayer enables us "to hold vulnerability and personal empowerment together." This constitutes a "power-in-vulnerability" or a "right" form of vulnerability which empowers (through contemplation).[60]

---

58 O'Leary, *Begin With the Heart*, 49.
59 Michael Welker, *God the Spirit* (Minneapolis, MN: Fortress Press, 1994), 311.
60 Coakley, *Powers and Submission*, 5.

She asks whether vulnerability could be seen as a strength,[61] and whether "true divine 'empowerment' occurs most unimpededly in the context of a special form of human vulnerability."[62] This "special form of vulnerability" refers to that which is embraced through a practice of contemplative prayer, which centres on "the defenceless prayer of silent waiting on God."[63] She contends that only by making space for God in this way, to allow ourselves to be invaded and converted by God, can we be fully empowered. Applied to the sisters, this would not refer to the self-abnegation of their earlier years, nor a silencing, but "the place of the self's transformation and expansion into God."[64]

I have already stated that I recognize some of the difficulties with applying the concept of *kenosis* to human self-giving.[65] However, my concern here is specifically the process by which the sisters have been able both to live self-gift, and develop their 'self' and draw on it as a resource. Stogdon recognizes the need "to have an adequate sense of self before one is able freely to give it away altruistically or spiritually (and without damaging self or others)."[66] Coakley's work identifies a place or process which would have enabled the ongoing conversion and transformation of the self. This, for Stogdon, is the prayer of union, "the giving of oneself in love to the purposes of God ... the assent to an ongoing transformation through a radical availability to the divine initiative."[67] The sisters' commitment to a self-denying love would have brought them to this place recognized as the result of their conversion. Schneiders understands this as the prayer of union, and what she sees as the goal of the spiritual life: "the deep wellspring of the selflessness ... profound poverty of spirit and total detachment from the ego that frees the true self for full union with God."[68] Identifying this as poverty of spirit perhaps expresses more appropriately the issue at stake here, which is recognition of "the deepening conversion that occurs through the life devoted to the single-hearted quest for God through union with Christ."[69]

---

61 Coakley, *Powers and Submission*, 25–29.
62 Coakley, *Powers and Submission*, 32.
63 Coakley, *Powers and Submission*, 33.
64 Coakley, *Powers and Submission*, 36.
65 See pages 133, 153 above.
66 Kate Stogdon, "'Nothing Was Taken From Me: Everything Was Given': Religious Life and Second Wave Feminism," in *A Future Full of Hope?*, ed. Gemma Simmonds (Dublin: Columba Press, 2012), 74.
67 Stogdon, "'Nothing Was Taken From Me,'" 74.
68 Schneiders, *Buying the Field*, 352.
69 Sandra Schneiders, *Selling All: Commitment, Consecrated Celibacy, and Community in Catholic Religious Life* (Mahwah, NJ: Paulist Press, 2001), 158.

At least half of the sisters spoke of a call to a practice of contemplative prayer, or "the defenceless prayer of silent waiting on God,"[70] which has strengthened with age. Sr. Jayne, in saying "I want to be more contemplative in this stage of life" and no longer in full-time ministry, experiences a call to a different way of being. However, as Stogdon recognizes, "the resulting strong sense of self is not the end of the story."[71] This form of personal empowerment in God indicated by Coakley and Stogdon both makes possible and results from the forms of ministry explored in this and the previous chapters.

6.4.5 Raising Up the Ordinary

A further aspect of the question of sacramentality, which I have already explored from a number of perspectives, is the sisters' concern with the ordinary. In the sisters' language, there is a point at which the desire to be and to be seen as ordinary, and the understanding of religious life as a distinct life form, come together. This coming together in the sense of being Christ in the ordinary is the fruit of a lifetime of conversion, in the conforming of self to Christ.

The dualistic attitude towards the Church and the world of the pre-conciliar period, which might have prevented us from understanding these perspectives as incarnational, was finally addressed in the Second Vatican Council through the document *Gaudium et Spes* (1965, §§3, 16, 44) with its world-embracing theology and orientation.[72] Gregory Baum, himself a *peritus*[73] at the Council, summarized this unified understanding: "In Christ it is revealed that the locus of the divine is the human. In Him it is made manifest that God speaks in and through the words and gestures of people,"[74] and simultaneously addresses the worldly and the spiritual.

Sr. Pamela, in her second interview, offered three reflections on the relationship between the ordinary and the extraordinary. In the first, she revisited her 'extraordinary' experience of giving up teaching in school, and moving out to live in a shanty town under a Latin American dictatorship in the 1980s. In response to my feedback on embodiment, she framed this as incarnational: "We went into the shanty towns; that was called '*encarnándose*,' which was incarnational—incarnating—you see."

In this, she takes an extraordinary situation in her life and understands it as incarnating, that is, making God real and bringing God's presence into

---

70 Coakley, *Powers and Submission*, 34.
71 Stogdon, "'Nothing Was Taken From Me,'" 74.
72 O'Leary, *Begin With the Heart*, 45; James Sweeney, "Catholic Theology and Practice Today," in Sweeney et al., *Keeping Faith in Practice*, 11–25; and Schneiders, *Buying the Field*, 21–25.
73 *Peritus*: a theological adviser or consultant.
74 O'Leary, *Begin With the Heart*, 45, citing Baum.

that situation in an intentional and purposeful way. However, mostly the sisters reflect on the ordinary as extraordinary and in doing so, raise up the ordinary and the prosaic and sanctify it, particularly through the juxtaposition of encounters in Tesco with being the presence of God, reminding us of Orobator's "sacramentality of mundane events and moments of daily life."[75] Sr. Susan identifies the need, therefore, to be open to the extraordinariness of God's presence in everyday encounters, describing 'apostolic' as

> a focus on relationship with all who you encounter, so that you have to be much more aware that every encounter can be a meeting with the divine. ... I suppose it's a recognition of the presence of the divine in the world, in the very ordinary—the extraordinary as present in the ordinary.

In Sr. Pamela's second example, she views presence from the perspective of the ordinary, and feels moved to celebrate this rather than her diamond jubilee, because it was in the ordinary that she saw (to use her own word) the sacramental. She feels women religious underestimate the value of their ordinary lives, particularly after or because they have spent their lives fully occupied in recognizable ministries in schools, in parishes, and clinics.

> I think that we [religious] tend to underestimate the power, the influence, of our ordinary, everyday lives, and that it is the little things that we do to help one other in community life that makes life. At the beginning of this year, I celebrated my diamond jubilee, and what I wanted to celebrate was the 'ordinariness' of religious life—so I didn't want a big celebration. What I want to celebrate are the things that we do every day, all day, that make our life so worthwhile.

Her words exemplify O'Leary's "sacramental imagination" which allows us to perceive "God at work in all created reality, especially in human life and relationships, so that they carry the image of Christ."[76] He locates the emergence of the ordinary in the Second Vatican Council, stating "the theology of grace that informs Vatican II recovers 'the ordinary' as the realm of grace. ... Hence the aesthetic of holiness is not something exceptional but the same thing that is shaped in the realm of the domestic."[77] His recognition of "the domestic" has particular bearing on the sisters' contexts and calls to mind "Love and

---

75 Orobator, "A Global Sign of Outward Grace," 14.
76 O'Leary, *Begin With the Heart*, 176.
77 O'Leary, *Begin With the Heart*, 44.

Attention: Incarnateness," the first chapter in Soskice's 2007 work *The Kindness of God*.[78]

In this work, Soskice argues for an alternative to the received wisdom—which emphasizes silence and prayer and being set apart from the noise and demands of ordinary life—of what constitutes spiritual life. She claims that this traditional or received view of what will promote spiritual growth and enable self-mastery does not recognize the value of our paying attention to demands made on us by love in everyday life, particularly on those caring for others. Like Ross, she concludes that this "received spirituality" and the image of God it presupposes "disenfranchise[s] many people, and perhaps especially women," as it fails to reflect the reality of ordinary women's lives.[79] Her proposal is "to add the spiritual discipline of attention (*prosochē*) to self-mastery (*enkrateia*),"[80] and to recognize the worth of our responding to others both with loving attention and availability in everyday life, echoing Marcel's concept of *disponibilité*.

In Sr. Pamela's final example, she perceives the ordinary as ministry, as grace-filled, imbuing it with a sacramental meaning, pointing to, and making real, the presence of God. This insight into the sacredness of the ordinary has been formed by her mother's spirituality, and particularly her mother's experience of caring for her dying husband, as she told Sr. Pamela:

> "People kept praying; I could feel the prayer, and it was the prayer that kept me going, and I was very sad," she said, "because I couldn't pray, but everything I did was a prayer." She could see that her way of praying for my dad was getting his meals ready and looking after him and taking in his cup of tea and being patient when he was being snappy because he was ill. ... I think my mother was a very wise woman, and she found her service in the ordinary things.

She echoes Soskice's call to love and attention, particularly relevant to the orientation of the sisters in this study, through their availability for and to others: "It is by being at the disposal of another that we are characteristically drawn out of ourselves (*ecstasis*) and come to understand ourselves fully as selves."[81] LaCugna explains *ekstasis* as freedom, and ecstasy as being-in-transcendence,

---

78   Janet Martin Soskice, *The Kindness of God: Metaphor, Gender, and Religious Language* (Oxford: Oxford University Press, 2007), chap. 1.
79   Soskice, *Kindness of God*, 14.
80   Soskice, *Kindness of God*, 25.
81   Soskice, *Kindness of God*, 25.

taking us further out of ourselves and more fully and freely oriented towards others, in Trinitarian communion with them.[82]

6.5 Ministry to Each Other in Community: Sacramentality of Relationships

A second way in which elderly sisters continue to be apostolic is in their contribution to community. Within this, there is the more ordinary way of contributing to everyday domestic tasks where able, but also simply continuing to be a member of community, in relationship with their sisters, and all that entails in their everyday life together.

Although in the earlier section I focussed on the sacramental character of presence, sisters cannot be sacramental in a vacuum; they are signs pointing to God's presence for others. Timmerman addresses the Christian misconception that God can only be known in limited ways, and draws our attention to the sacramentality in human relationships, where we can experience God's presence for ourselves. She points to "a theology of God the Spirit understood as the divine *immanence* present in, with and under every encounter."[83] Her thinking about the sacramentality of relationships can clearly be applied to the way sisters are present to others, and see themselves as being the presence of God to others: "relationship … mediates the divine presence and power," both through ritual and "the ordinary actions of everyday life."[84] What she sees as specifically sacramental in relationships is the practical process or experience of "knowing relationships as sacramental and oneself as graced by them."[85]

As both Sr. Anne and Sr. Susan live in stable communities, it is hardly surprising that for them an important part of being apostolic in old age is simply continuing to be an active, contributing member of the community. As Sr. Susan says:

> I think being a member of this community and living this life, and joining in everything, genuinely sharing a life of prayer, the work, the things we do together, like choir, like entertaining, hospitality, all that sort of thing,

---

82 Catherine Mowry LaCugna, *God for Us: The Trinity and Christian Life* (New York: HarperSanFrancisco, 1991), 39.
83 Timmerman, "Sacramentality of Human Relationships," 19–20.
84 Timmerman, "Sacramentality of Human Relationships," 10.
85 Timmerman, "Sacramentality of Human Relationships," 12.

and welcoming and sharing ... the sharing of the space and being happy for that to happen [is important].

Sr. Anne here expands on the belief that the elderly or infirm in her congregation would never retire from religious life:

> As long as I'm physically and mentally able, there are contributions to community living that I can still exercise; there is the ministry of prayer and intercession, which is important, and there would still be the ministry of hospitality. So, I think to be apostolic is something to do with the way in which we *are* with people—people who try to follow 'the way'—we are people of 'the way,' and, to be as much as we can Easter people, people of hope; not always easy, but that's the ideal. ... As you know we have two elderly sisters who at the moment are pretty disabled because of their condition, so I think we would never retire from trying to be good community members, although our external apostolic ministry might well diminish.

There is a sense of contributing to and celebrating the domestic, but also of being in communion with others, and helping each other on her way to God—and this can continue until the end of life. As Sr. Beatrice affirms:

> We can be apostolic all the time—[the Foundress] says be real, be true, be united. That's what we should be, in community. We should help one another to have this apostolic thrust and not say we've done enough, we're tired. Of course we're tired.

When first asked, most sisters did not see caring for each other in community as a form of ministry. However, as more communities and indeed congregations comprise a majority of sisters who are very elderly, sisters have begun to see that increasingly this is a call to which they must respond. As Sr. Bernadette says of ministry for her time of life:

> It's a ministry inside the house: You can accept that and work on, either with the elderly there in helping care for them, or do what you've got to do like here with guests. Nevertheless, you're doing what you have to do, but you're doing it inside the house.

Sisters often have to adapt from being the ones helping others to become more fully themselves, to allowing themselves to be helped by a sister through whom a relationship reveals ever more of the face of God. Vacek identifies one challenge of infirmity in later life, to learn dependency: "Those who have lived their active lives caring for others as their way of cooperating with God now must cooperate with God by letting God take care of them through others."[86] This has particular relevance for this group of women. At an earlier age in religious life, sisters often retired at their silver jubilee and were cared for by younger sisters. In contrast, it is now common for elderly sisters who are still able to live relatively independently either to remain in their own small community, or to live in care communities which are increasingly comprised of the large percentage of the remaining sisters in a Province. In this, there is a new emerging form of ministry: that of caring for each other in elderly communities, and this can be understood in the context of both obedience and relinquishment. Sr. Maeve notes that her own congregation is only now beginning to acknowledge this, and that this is "new and kind of significant—charity begins at home."

She explains how, after a recent fall, she was cared for by her sisters, many of whom are equally elderly, and experienced their love in a new way. In this period of increasing dependency, the sisters' self-understanding of being apostolic serves them well as they age, as they give increasing value to 'being' because they can no longer do so much. Vacek sees finding new ways to care for others as one of the moral priorities for an earlier stage of old age,[87] but it is none the less what we see sisters continuing to do in this later stage of life.

6.6 Ministry with and for Their Carers

The third and final expression of ministry in old age which I will explore in this chapter is that of ministering to one's carers. Despite Sr. Kathleen's comment that caring for one's carers does not really constitute ministry, half of the sisters understand their relationship with those who care for them as offering an opportunity for a very context-specific form of ministry at the end of their lives. Even in their own state of increasing dependency, the sisters in Sr. Pamela's congregation's care community find meaning through this form of care.

> They see that they have an apostolate with the carers; the carers look after them, but they also look after the carers. Whenever there's a carer who has some kind of problem at home, they will find somebody down there who will listen to them.

---

86 Vacek, "Vices and Virtues," 172–73.
87 Vacek, "Vices and Virtues," 169.

When I asked Sr. Pamela if she thought the carers were aware of this two-way aspect of the relationship, she said, "I think some of them are. Yes, I do," highlighting the potential for a two-way relationship of gift.

I would now like to consider in some depth the experience of Sr. Dorothy, who moved into a care community in between her first and second interviews with me. Although she accepted the need to move, she was not expecting it to be easy. She wanted to offer her reflection that the move had been surprisingly positive, and I want to draw out a number of points from her reflections. First, she described the move as being 'missioned' to the care community. In reality, she would have agreed to the move, in discernment with her Superior and her own community; she was not 'sent.' However, the practice of being missioned, as with other sisters being sent out to any new ministry, gives the transition to a care home both a normalizing feel and also a deeper, theological meaning.

Second, Sr. Dorothy had expected the move to represent simply a loss of independence, but to her surprise:

> I've found that coming here—you lose certain freedoms, obviously, but you gain other sorts of freedoms. Just to give a concrete example: I didn't want to go onto a three-wheeled walker, and I found it infra dig and embarrassing for twenty-four hours, and I thought, "Oh, I've lost freedom." I haven't. It's much quicker; I've lost pain, and there are all sorts of advantages. And they can be psychological as well as on a spiritual level.

Sr. Dorothy here is obedient to the new physical limitations in which she finds herself, but also recognizes that she is being presented with a new opportunity. It is also an example of mutual recognition as explored by Ricoeur;[88] the helpers and the helped are recognizing each other for who they are and what they can offer.

A third element of Sr. Dorothy's experience was that she found a genuine community rather than a society of helpers and helped, the independent and the dependent.

> What I find about here is that I feel that we are all one, one sort of family, and that includes nurses, carers, cleaners—the lot. And some of us need help, and some need a lot of help, and some give it. ... It just strikes me as one group of people, and they have different roles in it ... but there's an equality.

---

88   Paul Ricoeur, *The Course of Recognition*, trans. David Pellauer (Cambridge, MA: Harvard University Press, 2005), chap. 3.

Thus, the experience of giving and taking and mutuality within relationship continues. Earlier in the chapter, I quoted Pellegrino's call for sisters to understand themselves as being in communion rather than in diminishment. The kind of communion she calls for across age, nationality, and international borders in increasing recognition of the transnationality of religious life may not be that meaningful for sisters who are housebound. The ministry of presence and care for each other in community may offer a more meaningful and appropriate model of communion. Sr. Jayne is able to see a specific role for religious in this context, as religious and religious life ages. A friend of hers lives in a care home and is intentionally

> aiming to spread God's love in a nursing home, being the best you can be in the circumstances, with some inner strength coming from God's grace and help, and she says to me sometimes: "I think this is what we should be aiming at."

Returning to Sr. Dorothy, this next excerpt shows her response to the opportunity to continue to be of service, in what could be described as an encounter with grace.

> Whereas I thought coming here was going to bring a good deal of diminishment—it hasn't. ... In fact, it's opened up ways of ministry that I'd never imagined, and my biggest surprise. I thought you see—coming here—to a care home—oh, you'd spend a lot of time praying or visiting the sick, but for me—while I'm still able-bodied, more or less, and able-minded—the staff are the ones to be enabled and encouraged, and I find this very, very interesting, and something that never crossed my mind, but they are all human beings and they have needs, and they all love to be listened to, and I just find that quite exciting, really. It isn't just dealing with the people going down, down, down all the time.

More specifically, she identifies the quality of what she can do with and for her carers.

> Well, I've ended up here at the end of my life, after a very busy ministry in school. I find now that I can't go out to people, but they can come in to me, and here, the staff—all have families, and troubles, and I think they need encouragement, and it is something I could do, and it's a sort of continuation of dealing with school—bringing out the potential—and I do believe that's still there and terribly, terribly important. So that's a big surprise to me.

Her final comment to me on this situation was "there's room for growth there," and the growth she was referring to was her own, as she noted "I just think it's exciting." This, for Cottingham, would be an illustration of engagement with the depth of the present which can be an indicator of the "idea of moral growth as a continuous learning process that is lifelong," and "the idea that age and its trials can afford scope for the deepening of that process."[89] He posits that this continuing moral development can continue right to the end of life, which I claim to see taking place among the sisters in this study.

6.7 Obedience of Detachment and Relinquishment

In the final section of this chapter, I want to explore being apostolic as sisters cross the threshold to the final stages of life, as referred to by Sr. Susan: "I think I'm on that borderland—things and possibilities declining and so on." In response to my questions, the sisters continued to assert their self-understanding as apostolic to the end. When I asked Sr. Anne in her second interview if she thought sisters could be apostolic to the very end of their lives, she said, "My answer would be yes, because at the heart of any apostolic living is the following of Christ." Sr. Pamela notes:

> Somehow your apostolate becomes simpler, more mundane ... in the sense that your apostolate is in your ordinary daily life and in the people you meet with, and that's how you do your apostolate. It's how you are with people.

I also pushed sisters a little further to ask if this is the case even though bedridden, and Sr. Dorothy responded with a clear yes, and, although in a minority, still identifies this as ministry.

> Yes, and it would be, for want of a better word, to suffer and to pray, and I think they would be conscious that that is what they are doing. I mean, your ministry will diminish as you're fading out, but I still think you would think of it as a ministry; I think so.

Referring back to her earlier words about a recently explored aspect of her congregation's apostolic charism "to live the incarnation by *being* God's merciful love," she was clear that this could be applied in a context of increasing infirmity.

---

89   Cottingham, "The Question of Ageing," 15.

> I thought this applied very well to people who are old and out of the active life altogether. We're not involved in any specific work, but you can bring God's merciful love in whatever situation you are in. And I think we did it when we were actively engaged, and it's something that you can go on doing ... no matter how little you can do.

A second element which emerged in the responses was the experience of a call towards detachment and relinquishment. Sr. Pamela talked about this final stage of life.

> There's a kind of ... what shall I say? ... detachment, if you like. ... I remember previously, sitting around this table as part of the team, and we'd talk about things, and I'd say, "Well, I really thought this was the best idea," so I would be there fighting for my bit. Whereas now it's not like that. I can say what I think, and whether you follow it or not, it doesn't really make any difference. It's kind of a detachment—comes with age, I suppose.

Sr. Bernadette shows an awareness that this is what God now wants of her.

> This is probably the last sacrifice God is asking of me ... to give everything up and become dependent—to be free to be able to say I'm here, and not able to do any more than that.

Sr. Jayne highlights the need for discernment to identify how to continue to serve.

> 'Apostolic,' that to me is the essence of following the Lord, being close to him and so on, and actually working for him as we did when we were younger and had the ability. The needs are still there, but maybe he is saying you have got to tackle them in a different way.

Schneiders argues that religious obedience takes different forms at different stages of life, depending on whether a sister is in formation, in active ministry, or in old age. She terms the nature of obedience during the period of a sister's life when she is in active ministry "relational" or "dialogical obedience" due to the ongoing discernment processes and relationships with which the sister must engage. She describes this form of obedience as formative, that is:

> the interaction between who we are, what we think ... our spontaneous attractions and repulsions, our experience and conclusions and what

enters into our minds and hearts on the words and concerns of others who, themselves, are being transformed by our contributions.[90]

While Schneiders observes that there is no particular cut-off point to one form of obedience and passing into the next, the form she claims is especially operative in old age focusses on relinquishment, rather than formative or even generative. She names this "unitive obedience" and sees its purpose—"to relinquish literally all in our life that is not God"[91]—as the focus on seeking union with the will of God becomes ever more single-minded. Schneiders views suffering, loss of independence, and the physical diminishment faced in old age as "a one-way journey,"[92] as there is no cure or recovery. Nothing can be done to revert or change this process—"it can only be engaged"[93]—and so the choice is not whether to accept or reject this, but how to engage with and respond to it. Sr. Jayne in her second interview explained:

> It is almost as if God says, "Look, I am grateful for what you have done, and I want you just to enjoy being with me." It is as simple as that, really. So it is the contemplative aspect of life, it's almost as if that side can swell and grow as your body diminishes.

The call to unitive obedience appears to be relational in terms of its focus on the prayerful union with God and the response to a call to relinquishment, and Schneiders sees this as "poverty of spirit actualized by unitive love ... the purpose and the final realization of the vow of evangelical poverty."[94] In this sense, it also reflects what Vacek calls the "virtue of detachment in later life," as he adds that "we must cease asserting our Yes to earthly life."[95] However, based on my engagement with the sisters' experiences and words, I believe that their world, although smaller, continues to be relational and dialogical, and even formative until the end. Sr. Dorothy, Sr. Maeve, and Sr. Martina continue to engage with, and minister to, others. Sr. Dorothy's decision to move into care came about as a result of discernment conducted with others. Vacek, in setting out what he calls the four moral priorities for the elderly to undertake, says that "persons must discern where in this rhythm God wants them to be,"[96]

---

90   Schneiders, *Buying the Field*, 585.
91   Schneiders, *Buying the Field*, 590.
92   Schneiders, *Buying the Field*, 589.
93   Schneiders, *Buying the Field*, 589.
94   Schneiders, *Buying the Field*, 352.
95   Vacek, "Vices and Virtues," 173, 174.
96   Vacek, "Vices and Virtues," 166.

reinforcing the sisters' experience that discernment continues to the latest stages of life.

Furthermore, the orientation towards and awareness of the needs of others continues well into old age and its stages of completion or relinquishment. Sr. Maeve explained in her second interview how she still keeps the needs of others in mind.

> Kidnapped people, you know, what they suffer and the dangers today. ... It is something that you are to try to get involved in some small way myself, even though at this time in my life. ... But I think it is good to try as much as I can to focus outward. That is what I am hoping to do.

Vacek identifies retirement as a time which "should first bring to mind ... new opportunities for serving others,"[97] and I would argue that this is exactly what we are seeing sisters in the study fulfilling. Vacek sees this as a task likely to be approached in the earlier stage of old age, and in earlier chapters I have shown how sisters took formal retirement from teaching or social work and then embarked on a new form of service. However, the sisters also demonstrate that this is a task they seek to undertake until the end of their lives. Although none of the sisters I interviewed were actually in the very final stage of their lives, they were still discussing how to be apostolic with their carers and those around them at the final stages of their lives, in continued obedience to their context and call.

6.7.1 Obedient to the End

In perhaps the most challenging question I put to sisters, I asked what hopes they had for themselves as they face possible loss of independence and, eventually, their own death. Both Sr. Jayne and Sr. Pamela hope that they would still be able to be turned towards the needs of others. Sr. Pamela explains:

> I would hope that I would be patient and gracious, and that I wouldn't be a testy patient, and that I wouldn't be a demanding patient. And I suppose that would be my ministry; my ministry would be that I would be gracious and caring to whoever was looking after me, and not demanding.

---

97   Vacek, "Vices and Virtues," 169.

Sr. Jayne adds her perspective:

> If you can, hopefully, in spite of whatever pain you've got, still be ready to listen to other people, to try and understand their problems, just to be cheerful even with them sometimes, at the end, when you're helpless and you have to be turned over, what can you do? You can be patient. I don't like saying "you can pray for people," because it sounds so vague, but you can think of them, and in that thinking, you're uniting with them—you don't want lots of words.

The sisters accept the possibility of suffering; they do not ask for it to be taken away, and they identify the possibility of life and grace amid suffering. Increasingly, the work may be inward and concerns their continuing moral growth, but it does not cease to be outward-oriented and relational and dialogical in nature. Their concern shifts from one of actively listening to the needs of carers and trying to respond and help, to one of concern for the impact of their illness and their physical needs on the carers in trying to reduce the burden that they might be: to make the interaction one of love. The sisters are indeed obedient to context, but in ways where Schneiders' forms of obedience for ministerial activity and old age clearly not only overlap, but run in parallel. Sr. Dorothy talks about being on one's bed of pain, and that even at this stage of life, it might still be possible to contribute in some way, although she is uncertain how.

> I think you still have something to contribute, but it's in a different way. But I do think you can still make a difference. Unless you're on your bed of pain, I think you can still make a difference … but you might not know you're making a difference; I'm sure they're contributing and I'm sure they're offering it up to—I'm sure, yes.

Sr. Anne is able to identify something more tangible; she hopes that the experience of suffering would somehow enable her to enter into the suffering of others, seeing it in some way as an empathic resource to offer to others.

> A Good Friday person—somebody who is being prepared for death, probably, and she has the unenviable experience of pain and the effects that has on a person, but at the same time, if she is able or if I were able, and this would be the ideal, and if it did happen to me, what I would want is that I somehow saw what it is that I am enduring as sharing in some

way with the passion of Christ, sharing therefore with the pain that so many other people experience, recognizing that even within a situation which is of intense suffering, God is there with you.

It has to be recognized that what the sisters offer now becomes less experiential and more hypothetical, but their ideal is still outward-oriented. Sr. Martina is perhaps the one sister in the study for whom the question is closest to the reality of her life in a care community. Although in her early nineties, she spoke about her concern to visit others in the care community who are weaker than she is. However, she acknowledges that her capacity is now less. Even though she is grateful for the gift of time to pray, this can also now be too demanding.

> I like to go into church and just sit there in front of the tabernacle and say nothing at all because sometimes I get tired praying and I'm just … just there, with the Lord, and praying. … The thing is, the nuns, when they're sick, many of them, because their mind and because of the situation, you don't pray—you don't see that they're capable of praying any more. They might say a few Hail Marys, some prayers that they know, and they may not. And all I can say is that you can offer up your future days and nights—what is to come—to our Lord and our Lady, so that you will continue to fulfil the promise you made.

Cottingham understands that "our task as human beings is to strive to do what is right, and to live in love and peace with our neighbours," and holds that being attentive to this task is "the key to true human flourishing."[98] He rightly asserts that this can apply to any stage of life, irrelevant of human physical capacity. Like Soskice, he sees love and the self-sacrifice it demands as the ultimate purpose of the human life. Vacek's concern is how to live this stage of life with meaning and purpose, enabling completion to take place, so that people at the final stage of their lives may "come to entrust themselves to Mystery."[99]

Sr. Martina's words above bring us back to what first called her to religious life: love of God and desire to serve others, and a promise to do so all her life. Then, as now, she made a commitment, and even though she has suffered through her own call to nurse on the missions being unfulfilled, she chose to stay faithful to her promise and to her search for God, on a journey of personal conversion, and call to conversion of others. At this point in the sisters' lives, their obedience is indeed more and more unitive in nature. They accept that

---

98 Cottingham, "The Question of Ageing," 14.
99 Vacek, "Vices and Virtues," 175.

all they can do is strive to be apostolic to the very end, enjoy God's presence if they are still able to, and trust that all will be well. Sr. Maeve, in her second interview, said:

> At this point in my life now … it is a very reflective time, and rightly so, and it wasn't that I didn't always have the Lord right at the centre, but more and more he is there from morning until night, and even during the night as well, because I know well that there isn't that much left for me, you know, so that sort of stills me.

6.8   Conclusion

Cottingham argues that "meaningfulness is an essential ingredient of true human flourishing,"[100] and that old age offers an opportunity for integration of the various aspects and experiences of a life. He writes, "The process of moving towards old age emerges as a vital part of the fullest human flourishing," for it is that particular process which, if we are fortunate, "allows space for there to be a sense of meaning and connection over the entire span of a life."[101] The sisters featured in this book have had this opportunity, but in fact, for them, meaning ultimately lies in the paschal cycle and resurrection: their hope is found in grace encountered within the challenges of physical diminishment and ageing.

It is also clear that even sisters who are apostolic to the end face challenges in making sense of their lives. There is an opportunity to develop a more robust theological underpinning to support sisters in finding meaning in their later years when their call to continue to respond to the apostolic impulse may be challenged by physical limitation and inactivity. This could comprise recognizing and exploring the three emerging forms of ministry. It is particularly important for this to be articulated more clearly in this time of transition in the history of apostolic religious life, both within congregations and the Church more broadly, and that this contribution is understood more explicitly to be part of the mission of the Church.

---

100   Cottingham, "The Question of Ageing," 7.
101   Cottingham, "The Question of Ageing," 7.

CHAPTER 7

Theologies That Speak to All?

7.1 Theology for Ageing Religious or for Apostolic Religious Life More Widely?

In identifying theologies of ministry among the older apostolic sisters with whom I have worked, I have been heavily influenced by James Sweeney's work on the necessity of understanding the fundamental impulse of apostolic religious life. I brought the concern for *koinonia* and presence which I also found in British literature on the topic into conversation with the women's lived experience and theologies. I recognized and worked with the concept of self-gift as a unifying feature of the theological concepts operant in their narratives: availability, communion, and gift as reciprocity and mutuality. In recognizing that these concepts underpin the three emerging forms of ministry I identified, I have formed them into a theology which gives expression to the lived experience of the sisters in a context of social diminishment and increasing physical constraints. The ministry of presence, in particular, is understood as both sacramental and incarnational as it makes real that which it signifies, through both presence and relationships.

In these theological expressions, I have heard much that has resonance for women's apostolic or ministerial religious life more widely, particularly in relation to a number of challenges currently facing this form of religious life. The primary ones would be the question of identity: dealing with unhelpful dualisms and the vexed question of the decline in membership of religious congregations, and whether this actually constitutes a form of diminishment.

Establishing a new identity continues to be an unresolved issue for post-institutional apostolic religious life, particularly for the majority of sisters who no longer wear a habit and can be identified as sisters only by a ring or small congregational symbol. Visibility is further reduced by the loss of corporate ministries and the shift to individualized ministries. Nevertheless, I found that the sisters I worked with have a clear identity in their being with and being for others. I found this expressed in the three forms of ministry I have highlighted, along with a strong orientation towards others which continues and even strengthens into old age. Within the ministry of presence to each other and with and to their carers, 'presence' is understood as both a form of ministry through accompanying and being present to, and a way of being. In this, the women have been formed by the life itself, and, therefore, this constitutes a defining element of apostolic religious life for women, and contributes to a new articulation of the theology of apostolic or active religious life, in old age and more widely.

The sisters' apostolic identity can clearly be understood in terms of being with and being for others for the sake of the kingdom. This takes their self-understanding as religious beyond being defined by employment or a specific task, integrating self with becoming and being apostolic, so that the self each sister has become as they continue to follow and are conformed to Christ comprises their key resource. This narrated self is the well from which they draw, forged by their relationship with God and their commitment to, and journey of, conversion so that what they employ is the true self, which Schneiders sees as having been transformed through the prayer of union.[1] Furthermore, how they have become apostolic *as themselves* shapes their own understanding of what 'apostolic' means. Their growing concern for self has been fundamental to their understanding and practice of being apostolic as an exercise of self and presence as they have aged. This transition to/acquiring of a new identity seems to have been particularly striking where the identity linked to outward or active forms of ministry associated with work, or when a role diminishes, suggesting a characteristic at the heart of apostolic religious life unrelated to ministerial activity and not just for the later stages of life.

A second area where these older women's theologies of ministry may have a contribution to make to expressions of religious life more broadly is in confronting various artificial binaries and dualisms associated with religious life: contemplative and active; being and doing; thinking and acting; priest and prophet; ordinary and extraordinary. The sisters in their lived experience overcome these artificial binaries, with their rejection of the association between defined work and 'apostolic', between work and identity, and, indeed, work and worth—and this, despite their initial and, in some cases, lingering need to be useful.

The former 'institutional' (as opposed to 'post-institutional') identity often contained within it some elements of their ministry, as women religious, being instrumentalized by their own congregations and other Church institutions. Understanding the centrality of the self to the process of becoming apostolic also attends to my own unease about religious life having or being ascribed a 'worthwhile' purpose, which may risk reintroducing a utilitarian or instrumentalized understanding of religious life. The life needs no purpose as such, other than the single-minded search for God. Religious life, through the journey of

---

[1] Sandra Schneiders, *Buying the Field: Religious Life in the New Millennium* (Mahwah, NJ: Paulist Press, 2013), 352.

conversion, enables sisters to become the women God called them to be. In turn, this self, transformed by openness to God, becomes their resource in their being with and for others, for the kingdom.

I observed a particular tension throughout the study as I repeatedly encountered the claim to, and affirmation of, ordinary life. I found sisters eager to be seen as ordinary and to live and witness among, and as, ordinary people, even though this may contribute to the loss of visibility of sisters.[2] One way of addressing the tension in the extra/ordinary binary may be through recognition of the role of the self. The sisters have come to understand that one of the primary ways in which they become apostolic is "through how we express our being," as noted by Sr. Susan. This brings the central emphasis of religious life back to how the sisters live and who they are in ordinary settings, rather than a central concern with what they do. Furthermore, the sisters may have come to be more aware of their 'self' as they experience religious life unconstrained by the structures and strictures of formal employment. Many still feel a sense of loss for expressions of their selves which never found voice, for the lack of opportunities to follow interests, and to use gifts which never bore fruit.

Both the sisters and I experienced difficulty in exploring and expressing their ambivalence towards old age, infirmity, and dependency, and it is here that different aspects of my findings come together in creative tension. On the one hand, I draw on Vanstone, Vacek, and the sisters themselves to argue for the theological value of 'undergoing' and dependency. At the same time, I am raising up three ways of being into ministry: presence for each other, and with and for carers, and, therefore, engaging in the same dynamic and reframing their being as doing. The sisters in their articulation, and I in my reinterpretation, celebrate the sacramental and extraordinary in the ordinary, raising up the small things of the ordinary and everyday into ministry. In doing so, there may be a risk of devaluing ministry. One way through this dilemma is to recognize that a narrating self can hold different experiences at once, including those that appear contradictory, such as active and contemplative, ordinary and extraordinary.

The third, and perhaps rather obvious, area where the experience and theologies of these women have a contribution to make to the theology of apostolic religious life more broadly is in relation to the current trend of falling and ageing membership of their congregations, and whether these can accurately

---

2   Other sisters I have spoken to strongly refute the idea that religious or religious life can be viewed as ordinary on any level, as sisters who are members of a religious order always have the order and its resources to fall back on and to care for them when they are vulnerable and in need.

be termed to be 'in diminishment.' I would like to consider this issue first in relation to sisters as individuals, and then turn to the institutional context.

Lumen Gentium (1964, §44)[3] and *Vita Consecrata* (1996, §§3, 29)[4] both state that religious life is ecclesial and constitutive of the Church, with the Code of Canon Law stating emphatically that it "belongs to the life and holiness of the Church" (CCL 574 §1) as a clear expression of the Church's mission.[5] My work has identified the contribution that those sisters who appear to be no longer in active ministry make to this mission. *Vita Consecrata* states that even at a late stage in life, "when for reasons of age or infirmity they have had to abandon their specific apostolate" (*VC*, §44), there is value in the sisters' ongoing mission.

> More than in any activity, the apostolate consists in the witness of one's own complete dedication to the Lord's saving will. ... The elderly are called in many ways to live out their vocation: by persevering prayer, by patient acceptance of their condition, and by their readiness to serve as spiritual directors, confessors or mentors in prayer. (*VC*, §44)

Vita Consecrata does indeed go some way to recognizing the continuing contribution of sisters in the later stages of their lives. However, I have found that their contribution is more complex and agentive than that outlined above. The sisters' way of continuing to be apostolic until the end of their lives by making active use of the formed, true self is a constitutive aspect of apostolic religious life and, therefore, of the church's own mission. The individual sisters in this study are not 'in diminishment' in theological terms.

I accept, as do they, that they experience social and physical diminishment, and that their context is one of deep institutional uncertainty and fragility. Nevertheless, these women began their religious lives by making a vowed commitment to search for God. Their words as presented in the final chapter of this book demonstrate that a central concern for them, up until the end

---

3 Pope Paul VI, *Dogmatic Constitution on the Church: "Lumen Gentium,"* November 21, 1964, https://www.vatican.va/archive/hist_councils/ii_vatican_council/documents/vat-ii_const_19641121_lumen-gentium_en.html.

4 Pope John Paul II, *Post-synodal Apostolic Exhortation: "Vita Consecrata,"* March 25, 1996, accessed November 23, 2015, http://w2.vatican.va/content/john-paul-ii/en/apost_exhortations/documents/hf_jp-ii_exh_25031996_vita-consecrata.html.

5 John Paul II, *Apostolic Constitution: "Sacrae Disciplinae Leges,"* January 25, 1983, https://www.vatican.va/content/john-paul-ii/en/apost_constitutions/documents/hf_jp-ii_apc_25011983_sacrae-disciplinae-leges.html; more commonly known as the 'Code of Canon Law' (http://www.vatican.va/archive/ENG1104/).

of their lives, is living out of this fidelity, in obedience, and articulating this through remaining apostolic until the very end of their lives. This constitutes a flourishing and fulfilling life;[6] they do not experience or indeed represent diminishment in terms of embodying their apostolic vocation and/or charism. I have not found the way in which they live their religious lives to be in diminishment, and therefore this is not an appropriate term to be applying to them as individual religious, either personally or spiritually

I turn now to the 'crisis' facing some parts and elements of the institutions of religious life to which I referred in the opening chapter of this book. By 1996, this reality had found its way into Vatican teaching documents relating to religious life, as seen in *Vita Consecrata*:

> What must be avoided at all costs is the actual breakdown of the consecrated life, a collapse which is not measured by a decrease in numbers but by a failure to cling steadfastly to the Lord and to personal vocation and mission. (*VC*, §63)

Pope Francis, as a member of a religious order, is very aware of the situation facing religious life. From the early days of his papacy, he has addressed religious repeatedly on this topic. He spoke to the Union of International Superiors General (UISG) Plenary Assembly in May 2013, and then declared 2014 the Year of Consecrated Life, which in turn prompted the publication of two teaching documents—"Rejoice" and "Keep Watch!"—by the Congregation for Institutes of Consecrated Life and Societies of Apostolic Life (CICLSAL).[7] His November 2014 Apostolic Letter to all Consecrated Peoples has provided much spiritual leadership, encouragement, and challenge to religious all over the world. Most recently, he spoke to members and theologians of the Claretian order,[8] encouraging them to guard against despondency in the face

---

6 Edward Collins Vacek, "Vices and Virtues of Old-age Retirement," *Journal of the Society of Christian Ethics* 30, no. 2 (2010): 161–82; and John Cottingham, "The Question of Ageing," *Philosophical Papers* 41, no. 3 (2012): 371–96.
7 Congregation for Institutes of Consecrated Life and Societies of Apostolic Life (CICLSAL), "Rejoice: A Letter to Consecrated Men and Women," February 2, 2014, https://www.vatican.va/roman_curia/congregations/ccscrlife/documents/rc_con_ccscrlife_doc_20140202_rallegratevi-lettera-consacrati_en.html; and CICLSAL, "Keep Watch! A Letter to Consecrated Men and Women Journeying in the Footsteps of God," September 8, 2014.
8 The Claretians, or Claretian Missionaries, have the official name of the 'Congregation of Missionary Sons of the Immaculate Heart of the Blessed Virgin Mary' and are a clerical order of missionaries founded in Spain by 1849 by Fr. Antonio María Claret y Clará.

of declining membership, reminding them that such a "spirit of defeat and pessimism are not Christian."[9]

Considering the full predicament of and outlook for individual congregations and, indeed, religious life more widely is beyond the scope of this book, as is the discussion of the word 'diminishment' in relation to religious life itself, even in the Global North. However, I have recognized that the stories of the individual sisters in this work are deeply affected by the reality of the decline in membership, particularly that of having few, if any, newer, younger sisters coming behind them in their communities, and that many orders currently present in the UK are facing closure in the coming decades. Despite this, the way in which they continue to be apostolic until the end of their lives, formed in and by their charism, would suggest that the charisms of their congregations are still alive and present among them, and often attractive to other parts of the Church.

National standing conferences of religious in the US and UK have drawn on the resources and leadership offered by Pope Francis to reframe the discourse and look to the future of religious life. Earlier, in chapter 6, I noted Sr. Mary Pellegrino's call to the Leadership Conference of Women Religious (LCWR) in the United States to reframe the narrative of diminishment to "a narrative of deepening communion."[10] In 2018 in the UK, Sr. Patricia Murray, Executive Secretary of the Union of International Superiors General (UISG) addressed the Conference of Religious of England and Wales (COREW), agreeing with Pope Francis that the health of religious life cannot and should not be determined by the number of members.[11] She encouraged her audience to embrace Pope Francis narrative of religious life as a call to encounter and communion.

> Pope Francis calls us to go forth to encounter others in clear and unequivocal ways. He says "leave your nests"; "go out through that door and meet

---

[9] Lisa Zengarini, "Pope to Claretians: Always Seek New Ways to Serve the Lord," *Vatican News*, November 7, 2022, https://www.vaticannews.va/en/pope/news/2022-11/pope-to-claretianum-always-seek-new-ways-to-serve-the-lord.html.

[10] Mary Pellegrino, "The Future Enters Us Long Before It Happens: Opening Space for an Emerging Narrative of Communion," presidential address for the Leadership Conference of Women Religious, Orlando, Florida, August 10, 2017, accessed September 14, 2017, https://lcwr.org/sites/default/files/calendar/attachments/2017_lcwr_presidential_address_-_mary_pellegrino_csj.pdf.

[11] Pat Murray, "Conversation 1: New and Old Wineskins," address delivered to the Annual General Meeting of the Conference of Religious of England and Wales, May 24, 2018, https://www.corew.org/news/2018/5/24/cor-agm-2018-Sr.-pat-murray-ibvm.

the people"; "go out on the streets"; "go to the frontiers"; "leave the centre and travel towards the peripheries"; "reach the fringes of humanity."[12]

In his November 2022 address to the Claretians referred to above, Pope Francis said, "Religious life is understood only by what the Spirit does in each of the people called. There are those who focus too much on the external—the structures, the activities—and lose sight of the superabundance of grace in people and communities." He continued, "Do not tire of going to the frontiers, even to the frontiers of thought; of opening paths, of accompanying, rooted in the Lord to be bold in mission."[13]

I argue in this book that the fundamental orientation I have found among the ageing sisters I spoke to addresses this challenge. These are women accompanying each other in their final years, and often moments, as they, their communities, and often their congregations, face death, passing through the final years of their history, spiritual heritage, and traditions, holding the future of their individual charisms and the future of religious life in hope. This is indeed frontier country, requiring them to be bold in mission.

Turning back to the United States, LCWR leaders have spoken about the "unprecedented transformation of religious life."[14] In an interview with Global Sisters Report in November 2022, Sr. Carol Zinn, Executive Director of the LCWR identified the changes currently taking place as the biggest issue facing their membership. Zinn claims hopefully that "clearly, something else is emerging" but, unsurprisingly, cannot identify what form that might take. Timothy Radcliffe, in his 2018 piece, wrote that "periodically new forms of religious life unexpectedly burst into life," but followed this with "I have not so far spotted any radically innovatory forms of religious life emerging today."[15] This unknown future calls for great reserves of hope, and is another frontier or periphery.

However, both Zinn and Radcliffe agree that there needs to be a refocussing on the real meaning of religious life: what makes the life distinctive. Zinn identified a role for the LCWR in helping the membership "focus on what religious

---

12   Pat Murray, "Conversation 2: The Emergence of New Narratives—of Encounter," address delivered to the Annual General Meeting of the Conference of Religious of England and Wales, May 24, 2018, https://www.corew.org/news/2018/5/24/cor-agm-2018-Sr.-pat-murray-ibvm.
13   Zengarini, "Pope to Claretians."
14   Dan Stockman, "LCWR Leaders Talk about Unprecedented Transformation of Religious Life," *Global Sisters Report,* January 12, 2023, https://www.globalsistersreport.org/news/lcwr-leaders-talk-about-unprecedented-transformation-religious-life.
15   Timothy Radcliffe, "Religious Life: Candlemas Time?," in *Envisioning Futures for the Catholic Church,* ed. Staf Hellemans and Peter Jonkers (Washington, DC. Council for Research in Values and Philosophy, 2018), 327.

life really means." She then made a comment which speaks directly to the experience of the sisters in my study:

> Sisters need to focus on religious life itself, not just their ministry, which is only a fruit of their vocation. "I am a sister until I draw my last breath, not until I can't physically do my ministry anymore."

Sr. Jane Herb, past-president of the LCWR, said, in the same group interview, that there needs to be a change in how religious life is viewed from "a ministry of doing to a ministry of being." This is both a helpful and unhelpful statement. It is helpful in drawing the focus away from an understanding of religious as active and useful to a deeper meaning of the life, but unhelpful as it re-emphasizes the artificial dualism between doing and being that I and the sisters in this book have found to represent a barrier to be overcome.

Speaking to Dan Stockman, Zinn identified a central dilemma facing religious life today, and one that touches on all the questions of identity, purpose, and what makes religious life distinctive. Newer, younger sisters are aware that the call and opportunities to ministry in apostolic or ministerial religious life today are not unique to religious. One does not have to enter religious life to fight racism, work with the homeless, or go to the 'frontiers' of refugee crises in southern Europe, the southern United States, or the beaches of southern England, to support and serve those seeking asylum. However, these young women "joined religious life because they wanted that communal, spiritual life as well. ... 'So what is it in [religious life] that a 35-year-old woman joins this life, when she could go to the border herself?' Zinn asked. 'It's the contemplative discernment. The transformation of consciousness that is this life.'"[16]

What Zinn calls "transformation of consciousness," I have called 'becoming apostolic' as oneself, in a lifelong process of conversion; becoming fully oriented towards others, a being with and being for others. Religious do indeed need to be wary of becoming too inward-looking or 'navel-gazing,' a tendency which can beset any institution experiencing such radical change or even the temptation to become self-centred or too individualistic. The CICLSAL document "Rejoice" calls on religious "to undertake an exodus out of our own selves, setting out on a path of adoration and service."[17] I do not in any way contradict this with my emphasis on religious women who have become more fully themselves, and who remain firmly rooted in and draw on that self in order to minister to others. However, I believe that a paradigm of religious life which

---

16   Stockman, "LCWR Leaders Talk."
17   CICLSAL, "Rejoice." This draws on Pope Francis's address to the UISG Plenary Assembly in Rome on May 8, 2013.

locates identity and worth in degrees of usefulness, or engagement in purposeful activity as the central defining characteristic of a woman religious, is harmful and does not prepare her for any form of diminishment on an individual or institutional level, or the uncertainty facing religious life. What does form her is a single-minded focus on a relationship with God and a desire for and commitment to lifelong conversion.

Radcliffe highlights the radicality which, for him, defines religious life, referring to "the radical choice: the summons to adventure." He reports that millennials consulted about religious life say they see it "as a radical decision to follow Christ," but notes, "Only if we can articulate such a radical call, the gift of one's life in the perilous adventure of following Christ, we are going to attract vocations who will set the world alight."[18] He goes on to say that "the adventure takes many forms," and writes of religious being called to abide "in desolate places."[19]

Sr. Rebecca Ann Gemma[20] claimed that many sisters view prayer life as something of a 'Plan B' for when their physical ministry is done, when it should be so much more than that. Radcliffe agrees that prayer in religious life has to represent more than what you fall back on when you 'retire'; it is part of the radicality—its root. He acknowledged this challenge when he wrote "the religious of the future will need a deeper sense of identity than that given by the habit."[21] For him, the only possible identity for religious is "an identity as disciples, always attentive to the summons of the Lord ... deepened and clarified as we hear the one who continues to call us every morning."[22] This is the identity of the twelve 'tall trees' in my work, one that has been forged and formed in the narratives of conversion, and in a life of seeking God. It is one that equips them to respond to a call to wake up the world, and to abide in the most desolate of places, including that of facing their own death, and the loss of much of what they hold dear.

7.2 Theology of Religious Life or Theology for All Those Ageing?

Although this work engages with the theology of religious life, it has applications and meaning beyond the practical and theoretical implications for women religious. These resonances takes several forms.

---

18 Radcliffe, "Religious Life: Candlemas Time?," 314.
19 Radcliffe, "Religious Life: Candlemas Time?," 315, 316.
20 Sr. Rebecca Ann Gemma is another sister in the same group interview with Dan Stockman.
21 Radcliffe, "Religious Life: Candlemas Time?," 310.
22 Radcliffe, "Religious Life: Candlemas Time?," 327.

The first is through what Graham calls "an insistence on the primacy of lived experience."[23] Practical and pastoral theology and feminist research methodologies justify such an approach, particularly where women's voices have not been brought to bear on a concrete situation which defines and shapes their lives and identities, as is the case with women religious and the Church. Bennett Moore acknowledges this as a principle informing her work on feminist pastoral theology:

> to start from life experience and to move to a theorizing of that experience and to a critique of existing theory.[24]

This is the journey undertaken in this study. Although informed by theological theory, my perspectives have been rooted in, and formed by, the sisters' lived experience. I have brought existing theology of ministry in religious life into conversation with the sisters' theological perspectives and used the latter to critique theory.

A further contribution is my finding that the sisters' orientation of being with and being for others continues late in their lives. The most immediate audience for this finding is their own congregations and the Church. However, I, like Woodward, claim a wider audience and consideration beyond the vowed life: "As Practical Theologians we should be concerned to know more about how faith shapes us as humans. Does my faith help me to understand the world around me? Does faith contribute to my aspiration to age well?"[25] Vacek argues that the Christian tradition has a responsibility to contribute to thinking about "elderly spirituality" and to help "shape an ethical vision" for later life.[26] However, although the works cited in this study which deal specifically with ageing refer to continuing opportunities to engage with and give to others in later life,[27] none opens up the notion of self-gift as has been done in this book. While encouraging all elderly people to work towards the total self-gift sought by religious is unrealistic and unnecessary, I believe the way in which the sisters continue to orient themselves towards others offers guidance for ordinary people of Christian faith, or of other faiths and none. This work, therefore, contributes to discussions about the role and realistic possibilities

---

23 Elaine Graham, "Feminist Theory," in *The Wiley-Blackwell Companion to Practical Theology*, ed. Bonnie J. Miller-McLemore (Chichester: Wiley-Blackwell, 2012), 202.

24 Zoe Bennett Moore, *Introducing Feminist Perspectives on Pastoral Theology* (London: Sheffield Academic Press, 2002), 138.

25 James Woodward, *Valuing Age: Pastoral Ministry with Older People* (London: SPCK, 2008), 190.

26 Vacek, "Vices and Virtues," 165.

27 Woodward, *Valuing Age*; Vacek, "Vices and Virtues"; and Cottingham, "The Question of Ageing."

for either continuing to be, or becoming oriented to, the presence and needs of others. Many of the issues faced by sisters in relation to old age certainly affect the wider ageing population.[28] The meaning the sisters have found in ageing, which is separated from a need for purpose, and the way in which they continue to be with and for others until the end through the gift of time, availability, and presence, have much to offer others.

First, the sisters show that moral growth over a lifetime does not end with old age: later life is more than sitting back and reflecting over a life well-lived, if indeed it has been. In being offered, and taking up, opportunities to be present to others, life can continue to be generative in providing continued moral and spiritual growth. I dispute neither Woodward's[29] nor Schneiders' insistence that the time comes for relinquishment,[30] but the sisters show that there is a period when relinquishment can be lived alongside continuing to love. Love is the purpose of human life, and the study has shown that love requires the giving of self in some form—whether we call that self-sacrifice or self-gift—and even in the final giving up of self to God so that giving of self to others can continue.

Second, although this study does not specifically treat suffering, it is not unreasonable to ask whether we can expect to give of ourselves while becoming dependent on others or undergoing the suffering and debilitating illnesses of old age. Again, the study provides a very concrete example of possibilities of love amid suffering in how the sisters understand themselves as ministering to their carers, identifying the reciprocity and mutuality in giving and receiving care.

What we see in the sisters is the fruit of *sequela Christi* lived to the end, even through their suffering. Christ's own suffering and passion, totally centred on self-gift, is a model for the women and, indeed, for any Christian. We may not be able to prevent the failings, pain, and ill-health of old age, but they can be lived with love, and in a way that constitutes a continuing generative and flourishing life.

The sisters' voices demonstrate how God's grace is encountered right until the end. It is experienced through careful, prayerful attentive listening through and with presence to others. There will come a time of dependency for most of us when we have to 'undergo,' and in that time, these experienced guides have much to teach us about finding meaning when we may experience loss of purpose.

---

28 Janet Eldred, "Community, Connection and Caring: Towards a Christian Feminist Practical Theology of Older Women" (PhD diss., University of Leeds, 2002), accessed June 24, 2015, http://etheses.whiterose.ac.uk/642/; and Vacek, "Vices and Virtues," 161–82.
29 Woodward, *Valuing Age*, 195.
30 See pages 135, 165 above.

Bibliography

Allen, John. "Notes on the LCWR Overhaul." *National Catholic Reporter*, April 27, 2012. https://www.ncronline.org/blogs/all-things-catholic/notes-lcwr-overhaul.

Allen, Mary Prudence. "Communion in Community." In *The Foundations of Religious Life: Revisiting the Vision*, edited by the Council of Major Superiors of Women Religious, chap. 4. Notre Dame, IN: Ave Maria Press, 2009.

Alvesson, Mats, and Kaj Skoldberg. *Reflexive Methodology: New Vistas for Qualitative Research*. London: Sage, 2012.

Amaladoss, A. "The Religious in Mission." In *Consecrated Life Today: Charisms in the Church for the World*, edited by the Union of Superiors General, 127–39. Slough: St. Pauls, 1994.

Andrews, Molly, Corrine Squire, and Maria Tamboukou, eds. *Doing Narrative Research*. 2nd ed. London: Sage, 2013.

Annuarium Statisticum Ecclesiae/Statistical Yearbook of the Church 2020. Città del Vaticano: Libreria Editrice Vaticana, 2022.

Annuarium Statisticum Ecclesiae/Statistical Yearbook of the Church 2006. Città del Vaticano: Libreria Editrice Vaticana, 2008.

Anspach, Mark Rogin. *À charge de revanche: Figures élémentaires de la réciprocité*. Paris: Seuil, 2002.

Arber, Sara, and Jay Ginn. *Gender and Later Life: A Sociological Analysis of Resources and Constraints*. London: Sage, 1991.

Arbuckle, Gerald A. *Out of Chaos: Refounding Religious Life*. London: Geoffrey Chapman, 1987.

Aschenbrenner, George A. "Active and Monastic: Two Apostolic Lifestyles." *Review for Religious* 45, no. 5 (1986): 653–68. http://cdm.slu.edu/cdm/singleitem/collection/rfr/id/298/rec/11. Accessed September 19, 2015.

Atkinson, Rowland, and John Flint. "Accessing Hidden and Hard-to-reach Populations: Snowball Research Strategies." *Social Research Update* 33 (2001). http://Sr.u.soc.surrey.ac.uk/SR.U33.pdf. Accessed December 20, 2015.

Augustine. *Confessions*. Translated by R. S. Pine-Coffin. London: Penguin, 1961.

Badcock, Gary D. *The Way of Life*. Grand Rapids, MI: Eerdmans, 1998.

Ballard, Paul H., and John Pritchard. *Practical Theology in Action: Christian Thinking in the Service of Church and Society*. London: SPCK, 1996.

Balls, P. "Phenomenology in Nursing Research: Methodology, Interviewing and Transcribing." *Nursing Times*, August 13, 2009. http://www.nursingtimes.net/phenomenology-in-nursing-research-methodology-interviewing-and-transcribing/5005138.article. Accessed August 14, 2015.

Barrett, Mark. "Consider Your Call: A Theology of Monastic Life Today (1978): A Post-conciliar Process of Reflection on Monastic Identity." In *A Future Built on Faith: Religious Life and the Legacy of Vatican II*, edited by Gemma Simmonds, chap. 2. Dublin: Columba Press, 2014.

Bauman, Michelle. "Vatican Announces Reform of US Women's Religious Conference." CAN/EWTN News, April 18, 2012. https://www.catholicnewsagency.com/news/24757/vatican-announces-reform-of-us-womens-religious-conference.

Bazeley, Paul. *Qualitative Data Analysis: Practical Strategies*. London: Sage, 2013.

BBC Radio 4. "Where Have All the Good Nuns Gone?" *Woman's Hour*. Radio broadcast, November 12, 2013. http://www.bbc.co.uk/programmes/b03h2rdn. Accessed November 3, 2015.

Bell, Judith. *Doing Your Research Project*. 5th ed. Buckingham: Open University Press, 2010.

Bennett Moore, Zoe. *Introducing Feminist Perspectives on Pastoral Theology*. London: Sheffield Academic Press, 2002.

Bernstein, Marcelle. *Nuns*. Great Britain: Fount, 1976.

Berrelleza, Erick, Mary L. Gautier, and Mark M. Gray. *Population Trends Among Religious Institutes of Women*. Washington, DC: Georgetown University/Center for Applied Research in the Apostolate, 2014.

Blundell, Boyd. *Paul Ricoeur Between Theology and Philosophy*. Bloomington, IN: University of Indiana Press, 2010.

Bolton, Gillie. *Reflective Practice: Writing and Professional Development*. London: Sage, 2010.

Boner. J. "Our Weakness is Our Strength." In *Sharing the Joy of the Gospel: Identity and Missionary Conversion*, edited by J. C. R. Garcia Paredes, 33–43. Madrid: Claret, 2014.

Braun, Virginia, and Victoria Clarke. "Using Thematic Analysis in Psychology." *Qualitative Research in Psychology* 3, no. 2 (2006): 77–101. http://dx.doi.org/10.1191/1478088706qp063oa.

Brock, Megan P. "Resisting the Catholic Church's Notion of the Nun as Self-sacrificing Woman." *Feminism and Psychology* 20, no. 4 (2010): 473–90.

Brock, Megan P. "Force of Habit: The Construction and Negotiation of Subjectivity in Catholic Nuns." PhD diss., University of Western Sydney, 2007. http://researchdirect.uws.edu.au/islandora/object/uws:2379. Accessed January 15, 2015.

Brouard, Susanna. "Using Theological Action Research to Embed Catholic Social Teaching in a Catholic Development Agency." PhD diss., Anglia Ruskin University, 2015. http://arro.anglia.ac.uk/580464/1/FullThesis%20Susanna%20Brouard.pdf. Accessed November 24, 2016.

Brown, Lyn Mikel, and Carol Gilligan, eds. *Meeting at the Crossroads: Women's Psychology and Girls' Development*. Harvard: Harvard University Press, 1992.

Brown, Sally A. "Hermeneutical Theory." In *The Wiley-Blackwell Companion to Practical Theology*, edited by Bonnie J. Miller-McLemore, chap. 10. Chichester: Wiley-Blackwell, 2012.

Bryman, Alan. *Social Science Research Methods*. Oxford: Oxford University Press, 2004.

Butler, Sara. "Apostolic Religious Life: A Public, Ecclesial Vocation." Address delivered to the "Apostolic Religious Life Since Vatican iII Reclaiming the Treasure; Bishops, Theologians, and Religious in Conversation" symposium, Stonchill College, Easton, MA, September 27, 2008. http://www.zenit.org/en/articles/sister-butler-at-symposium-on-consecrated-life.

Byrne, Anne, John Canavan, and Michelle Millar. "Participatory Research and the Voice-centred Relational Method of Data Analysis: Is it Worth it?" *International Journal of Social Research Methodology* 12, no. 1 (2009): 67–77.

Calasanti, Toni M. "Theorizing Age Relations." In *The Need for Theory: Critical Approaches to Social Gerontology for the 21st Century*, edited by Simon Biggs, Ariela Lowenstein, and Jon Hendricks, 199–218. Amityville, NY: Baywood, 2003.

Cameron, Helen, and Catherine Duce. *Researching Practice in Ministry and Mission: A Companion*. London: SCM Press, 2013.

Cameron, Helen, Deborah Bhatti, Catherine Duce, James Sweeney, and Clare Watkins. *Talking about God in Practice*. London: SCM Press, 2010.

Campbell-Jones, Suzanne. *In Habit: An Anthropological Study of Working Nuns*. London: Faber and Faber, 1979.

Carr, Anne E. "The New Vision of Feminist Theology: Method." In *Freeing Theology: The Essentials of Theology in Feminist Perspective*, edited by Catherine Mowry LaCugna, chap. 1. New York: HarperCollins, 1993.

Casey, Michael. *Sacred Reading: The Ancient Art of Lectio Divina*. Liguori, MI: Liguori Publications, 1996.

Catholic Church. *Catechism of the Catholic Church*. November 4, 2003. http://www.vatican.va/archive/ENG0015/_INDEX.HTM. Accessed January 18, 2018.

Catholic Church. *Code of Canon Law*. January 25, 1983. http://www.vatican.va/archive/ENG1104/. Accessed September 27, 2017.

Catholic Herald. "Number of Catholics in the World Grows by 15m in a Year." February 21, 2011. http://www.catholicherald.co.uk/news/2011/02/21/number-of-catholics-in-the-world-grows-by-15m-in-a-year/. Accessed January 20, 2012.

Catholic Women Speak Network, ed. *Catholic Women Speak: Bringing Our Gifts to the Table*. Mahwah, NJ: Paulist Press, 2015.

Chittister, Joan. *The Fire in these Ashes: A Spirituality of Contemporary Religious Life*. Kansas City, MI: Sheed and Ward, 1995.

Chittister, Joan. "Religious Life in Contemporary Society: Woman: Icon, Rebel, Saint?" Recorded talk given at Baden Powell House, June 5, 1993. Catholic Communications Centre.

Ciardi, Fabio. "Fraternal Life in Common." In *Consecrated Life Today: Charisms in the Church for the World*, edited by the Union of Superiors General, 153–86. Slough: St. Pauls, 1994.

Claretian Teaching Materials. "Paper 2: The Theme of Consecration in the Renewal Process of Religious Life." No date. http://www.icla.org.ph. Accessed June 16, 2012.

Coakley, Sarah. *Powers and Submission: Spirituality, Philosophy and Gender*. Oxford: Blackwell, 2002.

Coffey, Mary Finbarr. "The Complexities and Difficulties of a Return *ad fontes*." In *A Future Full of Hope?*, edited by Gemma Simmonds, chap. 2. Dublin: Columba Press, 2012.

Cohen, Louis, Lawrence Manion, and Keith Morrison. *Research Methods in Education*. 5th ed. London: Routledge Falmer, 2000.

Collins, Gregory. "Giving Religious Life a Theology Transfusion." In *A Future Full of Hope?*, edited by Gemma Simmonds, chap. 1. Dublin: Columba Press, 2012.

Collins, Peter J. "Connecting Anthropology and Quakerism: Transcending the Insider/Outsider Dichotomy." In *Theorising Faith: The Insider/Outsider Problem in the Study of Ritual*, edited by Elisabeth Arweck and Martin D. Stringer, chap. 5. Birmingham: Birmingham University Press, 2002.

Collinson, Diané. *Fifty Major Philosophers: A Reference Guide*. New York: Routledge, 1987.

Conde-Frazier, Elizabeth. "Participatory Action Research: Practical Theology for Social Justice." *Religious Education* 101, no. 3 (2006): 321–29.

Congregation for Institutes of Consecrated Life and Societies of Apostolic Life (CICLSAL). "Apostolic Visitation Final Report." September 8, 2014. http://usccb.org/beliefs-and-teachings/vocations/consecrated-life/apostolic-visitation-final-report.cfm. Accessed January 9, 2015.

Congregation for Institutes of Consecrated Life and Societies of Apostolic Life (CICLSAL). "Keep Watch! A Letter to Consecrated Men and Women Journeying in the Footsteps of God." September 8, 2014.

Congregation for Institutes of Consecrated Life and Societies of Apostolic Life (CICLSAL). "Rejoice: A Letter to Consecrated Men and Women." February 2, 2014. https://www.vatican.va/roman_curia/congregations/ccscrlife/documents/rc_con_ccscrlife_doc_20140202_rallegratevi-lettera-consacrati_en.html.

Congregation for Institutes of Consecrated Life and Societies of Apostolic Life (CICLSAL). *Starting Afresh from Christ: A Renewed Commitment to Consecrated Life in the Third Millennium*. London: St. Pauls, 2002.

Conroy, Maureen. *Looking into the Well: Supervision of Spiritual Directors*. Chicago, IL: Loyola University Press, 1996.

Corbin, Juliet, and Anselm Strauss. *Basics of Qualitative Research*. London: Sage, 1990.

Cottingham, John. "The Question of Ageing." *Philosophical Papers* 41, no. 3 (2012): 371–96.
Council of Major Superiors of Women Religious, *Study Guide for the Foundations of Religious Life: Revisiting the Vision* (Notre Dame, IN: Ave Maria Press, 2015).
Council of Major Superiors of Women Religious, ed. *The Foundations of Religious Life: Revisiting the Vision*. Notre Dame, IN: Ave Maria Press, 2009.
Cresswell, John W. *Research Design: Qualitative, Quantitative and Mixed Method Approaches*. London: Sage, 2003.
Crotty, Michael. *Foundations of Social Research*. Thousand Oaks, CA: Sage, 1998.
Cummings, Kathleen Sprows. "Understanding U.S. Catholic Sisters Today." Washington, DC: FADICA, 2015. http://www.nationalcatholicsistersweek.org/_resources/FDC_001_Report.pdf. Accessed December 16, 2015.
Cummings, Kathleen Sprows. "The Vatican and American Catholic Sisters." *Religion in American History* (blog). July 16, 2009. http://uSr.eligion.blogspot.co.uk/2009/07/vatican-and-american-catholic-sisters.html. Accessed November 19, 2012.
Cunliffe, Ann L. "On Becoming a Critically Reflexive Practitioner." *Journal of Management Education* 28, no. 4 (2004): 407–26.
Daughton, Amy. *With and For Others: Developing Ricoeur's Ethics of Self Using Aquinas's Language of Analogy*. Fribourg: Academic Press Fribourg, 2016.
De Waal, Esther. *Seeking God: The Benedictine Way*. London: Fount, 1984.
Della Cava, Ralph. "Transnational Religions: The Roman Catholic Church in Brazil and the Orthodox Church in Russia." *Sociology of Religion* 62, no. 4 (2001): 535–50.
Denzin, Norman K., and Yvonna S. Lincoln, eds. *Handbook of Qualitative Research*. 3rd ed. London: Sage, 2005.
Denzin, Norman K., and Yvonna S. Lincoln, eds. *Collecting and Interpreting Qualitative Materials*. 2nd ed. London: Sage, 2003.
Doctrinal Commission of the Spanish Bishops Conference. "Critiquing Diarmuid O'Murchu's 'New World Order': Doctrinal Note on the Book 'Reframing Religious Life.'" March 15, 2006. http://www.zenit.org/en/articles/critiquing-diarmuid-o-murchu-s-new-world-order. Accessed December 4, 2015.
Donnelly, James S., Jr. "The Peak of Marianism in Ireland, 1930–60." In *Piety and Power in Ireland, 1760–1960: Essays in Honour of Emmet Larkin*, edited by Stewart J. Brown and David W. Miller, 252–83. Notre Dame, IN: University of Notre Dame Press, 2000.
Donovan, Agnes Mary, and Mary Elizabeth Wusinich. "Religious Consecration: A Particular Form of Consecrated Life." In *The Foundations of Religious Life: Revisiting the Vision*, edited by the Council of Major Superiors of Women Religious, chap. 1. Notre Dame, IN: Ave Maria Press, 2009.
Doucet, Andrea, and Natasha S. Mauthner. "Feminist Methodologies and Epistemologies." In *21st Century Sociology: A Reference Handbook*, edited by Clifton D. Bryant and Dennis L. Peck, 36–42. Thousand Oaks, CA: Sage, 2006.

Dunne, Gerard. "The Dominicans and Vocations." In *A Future Full of Hope?*, edited by Gemma Simmonds, chap. 7. Dublin: Columba Press, 2012.

Easterby-Smith, Mark, Richard Thorpe, and Andy Lowe. *Management Research: An Introduction*. 2nd ed. London: Sage, 2002.

Ebaugh, Helen Rose Fuchs. "Transnationality and Religion in Immigrant Congregations: The Global Impact." *Nordic Journal of Religion and Society* 23, no. 2 (2010): 105–19.

Ebaugh, Helen Rose Fuchs. *Out of the Cloister: A Study of Organizational Dilemmas*. Austin, TX: University of Texas Press, 1977.

Eldred, Janet. "Community, Connection and Caring: Towards a Christian Feminist Practical Theology of Older Women." PhD diss., University of Leeds, 2002. http://etheses.whiterose.ac.uk/642/. Accessed June 24, 2015.

Endean, Philip. *Karl Rahner and Ignatian Spirituality*. Oxford: Oxford University Press, 2001.

Etherington, Kim. *Becoming a Reflexive Researcher: Using Ourselves in Research*. London: Jessica Kingsley, 2005.

Fiand, Barbara. *Living the Vision: Religious Vows in an Age of Change*. New York: Crossroad, 1991.

Finch, Jo. "Innovation or Imitation? The Use of Voice-centred Relational Method in Social Work Research Methods." Presentation transcript, 2011. http://www.slideserve.com/benjamin/innovation-or-imitation-the-use-of-the-voice-centred-relational-method-in-social-work-research-methodsplymouth-plymouth. Accessed June 15, 2016.

Flanagan, Bernadette. "*Quaestio divina*: Research as Spiritual Practice." *The Way* 53, no. 4 (2014): 126–36.

Flannery, Tony. "The Death of Religious Life? Seven Years On." *The Furrow* 55, no. 2 (2004): 92–96.

Flannery, Tony. *The Death of Religious Life?* Dublin: Columba Press, 1997.

Fleming, David. *Draw Me into your Friendship: A Literal Translation and a Contemporary Reading of the Spiritual Exercises*. Saint Louis, MO: Institute of Jesuit Sources, 1996.

Fontana, Andrea, and James H. Frey. "The Interview: From Structured Questions to Negotiated Text." In *Collecting and Interpreting Qualitative Materials*. 2nd ed., edited by Norman J. Denzin and Yvonna S. Lincoln, chap. 2. London: Sage, 2003.

Fontana, Andrea, and Anastasia H. Prokos. *The Interview: From Formal to Postmodern*. Walnut Creek, CA: Left Coast Press, 2007.

Fox, Thomas C. "Stonehill Symposium Played a Role in Women Religious Study." *National Catholic Reporter*, November 4, 2009. https://www.ncronline.org/news/stonehill-symposium-played-role-women-religious-study.

Francis, Pope. *Apostolic Letter to All Consecrated People.* November 21, 2014. https://www.vatican.va/content/francesco/en/apost_letters/documents/papa-francesco_lettera-ap_20141121_lettera-consacrati.html. Accessed January 12, 2015.

Francis, Pope. *Evangelii Gaudium.* November 24, 2013. https://www.vatican.va/content/francesco/en/apost_exhortations/documents/papa-francesco_esortazione-ap_20131124_evangelii-gaudium.html.

Freeman, Lawrence. "These are Not Crazy, Dangerous Women. They are Deeply Loved and Respected." *The Tablet,* May 5, 2012, 11–12.

Fry, Timothy, ed. *The Rule of St. Benedict in English.* Collegeville, MN: Liturgical Press, 1982.

Gallagher, Clarence. "The Church and Institutes of Consecrated Life." *The Way Supplement* 50 (1984): 3–15.

Ganiel, Gladys, and Claire Mitchell. "Turning the Categories Inside-out: Complex Identifications and Multiple Interactions in Religious Ethnography." *Sociology of Religion* 67, no. 1 (2006): 3–21.

Garcia Paredes, J. C. R., ed. *Sharing the Joy of the Gospel: Identity and Missionary Conversion.* Madrid: Claret, 2014.

Garcia Paredes, J. C. R., ed. *The Future as Promise: Religious Life in the UK and Europe.* Madrid: Claret, 2012.

Gibbs, Graham R., and Celia Taylor. "How and What to Code." *Online QDA Web Site.* February 19, 2010. onlineqda.hud.ac.uk/Intro_QDA/how_what_to_code.php. Accessed June 15, 2015.

Gilbert, Joanna. "Young People in Search of Religious Vocation." In *A Future Full of Hope?,* edited by Gemma Simmonds, chap. 6. Dublin: Columba Press, 2012.

Gilligan, Carol. *In a Different Voice: Psychological Theory and Women's Development.* London: Harvard University Press, 1982.

Gilligan, Carol, Renee Spencer, Katherine Weinberg, and Tatiana Bertsch. "On the Listening Guide: A Voice-centred Relational Model." In *Qualitative Research in Psychology: Expanding Perspectives in Methodology and Design,* edited by Paul M. Camic, Jean E. Rhodes, and Lucy Yardley, chap. 9. Washington, DC: American Psychological Association, 2003.

Glaze, Jane. "PhD Study and the Use of a Reflective Diary." *Reflective Practice* 3, no. 2 (2002): 153–66. https://doi.org/10.1080/14623940220142307.

Gluck, Sherna Berger, and Daphne Patai, eds. *Women's Words: Oral History and Feminist Methodology.* New York: Routledge, 1991.

Goffman, Erving. "The Characteristics of Total Institutions." In *A Sociological Reader on Complex Organizations,* edited by Amitia Etzioni and Edward Lehman, 319–39. New York: Holt, Rinehart, and Winston, 1980.

Gottemoeller, Doris. "Living in Community: Continuing the Conversation." *Review for Religious* 64, no. 3 (2005): 269–80.

Graham, Elaine. "Feminist Theory." In *The Wiley-Blackwell Companion to Practical Theology*, edited by Bonnie J. Miller-McLemore, 193–203. Chichester: Wiley-Blackwell, 2012.

Graham, Elaine, Heather Walton, and Frances Ward. *Theological Reflections: Methods*. London: SCM Press, 2005.

Grey, Mary C. *Prophecy and Mysticism: The Heart of the Postmodern Church*. Edinburgh: T&T Clark, 1997.

Grey, Mary C. *Redeeming the Dream: Feminism, Redemption and Christian Tradition*. London: SPCK, 1989.

Gubrium, Jaber F. *Speaking of Life: Horizons of Meaning for Nursing Home Residents*. New York: De Gruyter, 1993.

Gubrium, Jaber F., and James A. Holstein, eds. *Handbook of Interview Research: Context and Method*. Thousand Oaks, CA: Sage, 2002.

Gubrium, Jaber F., and Andrea Sankar, eds. *Qualitative Methods in Aging Research*. Thousand Oaks, CA: Sage, 1994.

Guenther, Margaret. *Holy Listening: The Art of Spiritual Direction*. London: DLT, 1993.

Guigo II. *The Ladder of Monks and Twelve Meditations*. Translated by Edmund Colledge and James Walsh. Kalamazoo, MI: Cistercian Publications, 1978.

Hahnenberg, Edward P. *Awakening Vocation: A Theology of Christian Call*. Collegeville, MN: Liturgical Press, 2010.

Haker, Hille. "The Fragility of the Moral Self." *Harvard Theological Review* 97, no. 4 (2004): 359–81.

Haker, Hille. "Narrative and Moral Identity in the Work of Paul Ricoeur." In *Memory, Narrativity, Self and the Challenge to Think God: The Reception within Theology of the Recent Work of Paul Ricoeur*, edited by Maureen Junker-Kenny and Peter Kenny, 134–52. Munster: Lit Verlag, 2004.

Hall, Thelma. *Too Deep for Words: Rediscovering Lectio Divina*. Mahwah, NJ: Paulist Press, 1988.

Hampson, Daphne, ed. *Swallowing a Fishbone: Feminist Theologians Debate*. London: SPCK, 1996.

Hampson, Daphne. *Theology and Feminism*. Oxford: Blackwell, 1990.

Hanafin, Jonno. "Rules of Thumb for Awareness Agents." *Organization Development Practitioner* 36, no. 4 (2004): 24–28.

Hanafin, Jonno, and Mary Ann Rainey Tolbert. "The Use of Self in OD Consulting: What Matters is Presence." In *The NTL Handbook of Organization Development and Change: Principles, Practices, and Perspectives*, edited by Brenda B. Jones and Michael Brazzel, 69–82. San Francisco: Pfeiffer, 2006.

Handy, Charles. The *Empty Raincoat*. London: Arrow, 1994.

Harline, Craig. "Actives and Contemplatives: The Female Religious of the Low Countries Before and After Trent." *The Catholic Historical Review* 81, no. 4 (October 1995): 541–67.

Heifetz, Ronald, and Martin Linsky. *Leadership on the Line.* Boston, MA: Harvard Business School Press, 2002.

Herrick, Vanessa, and Ivan Mann, 1998. *Jesus Wept.* London: DLT, 1998.

Hesse-Biber, Sharlene. "The Practice of Feminist In-depth Interviewing." In *Feminist Research Practice: A Primer,* edited by Sharlene Hesse-Biber and Patricia Leavy, 113–47. Thousand Oaks, CA: Sage, 2007.

Hesse-Biber, Sharlene, and Patricia Leavy, eds. *Feminist Research Practice: A Primer.* Thousand Oaks, CA: Sage, 2007.

Hogan, Linda. *From Women's Experience to Feminist Theology.* London: Sheffield Academic Press, 1997.

Hornsby-Smith, Michael P., ed. *Catholics in England, 1950–2000: Historical and Sociological Perspectives.* London: Cassell, 1999.

Humphreys, M. Claire. Review of *The Nun in the World,* by Léon-Joseph Cardinal Suenens. *The Furrow* 14, no. 7 (1963): 469–72.

Hunter, Sally V. "Analysing and Representing Narrative Data: 'The Long and Winding Road.'" *Current Narratives* 1, no. 2 (2009): 44–54.

Hurd Clarke, Laura. "'We're not old!' Older Women's Negotiation of Aging and Oldness." *Journal of Aging Studies* 13, no. 4 (1999): 419–40.

Inglis, Tom. *Moral Monopoly: The Rise and Fall of the Catholic Church in Modern Ireland.* Dublin: University College Dublin Press, 1998.

Jack, Dana C., and Kathryn Anderson. "Learning to Listen: Interview Techniques and Analyses." In *Women's Words: Oral History and Feminist Methodology,* edited by Sherna Berger Gluck and Daphne Patai, 11–26. New York: Routledge, 1991.

Jamison, Christopher, ed. *The Disciples' Call: Theologies of Vocation from Scripture to the Present Day.* London: Bloomsbury, 2013.

Jamison, Christopher. "Compass in the Catholic Church: Finding a Path to Vocation Discernment." In *A Future Full of Hope?,* edited by Gemma Simmonds, chap. 5. Dublin: Columba Press, 2012.

John Paul II, Pope. *Post-synodal Apostolic Exhortation: "Vita Consecrata."* March 25, 1996. http://w2.vatican.va/content/john-paul-ii/en/apost_exhortations/documents/hf_jp-ii_exh_25031996_vita-consecrata.html. Accessed November 23, 2015.

John Paul II, Pope. *Essential Elements in the Church's Teaching on Religious Life as Applied to Institutes Dedicated to Works of the Apostolate.* May 31, 1983. http://www.vatican.va/roman_curia/congregations/ccscrlife/documents/rc_con_ccscrlife_doc_31051983_magisterium-on-religious-life_en.html. Accessed November 23, 2015.

John Paul II, Pope. *Apostolic Constitution: "Sacrae Disciplinae Leges."* January 25, 1983. https://www.vatican.va/content/john-paul-ii/en/apost_constitutions/documents/hf_jp-ii_apc_25011983_sacrae-disciplinae-leges.html.

Johnson, Elizabeth A. *She Who Is: The Mystery of God in Feminist Theological Discourse.* New York: Crossroad, 1997.

Johnson, Elizabeth A. "Discipleship: Root Model of the Life Called 'Religious.'" *Review for Religious* 42, no. 6 (1983): 864–72. http://cdm.slu.edu/cdm/singleitem/collection/rfr/id/259/rec/23. Accessed August 7, 2017.

Johnson, Helen. "The PhD Student as an Adult Learner: Using Reflective Practice to Find and Speak in Her Own Voice." *Reflective Practice* 2, no. 1 (2001): 53–63. https://doi.org/10.1080/14623940120035523.

Johnson, Mary, Patricia Wittberg, and Mary L. Gautier. *A New Generation of Catholic Sisters: The Challenge of Diversity*. New York: Oxford University Press, 2014.

Jones, Cathy. "What is Distinctive about Vocations to Religious Life?" In *The Disciples' Call: Theologies of Vocation from Scripture to the Present Day*, edited by Christopher Jamison, chap. 8. London: Bloomsbury, 2013.

Jones, Serene. *Feminist Theory and Christian Theology: Cartographies of Grace*. Minneapolis, MN: Augsburg Fortress Press, 2000.

Kaufman, Sharon. "In-depth Interviewing." In *Qualitative Methods in Aging Research*, edited by Jaber F. Gubrium and Andrea Sankar, chap. 8. Thousand Oaks, CA: Sage, 1994.

Keely, Vivienne. "Aspects of Mission in Religious Life Since the Second Vatican Council." In *A Future Built on Faith: Religious Life and the Legacy of Vatican II*, edited by Gemma Simmonds, 81–102. Dublin: Columba Press, 2014.

Kelly, L. *Sacraments Revisited: What Do They Mean Today?* London: DLT, 1998.

Kelly, Liz, Sheila Burton, and Linda Regan. "Researching Women's Lives or Studying Women's Oppression." In *Researching Women's Lives from a Feminist Perspective*, edited by Mary Maynard and June Purvis, chap. 2. London: Taylor and Francis, 1994.

Kilby, Karen. "The Seductions of Kenosis." In *Suffering and the Christian Life*, edited by Karen Kilby and Rachel Davies, 163–74. London: T&T Clark, 2020.

Kilby, Karen. "The Seductions of Kenosis." Paper presented at the international conference of the Centre for Catholic Studies on the theme of "Suffering, Diminishment, and the Christian Life," Ushaw College, University of Durham, January 10, 2018.

King, Nigel, and Christine Horrocks. *Interviews in Qualitative Research*. London: Sage, 2010.

Knott, Kim. "Insider/outsider Perspectives." In *The Routledge Companion to the Study of Religion*, edited by John R. Hinnells, chap. 13. London: Routledge, 2005.

Kvale, Steinar. *Interviews: An Introduction to Qualitative Research Interviewing*. Thousand Oaks, CA: Sage, 1996.

Labaree, R. V. "The Risk of 'Going Observationalist': Negotiating the Hidden Dilemmas of Being an Insider Participant Observer." *Qualitative Research* 2, no. 1 (2002): 97–122.

LaCugna, Catherine Mowry, ed. *Freeing Theology: The Essentials of Theology in Feminist Perspective*. New York: HarperCollins, 1993.

LaCugna, Catherine Mowry. *God for Us: The Trinity and Christian Life*. New York: HarperSanFrancisco, 1991.

Lanslots, D. I. *Handbook of Canon Law for Congregations of Women under Simple Vows.* New York: Fr. Pustet, 1922.

Llewellyn, Dawn. "Maternality Matters: Self-disclosure, Reflexivity, Participant Relationships and Researching Motherhood." Paper presented at "The Faith Lives of Women and Girls" symposium, The Queen's Foundation, University of Birmingham, October 25, 2014.

Lofland, John, and Lyn H. Lofland. *Analyzing Social Settings.* Belmont, CA. Wadsworth, 1984.

Lunn, Julie. "Paying Attention: The Task of Attending in Spiritual Direction and Practical Theology." *Practical Theology* 2, no. 2 (2009): 219–22.

McAinsh, Ronald J. *Living the Consecrated Life in the Third Millennium.* Chawton, UK: Redemptorist Publications, 2014.

McBrien, Richard P. *Catholicism.* Minneapolis, MN: Winston Press, 1980.

Maccise, C. "The Foundation and Development of Theology of Consecrated Apostolic Life: Insights and Problems." Address delivered to the Union of International Superiors General, Rome, 2011. vcd.pcn.net/en/index.php?option=com_docman&task=doc. Accessed January 24, 2015.

McDade, John. "Catholic Theology in the Post-Conciliar Period." In *Modern Catholicism: Vatican II and After*, edited by Adrian Hastings, 422–43. London: SPCK, 1991.

McDougall, Joy Ann. "The Return of Trinitarian Praxis? Moltmann on the Trinity and the Christian Life." *Journal of Religion* 83, no. 2 (2003): 177–203. https://doi.org/10.15757/kpjt.2014.46.3.009. Accessed April 14, 2016.

McElwee, Joshua J. "Visitation Report Takes Mostly Positive Tone towards U.S. Sisters." *National Catholic Reporter*, December 16, 2014. http://globalsisters.report.org/visitation-report-takes-mostly-positive-tone-towards-us-sisters-16701. Accessed December 16, 2014.

McKenna, Yvonne. "Entering Religious Life, Claiming Subjectivity: Irish Nuns, 1930s–1960s." *Women's History Review* 15, no. 2 (2006): 189–211. http://0-www.tandfonline.com.wam.leeds.ac.uk/doi/pdf/10.1080/09612020500529598?needAccess=true. Accessed August 30, 2016.

McKenna, Yvonne. "Forgotten Migrants: Irish Women Religious in England, 1930s–1960s." *International Journal of Population Geography* 9, no. 4 (2003): 295–308.

McLoughlin, David, and Gemma Simmonds. "Pastoral and Practical Theology in Britain and Ireland: A Catholic Perspective." In *Keeping Faith in Practice: Aspects of Catholic Pastoral Theology*, edited by James Sweeney, Gemma Simmonds, and David Lonsdale, chap. 2. London: SCM Press, 2010.

McNamara, Jo Ann Kay. *Sisters in Arms: Catholic Nuns through Two Millennia.* Cambridge, MA: Harvard University Press, 1996.

Maher, Mary. "Called and Sent: Reflections on a Theology of Apostolic Religious Life Today." Address delivered to the Union of International Superiors General, Rome,

2011. http://vd.pcn.net/en/index.php?option=com_docman&Itemid=37. Accessed December 18, 2015.

Mahoney, Kathleen A. *Catholic Sisters in America: Trends and Opportunities*. Agoura Hills, CA: Conrad N. Hilton Foundation, 2010.

Malone, Mary T. *Women and Christianity*. Vol. 3, *From the Reformation to the 21st Century*. Dublin: Columba Press, 2003.

Malone, Mary T. *Women and Christianity*. Vol. 2, *The Medieval Period, AD 1000–1500*. Dublin: Columba Press, 2001.

Mangion, Carmen M. *Catholic Nuns and Sisters in a Secular Age: Britain 1945–90*. Manchester: Manchester University Press, 2020.

Mangion, Carmen M. "The Nuns' True Story." *The Tablet*, February 7, 2015, 8–9.

Mangion, Carmen M. "Women, Religious Ministry and Female Institution Building." In *Women, Gender and Religious Cultures in Britain, 1800–1940*, edited by Sue Morgan and Jacqueline de Vries, 72–93. London: Routledge, 2010.

Mangion, Carmen M. "The 'Mixed Life': Balancing the Active with the Contemplative." In *Gender, Catholicism and Spirituality: Women and the Roman Catholic Church in Britain and Europe, 1200–1900*, edited by Carmen M. Mangion and Laurence Lux-Sterritt, 165–79. Basingstoke: Palgrave McMillan, 2010.

Mangion, Carmen M. "Laying 'Good Strong Foundations': The Power of the Symbolic in the Formation of a Religious Sister." *Women's History Review* 16, no. 3 (2007): 403–15.

Mannion, Gerard, ed. *The Vision of John Paul II: Assessing His Thought and Influence*. Collegeville, MN: Liturgical Press, 2008.

Marcel, Gabriel. *The Mystery of Being*. Vol. 1, *Reflections on Mystery*. London: Holden, 1950.

Marcel, Gabriel. *The Mystery of Being*. Vol. 2, *Faith and Reality*. London: Harvill Press, 1951.

Marshall, Leni. "Aging: A Feminist Issue." *NWSA Journal* 18, no. 1 (2006): vii–xiii. http://www.academia.edu/999951/Aging_A_feminist_issue. Accessed November 6, 2013.

Mason, Jennifer. *Qualitative Researching*. London: Sage, 2002.

Mauthner, Natasha, and Andrea Doucet. "Reflexive Accounts and Accounts of Reflexivity in Qualitative Data Analysis." *Sociology* 37, no. 3 (2003): 413–31. https://www.academia.edu/2095691/Reflexive_accounts_and_accounts_of_reflexivity_in_qualitative_data_analysis. Accessed December 16, 2015.

Mauthner, Natasha, and Andrea Doucet. "Reflections on a Voice-centred Relational Method: Analysing Maternal and Domestic Voices." In *Feminist Dilemmas in Qualitative Research: Public Knowledge and Private Lives*, edited by Jane Ribbens and Rosalind Edwards, chap. 8. London: Sage, 1998.

Maynard, Mary. "Methods, Practice and Epistemology." In *Researching Women's Lives from a Feminist Perspective*, edited by Mary Maynard and June Purvis, chap. 1. London: Taylor and Francis, 1994.

Maynard, Mary, and June Purvis, eds. *Researching Women's Lives from a Feminist Perspective*. London: Taylor and Francis, 1994.

Meads, Helen. "Insider Research into 'Experiment with Light': Uncomfortable Reflexivity in a Different Field." *Quaker Studies* 11, no. 2 (2007): 282–98. http://www.academia.edu/152231/Meads_Helen._Insider_Research_into_Experiment_with_Light_Uncomfortable_Reflexivity_in_a_Different_Field. Accessed June 9, 2015.

Mellott, David M. *I Was and I Am Dust: Penitente Practices as a Way of Knowing*. Collegeville, MN: Liturgical Press, 2009.

Merkle, Judith. *A Different Touch: A Study of Vows in Religious Life*. Collegeville, MN: Liturgical Press, 1998.

Merton, Thomas. *New Seeds of Contemplation*. New York: New Directions, 2007.

Merton, Thomas. *Love and Living*. Edited by Naomi Burton Stone and Patrick Hart. New York: Farrar, Straus, and Giroux, 1979.

Metz, Johann Baptist. *Poverty of Spirit*. Mahwah, NJ: Paulist Press, 1968.

Mickens, R. "CDF Stands Firm after Meeting with US Religious Leaders in Rome." *The Tablet*, June 16, 2012, 24c.

Milbank, John. *The Future of Love: Essays in Political Theology*. London: SCM Press, 2009.

Miles, Matthew B., and A. Michael Huberman. *Qualitative Data Analysis: An Expanded Sourcebook*. 2nd ed. Thousand Oaks, CA: Sage, 1994.

Miller, Paula Jean. "The Spousal Bond." In *The Foundations of Religious Life: Revisiting the Vision*, edited by the Council of Major Superiors of Women Religious, 47–84. Notre Dame, IN: Ave Maria Press, 2009.

Miller-McLemore, Bonnie J., ed. *The Wiley-Blackwell Companion to Practical Theology*. Chichester: Wiley-Blackwell, 2012.

Moltmann, Jürgen. *The Spirit of Life: A Universal Affirmation*. Translated by Margaret Kohl. London: SCM Press, 1992.

Moon, Jennifer A. *A Handbook of Reflective and Experiential Learning: Theory and Practice*. Abingdon: Routledge Falmer, 2004.

Moschella, Mary Clark. "Ethnography." In *The Wiley-Blackwell Companion to Practical Theology*, edited by Bonnie J. Miller-McLemore, chap. 21. Chichester: Wiley-Blackwell, 2012.

Moschella, Mary Clark. *Ethnography as a Pastoral Practice: An Introduction*. Cleveland, OH: Pilgrim Press, 2008.

Murphy, Desmond. *The Death and Rebirth of Religious Life*. Alexandria, New South Wales: E. J. Dwyer, 1995.

Murray, Pat. "Conversation 2: The Emergence of New Narratives—of Encounter." Address delivered to the Annual General Meeting of the Conference of Religious of England and Wales, May 24, 2018. https://www.corew.org/news/2018/5/24/cor-agm-2018-Sr.-pat-murray-ibvm.

Murray, Pat. "Conversation 1: New and Old Wineskins." Address delivered to the Annual General Meeting of the Conference of Religious of England and Wales, May 24, 2018. https://www.corew.org/news/2018/5/24/cor-agm-2018-Sr.-pat-murray-ibvm.

Myrdal, Alva, and Viola Klein. *Women's Two Roles: Home and Work*. London: Routledge, 1956.

National Office of Vocations of the Catholic Bishops Conference of England and Wales and The Compass Project. *Religious Life in England and Wales: Executive Summary*. London: Compass Project, 2010.

New York Province of the Society of Jesus. *A Jesuit Approach to Aging*. 2006. http://nysj.org/s/316/images/editor_documents/content/Diminishment%20is%20a%20word%20we%20hear%20often%20these%20days.%20%20We%20hear%20i/Aging.pdf. Accessed November 25, 2012.

Nouwen, Henri. *Gracias: A Latin American Journal*. New York: HarperCollins, 1987.

Nygren, David J., and Miriam D. Ukeritis. "The Religious Life Futures Project: Executive Summary." *Review for Religious* 52, no. 1 (1993): 6–55.

O'Brien, Anne. "Catholic Nuns in Transnational Mission, 1528–2015." *Journal of Global History* 11 (2016): 387–408. https://doi:10.1017/S1740022816000206.

O'Brien, Susan. *Leaving God for God: The Daughters of Charity of St. Vincent de Paul in Britain, 1847–2017*. London: DLT, 2017.

O'Brien, Susan. "'Yes, But What Do You Do?' What is Distinctive about the Exercise of Ministry by Religious?" Paper presented at the Compass Catholic Vocations Projects study day, St. Mary's Church, Moorfields, London, June 6, 2015.

O'Brien, Susan. "Sisters of the Third Sector: Working Identities, Constructs and Relationships." Paper presented at "The Nun in the World" symposium, University of Notre Dame's Global Gateway, London, May 5–7, 2015.

O'Brien, Susan. "A Note on Apostolic Religious Life." In *The Disciples' Call: Theologies of Vocation from Scripture to the Present Day*, edited by Christopher Jamison, 155–66. London: Bloomsbury, 2013.

O'Brien, Susan. "Religious Life for Women." In *From Without the Flamian Gate: 150 Years of Roman Catholicism in England and Wales, 1850–2000*, edited by V. Alan McClelland and Michael Hodgetts, chap. 5. London: DLT, 1999.

O'Leary, Daniel. *Begin With the Heart: Recovering a Sacramental Vision*. Dublin: Columba Press, 2008.

O'Murchu, Diarmuid. "First and Foremost Lay People?" *Religious Life Review* 54, no. 290 (2015): 7–18.

O'Murchu, Diarmuid. *Consecrated Religious Life: The Changing Paradigms*. Manila: Orbis, 2005.

O'Murchu, Diarmuid. *Reframing Religious Life: An Expanded Vision for the Future*. Slough: St. Pauls, 1995.

O'Murchu, Diarmuid. *Religious Life: A Prophetic Vision*. Notre Dame, IN: Ave Maria Press, 1991.

O'Murchu, Diarmuid. *The Seed Must Die*. Dublin: Veritas, 1980.

Orobator, Agbonkhianmeghe E. "A Global Sign of Outward Grace: The Sacramentality of the World Church in the Era of Globalisation." *Catholic Theological Society of America Proceedings* 67 (2012): 14–22.

Orsi, Robert. *Between Heaven and Earth: The Religious Worlds People Make and the Scholars Who Study Them*. Oxford: Princeton University Press, 2005.

Patai, Daphne. "When Method Becomes Power." In *Power and method. Political Activism and Educational Research*, edited by Andrew Gitlen, 61–73. New York: Routledge, 1994.

Paul VI, Pope. *Apostolic Letter: "Ecclesiae Sanctae."* August 6, 1966. https://www.vatican.va/content/paul-vi/en/motu_proprio/documents/hf_p-vi_motu-proprio_19660806_ecclesiae-sanctae.html.

Paul VI, Pope. *Pastoral Constitution on the Church in the Modern World: "Gaudium et Spes."* December 7, 1965. http://www.vatican.va/archive/hist_councils/ii_vatican_council/documents/vat-ii_const_19651207_gaudium-et-spes_en.html.

Paul VI, Pope. *Decree on the Adaptation and Renewal of Religious Life: "Perfectae Caritatis."* October 28, 1965. http://www.vatican.va/archive/hist_councils/ii_vatican_council/documents/vat-ii_decree_19651028_perfectae-caritatis_en.html. Accessed April 15, 2012.

Paul VI, Pope. *Dogmatic Constitution on the Church: "Lumen Gentium."* November 21, 1964. http://www.vatican.va/archive/hist_councils/ii_vatican_council/documents/vat-ii_const_19641121_lumen-gentium_en.html.

Pellauer, David. *Ricoeur: A Guide for the Perplexed*. London: Continuum, 2007.

Pellegrino, Mary. "The Future Enters Us Long Before It Happens: Opening Space for an Emerging Narrative of Communion." Presidential address for the Leadership Conference of Women Religious, Orlando, Florida, August 10, 2017. https://lcwr.org/sites/default/files/calendar/attachments/2017_lcwr_presidential_address_-_mary_pellegrino_csj.pdf. Accessed September 14, 2017.

Phoenix, Ann. "Analysing Narrative Contexts." In *Doing Narrative Research*. 2nd ed., edited by Molly Andrews, Corinne Squire, and Maria Tamboukou, chap. 3. London: Sage, 2013.

Pillow, Wanda. "Confession, Catharsis, or Cure? Rethinking the Uses of Reflexivity as Methodological Power in Qualitative Research." *International Journal of Qualitative Studies in Education* 16, no. 2 (2003): 175–96.

Potthoff, Harvey H. "Good Aging: A Christian Perspective." December 1990. http://www.religion-online.org/showarticle.asp?title=298. Accessed November 20, 2012.

Poulsom, Martin. "Sustaining Presence: Religious Life in the Midst of Creation." In *A Future Full of Hope?*, edited by Gemma Simmonds, chap. 3. Dublin: Columba Press, 2012.

Power, David N. "Sacramental Abundance: An Economy of Gift." *The Way Supplement* 94 (1999): 90–99.

Radcliffe, Timothy. "Religious Life: Candlemas Time?" In *Envisioning Futures for the Catholic Church*, edited by Staf Hellemans and Peter Jonkers, chap. 9. Washington, DC: Council for Research in Values and Philosophy, 2018.

Radcliffe, Timothy. Foreword to *A Future Full of Hope?*, edited by Gemma Simmonds, 7–10. Dublin: Columba Press, 2012.

Radcliffe, Timothy. *Sing a New Song: The Christian Vocation*. Springfield, IL: Templegate, 1999.

Radford Ruether, Rosemary. *Sexism and God Talk*. London: SCM Press, 1983.

Radler, Charlotte. "*Actio et Contemplatio*/Action and Contemplation." In *The Cambridge Companion to Christian Mysticism*, edited by Amy Hollywood and Patricia Z. Zeckman, chap 12. New York: Cambridge University Press, 2012.

Raftery, Deirdre. "The Transnational Mobility of 19th Century Women Religious." Paper presented at the "'Too Small a World': Catholic Sisters as Global Missionaries" symposium, Cushwa Center for the Study of American Catholicism, University of Notre Dame, Indiana, April 6–8, 2017.

Raftery, Deirdre. "From Kerry to Katong: Transnational Influences in Convent and Novitiate Life for the Sisters of the Infant Jesus, c. 1908–1950." In *Education, Identity and Women Religious, 1800–1950: Convents, Classrooms and Colleges*, edited by Deirdre Raftery and Elizabeth M. Smyth, chap. 2. Abingdon: Routledge, 2016.

Raftery, Deirdre. "Teaching Sisters and Transnational Networks: Recruitment and Education Expansion in the Long Nineteenth Century." *History of Education* 44, no. 6 (2015): 717–28. https://www.researchgate.net/publication/283116476_Teaching _Sisters_and_transnational_networks_recruitment_and_education_expansion_in_the _long_nineteenth_century. Accessed August 7, 2017.

Raftery, Deirdre. "Rebels With a Cause: Obedience, Resistance and Convent Life, 1800–1940." *History of Education* 42, no. 6 (2013): 729–44. www.tandfonline.com .wam.leeds.ac.uk/doi/pdf/10.1080/0046760X.2013.826288?needAccess=true. Accessed August 10, 2017.

Rahner, Karl. *Foundations of Christian Faith: An Introduction to the Idea of Christianity*. Translated by William V. Dych. New York: Crossroad, 1978.

Ramazanoglu, Caroline, and Janet Holland. *Feminist Methodology: Challenges and Choices*. London: Sage, 2002.

Rapley, Elizabeth. *The Dévotes: Women and Church in Seventeenth-century France*. Montreal: McGill-Queen's University Press, 1990.

Reinharz, Shulamit. *Feminist Methods in Social Research*. Oxford: Oxford University Press, 1992.

Ribbens, Jane, and Rosalind Edwards, eds. *Feminist Dilemmas in Qualitative Research: Public Knowledge and Private Lives*. London: Sage, 1998.

Ricoeur, Paul. *The Course of Recognition*. Translated by David Pellauer. Cambridge, MA: Harvard University Press, 2005.

Ricoeur, Paul. "Approaching the Human Person." Translated by Dale Kidd. *Ethical Perspectives* 6, no. 1 (1999): 45–54.

Ricoeur, Paul. *Oneself as Another*. Translated by Kathleen Blamey. Chicago, IL: University of Chicago Press, 1992.

Ricoeur, Paul. "Life in Quest of Narrative." In *On Paul Ricoeur: Narrative and Interpretation*, edited by David Wood, chap. 2. London: Routledge, 1991.

Ricoeur, Paul. "Narrative Identity." In *On Paul Ricoeur: Narrative and Interpretation*, edited by David Wood, chap. 11. London: Routledge, 1991.

Ricoeur, Paul. *Time and Narrative*, vol. 1. Translated by Kathleen Mclaughlin and David Pellauer. Chicago, IL: University of Chicago Press, 1984.

Ricoeur, Paul. *Hermeneutics and the Human Sciences*. Translated and edited by John B. Thompson. New York: Cambridge University Press, 1981.

Rohr, Richard. *Hope against Darkness: The Transforming Vision of Saint Francis in an Age of Anxiety*. Cincinnati, OH: Franciscan Media, 2001.

Ross, Susan. *Extravagant Affections: A Feminist Sacramental Theology*. New York: Continuum, 2001.

Ross-Sheriff, Fariyal. "Aging and Gender, Feminist Theory and Social Work Practice Concerns." *Affilia: Journal of Women and Social Work* 23, no. 4 (2008): 309–11.

Rumsey, Patricia. "The Challenge of Community Today." In *A Future Built on Faith: Religious Life and the Legacy of Vatican II*, edited by Gemma Simmonds, chap. 5. Dublin: Columba Press, 2014.

Rutherford, Tom. *Population Ageing: Statistics*. Commons briefing paper SN/SG/3228. February 10, 2012. http://researchbriefings.parliament.uk/ResearchBriefing/Summary/SN03228#fullreport. Accessed December 9, 2017.

Ryan, Gery W., and H. Russell Bernard. "Techniques to Identify Themes." *Field Methods* 15, no. 1 (2003): 85–109. http://www.analytictech.com/mb870/Readings/ryan-bernard_techniques_to_identify_themes_in.htm. Accessed December 13, 2015.

Sacred Congregation for Religious and for Secular Institutes. "Essential Elements in the Church's Teaching on Religious Life as applied to Institutes Dedicated to Works of the Apostolate." May 31, 1983. https://www.vatican.va/roman_curia/congregations/ccscrlife/documents/rc_con_ccscrlife_doc_31051983_magisterium-on-religious-life_en.html.

Sacred Congregation for Religious and for Secular Institutes. "Directives for the Mutual Relations between Bishops and Religious in the Church." May 14, 1978. http://www.vatican.va/roman_curia/congregations/ccscrlife/documents/rc_con_ccscrlife_doc_14051978_mutuae-relationes_en.html.

Schenk, Christine. "It's Not All about Eve: Women in the Lectionary." In *Catholic Women Speak: Bringing Our Gifts to the Table*, edited by the Catholic Women Speak Network, 168–71. Mahwah, NJ: Paulist Press, 2015.

Schillebeeckx, Edward. *Christ the Sacrament of the Encounter with God*. New York: Sheed and Ward, 1963.
Schneiders, Sandra. "Engage the Future: Reflections on the Apostolic Visitation Report." *National Catholic Reporter*, December 18, 2014. https://www.globalsisters report.org/column/trends/engage-future-reflections-apostolic-visitation-report-17046. Accessed January 18, 2014.
Schneiders, Sandra. "Religious Life Evolving Faithful and Free." Paper presented to the Conference of Religious of Ireland, Dublin, April 25, 2014.
Schneiders, Sandra. *Buying the Field: Religious Life in the New Millennium*. Mahwah, NJ: Paulist Press, 2013.
Schneiders, Sandra. "The Radical Nature and Significance of Consecrated Life." UISG Bulletin 146 (2011): 22–29. http://www.uisg.org/public/Attachments/doc_semteol_schneiders_2011_en.pdf.
Schneiders, Sandra. "Religious Life as Prophetic Life Form." Pts. 1–5. *National Catholic Reporter*, January 4–8, 2010. http://ncronline.org. Accessed November 9, 2011.
Schneiders, Sandra. "Discerning Ministerial Religious Life Today." *National Catholic Reporter*, September 11, 2009. https://www.ncronline.org/news/discerning-ministerial-religious-life-today. Accessed November 9, 2012.
Schneiders, Sandra. "We've Given Birth to a New Form of Religious Life." *National Catholic Reporter*, February 27, 2009. http://ncronline.org/news/women/weve-given-birth-new-form-religious-life. Accessed November 13, 2012.
Schneiders, Sandra. *Selling All: Commitment, Consecrated Celibacy, and Community in Catholic Religious Life*. Mahwah, NJ: Paulist Press, 2001.
Schneiders, Sandra. *Finding the Treasure: Locating Catholic Religious Life in a New Ecclesial and Cultural Context*. Mahwah, NJ: Paulist Press, 2000.
Schneiders, Sandra. *New Wineskins: Re-imagining Religious Life Today*. Mahwah, NJ: Paulist Press, 1986.
Schön, Donald A. *The Reflective Practitioner: How Professionals Think in Action*. New York: Basic Books, 1991.
Seale, Clive. "Coding and Analysing Data." In *Researching Society and Culture*. 2nd ed., edited by Clive Seale, chap. 3. London: Sage, 2004.
Sexton, Catherine. "Still Life in Us Yet: In Search of a Narrative of Diminishment." Paper 2 in partial fulfilment of the Professional Doctorate in Practical Theology. Cambridge Theological Federation and Anglia Ruskin University, 2013.
Sexton, Catherine. "Figure and Ground: Vitality or Diminishment in Roman Catholic Women's Apostolic Orders in the United Kingdom?" Paper 1 in partial fulfilment of the Professional Doctorate in Practical Theology. Cambridge Theological Federation and Anglia Ruskin University, 2012.
Sexton, Catherine, and Gemma Simmonds. *Religious Life Vitality Project: Key Findings*. Report for the Conrad N. Hilton Foundation. London: Heythrop College, 2015.

Shammy, Eileen. *A Guide to the Spiritual Dimension of Care for People with Alzheimer's Disease and Related Dementia: More than Body, Brain and Breath*. London: Jessica Kingsley, 2003.

Shaw, Patricia. *Changing Conversations in Organizations: A Complexity Approach to Change*. London: Routledge, 2002.

Sheldrake, Philip. *Spirituality and Theology: Christian Living and the Doctrine of God*. London: DLT, 1998,

Shenton, Andrew K. "Strategies for Ensuring Trustworthiness in Qualitative Research Projects." *Education for Information* 22 (2004): 63–75. http://www.angelfire.com/the force/shu_cohort_viii/images/Trustworthypaper.pdf. Accessed June 17, 2015.

Silverman, David. *Interpreting Qualitative Data*. 4th ed. London: Sage, 2014.

Simmonds, Gemma. "Professed Religious Life." In *The Cambridge Companion to Vatican II*, edited by Richard R. Gaillardetz, 266–81. Cambridge: Cambridge University Press, 2020.

Simmonds, Gemma, ed. *A Future Built on Faith: Religious Life and the Legacy of Vatican II*. Dublin: Columba Press, 2014.

Simmonds, Gemma, ed. *A Future Full of Hope?* Dublin: Columba Press, 2012.

Simmonds, Gemma. "Religious Life: A Question of Visibility." In *A Future Full of Hope?*, edited by Gemma Simmonds, chap. 8. Dublin: Columba Press, 2012.

Simmonds, Gemma. "John Paul II and the Consecrated Life." In *The Vision of John Paul II: Assessing His Thought and Influence*, edited by Gerard Mannion, chap. 12. Collegeville, MN: Liturgical Press, 2008.

Simmonds, Gemma, and María Calderón Muñoz. *Religious Life: Discerning the Future*. Self-published, 2020.

Sisters of St. Joseph of Peace. *Constitutions of the Sisters of Saint Joseph of Peace*. Rome, 1994.

Slee, Nicola. "Feminist Qualitative Research as Spiritual Practice: Reflections on the Process of Doing Qualitative Research." In *The Faith Lives of Women and Girls: Qualitative Research Perspectives*, edited by Nicola Slee, Fran Porter, and Anne Phillips, chap. 1. Farnham: Ashgate, 2013.

Slee, Nicola. *Women's Faith Development: Patterns and Processes*. Guildford: Ashgate, 2004.

Slee, Nicola, Fran Porter, and Anne Phillips, eds. *The Faith Lives of Women and Girls: Qualitative Research Perspectives*. Farnham: Ashgate, 2013.

Smith, Jonathan A. "Evaluating the Contribution of Interpretative Phenomenological Analysis." *Health Psychology Review* 5, no. 1 (2011): 9–27. http://o-www.tandfon line.com.wam.leeds.ac.uk/doi/pdf/10.1080/17437199.2010.510659. Accessed July 10, 2015.

Smith, Jonathan A., Paul Flowers, and Michael Larkin. *Interpretive Phenomenological Analysis: Theory, Method and Research*. London: Sage, 2009.

Smith, Ted A. "Theories of Practice." In *The Wiley-Blackwell Companion to Practical Theology*, edited by Bonnie J. Miller-McLemore, chap. 23. Chichester: Wiley-Blackwell, 2012.

Soelle, Dorothee. *The Silent Cry: Mysticism and Resistance*. Translated by Barbara Rumscheidt and Martin Rumscheidt. Minneapolis, MN: Augsberg Fortress, 2001.

Soskice, Janet Martin. *The Kindness of God: Metaphor, Gender, and Religious Language*. Oxford: Oxford University Press, 2007.

Spadaro, Antonio. "'Wake up the World!' Conversation with Pope Francis about the Religious Life." Translated by Donald Maldari. Original text in Italian in *La Civiltà Cattolica* 165, no. 1 (2014): 3–17.

Spencer, Stephanie. *Gender, Work and Education in Britain in the 1950s*. Basingstoke: Palgrave Macmillan, 2005.

Squire, Corinne. "From Experience-centred to Socio-culturally Oriented Approaches to Narrative." In *Doing Narrative Research*. 2nd ed., edited by Molly Andrews, Corinne Squire, and Maria Tamboukou, chap. 2. London: Sage, 2013.

Stanley, Liz, and Sue Wise. *Breaking Out Again: Feminist Ontology and Epistemology*. London: Routledge, 1993.

Stark, Roger, and Roger Finke. *Acts of Faith: Explaining the Human Side of Religion*. Berkeley, CA: University of California Press, 2000.

Stockman, Dan. "LCWR Leaders Talk about Unprecedented Transformation of Religious Life." *Global Sisters Report*, January 12, 2023. https://www.globalsistersreport.org/news/lcwr-leaders-talk-about-unprecedented-transformation-religious-life.

Stockman, Dan, and Dawn Cherie Araujo. "Women Religious and Others React to Apostolic Visitation Report Release." *National Catholic Reporter*, December 16, 2014. http://globalsistersreport.org/women-religious-and-others-react-apostolic-visitation-report-release-16781. Accessed December 16, 2014.

Stogdon, Kate. "'Nothing Was Taken From Me: Everything Was Given': Religious Life and Second Wave Feminism." In *A Future Full of Hope?*, edited by Gemma Simmonds, chap. 4. Dublin: Columba Press, 2012.

Strauss, A. L. *Qualitative Analysis for Social Scientists*. Cambridge: Cambridge University Press, 1987.

Suenens, Léon Joseph. *The Nun in the World: New Dimensions in the Modern Apostolate*. London: Burns and Oates, 1962.

Sweeney, James. "Religious Life Looks to the Future." In *A Future Full of Hope?*, edited by Gemma Simmonds, chap. 9. Dublin: Columba Press, 2012.

Sweeney, James. "Catholic Theology and Practice Today." In *Keeping Faith in Practice: Aspects of Catholic Pastoral Theology*, edited by James Sweeney, Gemma Simmonds, and David Lonsdale, chap. 1. London: SCM Press, 2010.

Sweeney, James. "Prophets and Parables: A Future for Religious Orders." *Informationes Theologiae Europae: Internationales ökumenisches Jahrbuch für Theologie* 4 (2001): 273–92.

Sweeney, James. "Religious Life after Vatican II." In *Catholics in England, 1950–2000: Historical and Sociological Perspectives*, edited by Michael P. Hornsby-Smith, chap. 14. London: Cassell, 1999.

Sweeney, James, Gemma Simmonds, and David Lonsdale, eds. *Keeping Faith in Practice: Aspects of Catholic Pastoral Theology*. London: SCM Press, 2010.

Swinton, John. "What's Love Got to Do With It? Some Practical Theological Reflections on the Use of Different Kinds of Knowledge for the Purposes of Divine Love." Paper presented at the Annual Student Day Conference of the British and Irish Association of Practical Theology, The Queen's Foundation, University of Birmingham, April 17, 2017.

Swinton, John. "Where is your Church? Moving Toward a Hospitable and Sanctified Ethnography." In *Perspectives on Ecclesiology and Ethnography*, edited by Pete Ward, chap. 4. Cambridge: Eerdmans, 2012.

Swinton, John. "Disability, Ableism and Disablism." In *The Wiley-Blackwell Companion to Practical Theology*, edited by Bonnie J. Miller-McLemore, chap. 42. Chichester: Wiley-Blackwell, 2012.

Swinton, John. *Dementia: Living in the Memories of God*. Cambridge: Eerdmans, 2012.

Swinton, John. "'Who is the God We Worship?' Theologies of Disability; Challenges and New Possibilities." *International Journal of Practical Theology* 14, no. 2 (2011): 273–307.

Swinton, John. "The Body of Christ has Down's Syndrome: Theological Reflections on Vulnerability, Disability, and Graceful Communities." *Journal of Pastoral Theology* 13, no. 2 (2003): 66–78. http://www.abdn.ac.uk/cshad/TheBodyofChristHasDownSyndrome.htm. Accessed January 21, 2013.

Swinton, John, and Harriet Mowat. *Practical Theology and Qualitative Research*. Canterbury: SCM Press, 2006.

Tattam, Helen. "Atheism, Religion, and Philosophical 'Availability' in Gabriel Marcel." *International Journal of the Philosophy of Religion* 79, no. 1 (2016): 19–30. https://doi.org/10.1007/s11153-015-9547-9.

Taylor, Charles. *A Secular Age*. Cambridge, MA: Belknap Press of Harvard University Press, 2007.

Taylor, Charles. *Sources of the Self: The Making of the Modern Identity*. Cambridge: Cambridge University Press, 1989.

Timmerman, Joan H. "The Sacramentality of Human Relationships." *The Way Supplement* 94 (1999): 9–21.

Tobin, Joseph. "How Did We Get Here? The Renewal of Religious Life in the Church Since Vatican II." In *A Future Built on Faith: Religious Life and the Legacy of Vatican II*, edited by Gemma Simmonds, chap. 1. Dublin: Columba Press, 2014.

Tobin, Joseph. "The View from Roma." In *The Future as Promise: Religious Life in the UK and Europe*, edited by J. C. R. Garcia Paredes. Madrid: Claret, 2012.

Todd, Selina, and Hilary Young. "Baby-boomers to 'Beanstalkers': Making the Modern Teenager in Post-war Britain." *Cultural and Social History* 9, no. 3 (2012): 451–67.

Tracy, David. *The Analogical Imagination: Christian Theology and the Culture of Pluralism*. New York: Crossroad, 1981.

Trzebiatowska, Marta. "When Reflexivity is not Enough: Doing Research with Polish Catholics." *Fieldwork in Religion* 5, no. 1 (2010). https://www.academia.edu/11506267/When_reflexivity_is_not_enough_researching_Polish_Catholics. Accessed June 17, 2015.

Um, M. Maximilia. "Evangelical Mission." In *The Foundations of Religious Life: Revisiting the Vision*, edited by the Council of Major Superiors of Women Religious, chap. 5. Notre Dame, IN: Ave Maria Press, 2009.

Union of Superiors General, ed. *Consecrated Life Today: Charisms in the Church for the World*. Slough: St. Pauls, 1994.

Vacek, Edward Collins. "Vices and Virtues of Old-age Retirement." *Journal of the Society of Christian Ethics* 30 (2010): 161–82.

Vanstone, William Hubert. *The Stature of Waiting*. London: DLT, 1982.

Van Heijst, Annelise. *Models of Charitable Care: Catholic Nuns and Children in their Care in Amsterdam, 1852–2002*. Boston, MA: Brill Academic, 2008.

Veling, Terry A. "Listening to 'The Voices of the Pages' and 'Combining the Letters': Spiritual Practices of Reading and Writing." *Religious Education* 102, no. 2 (2007): 206–22. https://www.academia.edu/227483/Spiritual_Practices_of_Reading_and_Writing?auto=download. Accessed January 27, 2017.

Veling, Terry A. *Practical Theology: "On Earth as it is in Heaven."* Maryknoll, NY: Orbis, 2005.

Volf, Miroslav. *Exclusion and Embrace: A Theological Exploration of Identity, Otherness and Reconciliation*. Nashville, TN: Abingdon Press, 1996.

Walsh, Barbara. *Roman Catholic Nuns in England and Wales, 1800–1937: A Social History*. Dublin: Irish Academic Press, 2002.

Ward, Frances. *Lifelong Learning: Theological Education and Supervision*. London: SCM Press, 2005.

Watkins, Clare. *Disclosing Church: An Ecclesiology Learned from Conversations in Practice*. London: Routledge, 2020.

Watkins, C., and H. Cameron. "Epiphanic Sacramentality: An Example of Practical Ecclesiology Revisioning Theological Understanding." In *Explorations in Ecclesiology and Ethnography*, edited by C. B. Scharen, chap. 4. Cambridge: Eerdmans, 2012.

Weber, Max. *The Sociology of Religion*. Translated from German and edited by Ephraim Fischoff. Boston, MA: Beacon Press, 1963.

Welker, Michael. *God the Spirit*. Minneapolis, MN: Fortress Press, 1994.

White, Teresa. *A Vista of Years: History of the Society of the Sisters Faithful Companions of Jesus 1820–1993*. N.p.: Society of the Sisters Faithful Companions of Jesus, 2013.

Wickramasinghe, Maithree. *Feminist Research Methodology: Making Meanings of Meaning-making*. New York: Routledge, 2010.

Wittberg, Patricia. "The Challenge of Reconfiguration: New Opportunities for Religious Congregations." *Human Development* 30, no. 3 (2009): 14–22.

Wittberg, Patricia. *From Piety to Professionalism and Back*. Oxford: Lexington, 2006.

Wittberg, Patricia. *Pathways to Re-creating Religious Communities*. NJ: Paulist Press, 1996.

Wittberg, Patricia. *The Rise and Fall of Catholic Religious Orders: A Social Movement Perspective*. Albany, NY: SUNY Press, 1994.

Wittberg, Patricia. *Creating a Future for Religious Life*. NJ: Paulist Press, 1991.

Wood, David, ed. *On Paul Ricoeur: Narrative and Interpretation*. London: Routledge, 1991.

Woodward, James. *Valuing Age: Pastoral Ministry with Older People*. London: SPCK, 2008.

Woodward, James, Stephen Pattison, and John Patton, eds. *The Blackwell Reader in Pastoral and Practical Theology*. Oxford: Blackwell, 2000.

Wright, Mary. *Mary Ward's Institute: The Struggle for Identity*. Sydney: Crossing Press, 1997.

Wuthnow, Robert, and Stephen Offutt. "Transnational Religious Connections." *Sociology of Religion* 69, no. 2 (2008): 209–32.

Zagano, Phyllis. "A Very Public Rebuke." *The Tablet*, April 28, 2012, 4–5.

Zengarini, Lisa. "Pope to Claretians: Always Seek New Ways to Serve the Lord." *Vatican News*, November 7, 2022. https://www.vaticannews.va/en/pope/news/2022-11/pope-to-claretianum-always-seek-new-ways-to-serve-the-lord.html.

Zizioulas, John D. *Being in Communion: Studies in Personhood and the Church*. Crestwood, NY: St. Vladimir's Seminary Press, 1985.

Index

activism 122–123
ageism 140
agency 95, 99–104
aggiornamento 5, 20, 67, 99
anti-Catholicism 15
apostolates. *See* ministry and apostolates
apostolic
    as evangelization 115–116
    definitions of 1n2, 24
    understanding of 39, 66, 89, 114–120, 135–144, 156, 160, 171
apostolic impulse 21, 23, 29, 56, 62, 74–75, 82
apostolic religious life
    and British discourse 15–21
    and Vatican II 4–6
    as ministerial 80
    distinctiveness of 176, 178
    in the United States 9–15
    mystics 20
    observant model 20
    progressive 11, 13–14, 19
    prophetic model 20–21
    theology of 18, 22, 170–180
    traditional 11, 14, 19
Apostolic Visitation to Institutes of Women Religious in the US (2014) 10, 20
attention 157
authenticity 85, 89, 104–111, 148, 171–172, 177
authority 1n2, 29, 100
availability 25, 112, 116–120, 128, 133, 146–147, 157, 180

becoming 2, 24, 84, 86–89, 112, 117, 119, 171, 177
Beguine movement, the 2
Bennett Moore, Zoe 140, 179
Braun, Victoria 54
Brock, Megan P. 89, 92–93
Butler, Sara 11–12

Canon Law 3–4, 38, 173
Casey, Michael 49–51
Chittister, Joan 11, 15

Church
    and religious life 20–21, 62, 95, 173, 179
    and women religious 8–9, 18–19, 29, 47, 58, 89, 94, 171, 173, 179
Claretian order, the 17, 23, 174
Clarke, Victoria 54
Coakley, Sarah 142, 153–155
Collins, Gregory 18, 130, 133
communion 118, 122, 130, 133, 141, 146–147, 151, 159, 162. *See also* koinonia; relationships
community 2, 8, 12–14, 77, 88–89, 130, 144–146, 148, 158–160, 162
    and living independently 92–94, 160
Compass Project, the 7
Conditae a Christo (1900) 3, 8, 39n61, 68, 78
Normae (1901) 3
Conference of Religious of England and Wales (COREW) 16, 175
Congregation for Institutes of Consecrated Life and Societies of Apostolic Life (CICLSAL) 10, 174, 177
congregations 64, 89, 95, 97, 100, 171–172, 179
    and post-institutional religious life 2
Connelly, Cornelia 79n51, 152n56
Conroy, Maureen 41–42
contemplative enquiry 41
conversion 24, 56, 103, 121, 155, 172, 177
Cottingham, John 163, 168–169
Council of Major Superiors of Women Religious (CMSWR) 10, 12–14

data collection and analysis. *See also* methodology; Voice-Centred Relational Method (VCRM) 26
    interviews 37, 41–43
    Listening Method, the 44
    sampling 38–39
    thematic analysis 54–55
    thematic coding 43–44, 46
Daughters of Charity, the 38, 68, 146
dependency 164, 180
detachment 164–165

INDEX

diminishment 22, 33, 114, 141–142, 144
  institutional 2, 6, 19, 173. *See also* relinquishment
  numerical 4, 6–7, 10, 19, 22, 33, 81, 135, 143, 172, 175
  physical. *See* infirmity
  social 1, 25, 81, 148, 173
discernment 42, 52, 67, 99–105, 165–166
disponibilité 146
distinctive dress 6, 8, 12, 14, 90–91
Doucet, Andrea 46–48

Ecclesiae Sanctae (1966) 5–6, 82n58
ecclesiology 12, 20–21
epistemology 29–31
  theological 52
Essential Elements in the Church's Teaching on Religious Life (1983) 12
Evangelii Gaudium (2013) 152
evangelization 115–116

families 57, 61–62, 89
feminism 11, 28–31, 37, 43, 151, 153, 179
Flannery, Tony 60, 69
Flaxman, Radegunde 79n51, 152n56
freedom 86–89, 101, 107–110
fulfilment 60, 84, 94–97, 102–103

Gaudium et Spes (1965) 5, 13, 70, 149, 155
gender 80–81, 140
  gender stereotypes 62
gift-giving 124–128
Gilligan, Carol 44

Hahnenberg, Edward P. 57, 86–87, 89, 103, 105, 121–122, 134
hermeneutical phenomenology 26–29
Hogan, Linda 29–31
hospitality 117, 119–120

identity 2, 6, 35, 78, 80–81, 83–111, 117, 120, 124, 139, 171, 178
  being for 24, 112, 114, 117, 171, 179–180
  being with 24, 112, 114, 117, 171, 179–180
  definition of 88–89
  externally ascribed 89–92
  internally ascribed 92–94
  modern 84–85
  post-institutional 6–9, 81, 171

Ignatian spirituality
  rules for discerning the movement of the spirits 42–43
image of God 20, 104–105, 130
incarnational theology 151–155
Independent Inquiry into Child Sexual Abuse (IICSA) 16
Infant Jesus sisters, the 146
infirmity 1–2, 22, 25, 81, 112–114, 123–124, 134–135, 137–139, 142, 148, 159–160, 163, 165, 167, 169, 172–173, 180
insider/outsider binary 33–35
Institute of the Blessed Virgin Mary (IBVM) 2
  renaming 2n5
intersubjectivity 114, 118, 129, 147
Ireland 9, 15, 38–39, 57–62

Justice in the World (1971) 69

kenosis 133–134, 153–154
Kilby, Karen 133
koinonia 130, 132. *See also* communion; relationships

LaCugna, Catherine Mowry 130, 133, 157
laity 5, 18, 86, 106
Leadership Conference of Women Religious (LCWR) 10–12, 21, 29, 141, 175–176
Lectio Divina 24, 36, 42, 48–54
  parallels with VCRM 49–50
liberation theology 69, 71, 122
listening 117, 120, 146–148, 167
  holy listening 24, 36, 48–54
Lumen Gentium (1964) 5, 12–13, 18, 173

Mangion, Carmen M. 3, 108
Marcel, Gabriel 117–118, 125, 128, 134, 146–147, 151, 157
Mauthner, Natasha 46–48
McKenna, Yvonne 60, 62
meaning, finding and making 19, 22–23, 27, 35, 43, 46, 49, 52, 56–67, 114, 119, 136, 138–139, 145, 149, 160, 168–169, 180
Merton, Thomas 41, 104
methodology 26–55. *See also* data collection and analysis
  feminist 26, 28–31, 53, 179

Milbank, John   125–129
ministry
    and apostolates   67–69, 74, 76, 78, 81–82, 124
    as activity   75–79, 82
    as contemplative   64, 78
    as gift   25, 123–134
    as incarnational presence   25, 135, 151–155
    as sacramental presence   25, 135, 149–151
    as service   64–65, 80, 120, 124
    of prayer   138, 144, 155, 168, 178
    of presence   25, 75, 105, 134, 138, 144–158, 170, 180
    recognizable ministry   77, 81
    reviews of   68
    to carers   25, 144, 160–163, 167, 170, 172, 180
    to each other   25, 144, 148, 158–160, 170, 172
missions   1n2, 57, 59–63, 70, 161
Moltmann, Jürgen   121–122, 129–130, 133–134
Murray, Patricia   175
Mutuae Relationes (1978)   20
mutuality   25, 127–129, 134, 147, 180

narratives   35, 43, 45–47, 50–54, 56–57, 67, 88–89, 94–95, 99, 171
    metanarratives   31
nuns
    difference from sisters   1n1

O'Brien, Susan   4, 38–39, 59, 68, 80
O'Leary, Daniel   150, 153, 156
O'Murchu, Diarmuid   15
obedience   96–97, 99–104, 135, 142, 160, 163–169
old age   2, 22, 25, 112–169, 172
    and dependency   138, 142–144, 160, 172
    and inactivity   136–142, 169. *See also* ministry as activity; ministry as service
    and retirement   1, 8, 102, 112, 136, 160
open friendship   122, 129–130
openness towards others   120–123
ordinary, the   85–86, 106–107, 120, 131–132, 155–158, 172
Orobator, Agbonkhianmeghe E.   151, 156
Orsi, Robert   34

Pellegrino, Mary   141, 162, 175
Perfectae Caritatis (1965)   5, 13, 68, 78
Pope Francis   151–152, 174–175
Poulsom, Martin   20
practice-engaged theology   24, 33, 36–37, 51, 53
prayer. *See* ministry of prayer
preferential option for the poor   12, 71, 146
presence   2, 55, 170, 180
    of God   25, 41–43, 53, 105, 144, 152–153, 155, 157–158. *See also* ministry of presence; ministry of incarnational presence; ministry of sacramental presence   25
Presentation sisters, the   58
prophetic witness   84, 100–101, 123
purpose   2, 6, 77, 136–140, 149, 171, 180

Radcliffe, Timothy   19, 176, 178
Radford Ruether, Rosemary   31
reciprocity   25, 114, 124, 128–132, 134, 147, 180
reflexivity   26, 31–33, 45, 47
relationships   46, 73, 114, 117–118. *See also* communion; *koinonia*
    as sacramental   158–160
    with God   65–66
Religious Life Institute (RLI)   14, 16–17, 20
Religious Life Vitality Project, the   33
relinquishment   114, 135, 142, 160, 164–166, 180
resistance   89–94
ressourcement   20, 68
retirement. *See* old age and retirement   1
Ricoeur, Paul   27, 31, 53, 111, 125–126, 161
Ross, Susan   151, 157

sacramental theology   149–151, 158–160
Sacred Reading. *See* Lectio Divina
Schillebeeckx, Edward   149–150
Schneiders, Sandra   11–15, 22–23, 25, 65–66, 68–69, 80–82, 86, 95, 100–101, 103, 110, 112–113, 123–124, 127, 129, 133–134, 141–142, 154, 164–165, 167, 171, 180
Second Vatican Council. *See* Vatican II
self-denial   84, 96–97, 108, 110–111
self-gift   2, 25, 65, 110–112, 114, 116, 123, 127–129, 132–134, 142, 149, 153–154, 179–180

INDEX

self, the   2, 24, 83–111, 147, 154–155, 171–172
self-worth   136–140, 178
service. *See* ministry as service
sexism   29–30
Sexton, Catherine   141
Simmonds, Gemma   14–16, 18, 21
sisters. *See also* women religious
    and nursing   8, 62–63
    and office work   63
    and teaching   8, 15, 62–63, 67, 70–72, 95–97
    difference from nuns   1*n*1
    lay sisters   39
    participants' profiles   39, 57–58, 95
    relationship with God   65–66
Sisters of Mercy, the   58
Sisters of the Cross and Passion, the   146
Slee, Nicola   29, 43–44, 48–49, 53
social justice   64, 69, 71, 73
social sciences, role of   36, 53
    psychology   100
Soskice, Janet Martin   157, 168
spiritual direction   36*n*51, 41–43
Starting Afresh from Christ (2002)   107
Stogdon, Kate   154–155
Stonehill Symposium (2008)   11
stories. *See* narratives
Sweeney, James   17–20, 29, 53, 74, 82, 132, 147, 170
Swinton, John   28, 32, 142

talent-stripping   97–98
Taylor, Charles   84–85, 88–90, 104–106
Theological Action Research   36*n*49
theological self-understanding   1–2
thwarted desires   84, 94–95, 97–99, 103, 107–108
Timmerman, Joan H.   150, 158
total institution   8, 86, 97, 100
Trinitarian theology   121, 128–133
    perichoresis   128, 130, 132, 134

Union of International Superiors General (UISG)   174
United Kingdom, the
    and the United States   9–10
United States, the   9–14, 175–176
    and the United Kingdom   9–10
universities
    in the United Kingdom   15, 62
    in the United States   9
Ursuline order, the   2
usefulness   65, 136, 171, 178

Vacek, Edward Collins   135, 139–140, 143, 148, 160, 165–166, 168, 172, 179
Van Heijst, Annelies   69
Vanstone, William Hubert   142–143, 172
Vatican II   4, 6, 17, 19, 68, 86, 106, 155–156
    and apostolic religious life   4–6
Veling, Terry A.   52–53
Vita Consecrata (1996)   20, 107, 118, 136–137, 151, 173–174
vocation   5, 26, 33, 40, 53, 56–66, 86–88, 112, 149
    dual calling   63
Voice-Centred Relational Method (VCRM)   24, 36, 43–48
    parallels with *Lectio Divina*   49–50
Volf, Miroslav   121–122, 133–134
vulnerability   117, 133, 142–144, 153–154

Watkins, Clare   24*n*94
Wittberg, Patricia   5, 8, 11, 65, 81
women religious. *See also* sisters
    and the Church   8–9, 18–19, 29, 47, 58, 89, 94, 171, 173, 179
women's experience, validity of   30–31, 151, 179
work ethic   75

Zinn, Carol   176–177